Please retu...
Holy Cross International Justice
403 Bertrand Annex, Saint Mary's
Notre Dame IN 46556-5018

W9-ARL-844

at Morning

America and the Crisis of the
Global Environment

NEW HAVEN AND LONDON

Copyright © 2004 by James Gustave Speth. All rights reserved. This book may not be reproduced, in whole or in part, including illustrations, in any form (beyond that copying permitted by Sections 107 and 108 of the U.S. Copyright Law and except by reviewers for the public press), without written permission from the publishers.

The following publishers have generously given permission to use quotations from copyrighted works. From *The Collected Poems of Wallace Stevens* by Wallace Stevens, copyright 1954 by Wallace Stevens and renewed 1982 by Holly Stevens. Used by permission of Alfred A. Knopf, a division of Random House, Inc. From *The Rain in the Trees* by W. S. Merwin, copyright © 1988 by W. S. Merwin. Used by permission of Alfred A. Knopf, a division of Random House, Inc. From *The Lorax* by Dr. Seuss, copyright © by Dr. Seuss Enterprises, L.P. 1971, renewed 1999. Used by permission of Random House Children's Books, a division of Random House, Inc. All rights reserved. From *Silent Spring* by Rachel Carson. Copyright © 1962 by Rachel L. Carson, renewed 1990 by Roger Christie. Reprinted by permission of Houghton Mifflin Company. All rights reserved. From "We Who Prayed and Wept" by Wendell Berry, from *Collected Poems: 1957– 1982*, by Wendell Berry. Reprinted by permission of North Point Press, a division of Farrar, Straus and Giroux, LLC. From "Bank of Bad Habits" written by Jimmy Buffett, Peter Mayer, Roger Guth, Russ Kunkel, and Jay Oliver © 1998 Little Flock Music (BMI)/Alsatian Music (BMI)/Administered by Bug Coral Reefer Music/MCA Music Publishing/Olas Music/Jay Oliver Music. All rights reserved. Used by permission.

Printed in the United States of America by R. R. Donnelley & Sons.

Library of Congress Cataloging-in-Publication data will be found at the end of this book.

A catalogue record for this book is available from the British Library.

This book was printed with soy-based ink on acid-free recycled paper that contains postconsumer fiber. The case was manufactured using acid-free recycled paper that contains postconsumer pulps and colors that are lignin- and carbon-free.

10   9   8   7   6   5   4   3   2

For Cameron
and
The students of the Yale School of Forestry & Environmental Studies

After the final no there comes a yes
And on that yes the future of the world depends. Wallace Stevens

Contents

Preface   ix

Prologue: 1980   I

Part One. Environmental Challenges Go Global . . .   II

  1. A World of Wounds   13

  2. Lost in Eden   23

  3. Pollution and Climate Change in a Full World   43

Part Two. . . . And the World Responds   75

  4. First Attempt at Global Environmental Governance   77

  5. Anatomy of Failure   98

Part Three. Facing Up to Underlying Causes   117

  6. Ten Drivers of Environmental Deterioration   119

  7. Globalization and the Environment   140

Part Four. The Transition to Sustainability   149

  8. Attacking the Root Causes   151

  9. Taking "Good Governance" Seriously   172

10. The Most Fundamental Transition of All   191

    Resources for Citizens   203

    List of Abbreviations   229

    Notes   233

    For Further Reading: A Bookshelf   269

    Index   277

Preface

As I write this preface, an unusually severe blizzard is bearing down on Connecticut. Yale is shutting down. My wife is worrying about the children driving, even though they have all been adults for years. The blizzard is forecast to continue through most of the night and to set records. It hardly seems the moment for me to begin fretting again about global warming, but I check the NASA Web-site, and there it is: the bitterly cold January we just suffered through in the Northeast was actually the second warmest January on record globally, going back to 1880. And only a fortnight ago, two Harvard scientists pointed out in an op-ed article in the *Boston Globe* that dramatically colder weather in the North Atlantic region is one possible consequence of global warming because the warming could disrupt the Gulf Stream. There is a lesson here. To get it right we should trust science more than our senses, but the science is complicated, often confusing, and sometimes counterintuitive.

It is easy to long for the clarity of the early days of the modern environmental movement when the problems could be seen and smelled and the villains were obvious. Those insults led me and others, fresh out of law school in 1969, to help found the Natural Resources Defense

Council. In dozens of lawsuits, we attacked air and water pollution, clear-cutting, strip-mining, stream channelization, and breeder reactors and generally partook in a great moment in American history when extraordinary progress was made in cleaning up and protecting the environment here at home. The 1970s were a wonderful decade for our American environment, beginning with the enactment of the National Environmental Policy Act under President Richard M. Nixon and culminating in President Jimmy Carter's protection of Alaskan lands. It was a bipartisan effort, with Democrats like Senator Ed Muskie joining with Republicans like Senator Howard Baker to compile an unmatched record of tough environmental legislation. As a result, air and water pollution have been much reduced in the United States, we did get the lead out (of gasoline), and we have built a remarkable system of parks, wilderness, and other protected areas. Many lakes and rivers have been revived, and forest cover in the United States has increased, not decreased. These successes underscored that America can protect its environment without wrecking its economy.

In the early 1970s the CBS Evening News with Walter Cronkite ran a series of environmental stories entitled "Can the World Be Saved?" The globe behind this title was firmly grasped by a hand that seemed to come from nowhere. I was never sure whether this hand was crushing our small planet or saving it, but I was sure at least that Cronkite was out to save it. He dramatically presented the much simpler environmental problems of that period to a huge audience and helped build the powerful environmental consciousness of the day.

Today, the question "Can the world be saved?" is more serious and legitimate than it was then. As we begin the new century, human activities are disrupting the great ecological systems and natural cycles that make our planet habitable, bountiful, and wondrous. Only our heightened care can save the world as we know it. So, the world is indeed in our hands, for good or for ill.

After working through the 1970s exclusively on domestic environmental issues, my realization that even larger challenges were massing on the global front came as a rude awakening. I was serving then as chair of President Carter's Council on Environmental Quality, and our efforts at CEQ to prepare the *Global 2000 Report to the President* brought home to me and others that there was a new agenda of global environmental challenges more threatening and difficult than the predominantly domestic concerns that motivated us in founding NRDC. Climate change, devastation of ocean fisheries, deforestation in the tropics, loss of species, land deterioration, and other unwanted processes were occurring on a frightening scale and pace. I remember thinking that we were building a fool's paradise here in America by concentrating on local environmental concerns while ignoring these global-scale ones.

Banished by the 1980 elections, the Carter administration never had a chance to tackle these problems. I was fortunate, however, to find support in 1982 from the MacArthur Foundation to launch a new organization dedicated to these issues, the World Resources Institute. Throughout my decade there and since, WRI has sought to bring global-scale environmental challenges to broad public attention and help find solutions to them. At WRI we were in the thick of the international process that gave rise to the plethora of environmental treaties of the 1980s and 1990s that I discuss in this book.

Superficially, this outpouring of international legislation was similar to the burst of domestic environmental legislation of the 1970s. But, unfortunately, the similarity stopped there. Whereas our national legislation was successful in curbing many environmental abuses domestically, efforts to protect the global environment have largely failed in the sense that the trends in environmental deterioration have not improved and that more of the same will not get us where we want to be in time to head off an era of unprecedented environmental decline. Big trouble is coming down the pike—and coming fast indeed. Thus, the sailor's warning in the title.

I hope this short book will be a wake-up call to those of us, including many in the environmental community, who may believe that all the international negotiations, treaties, and other agreements of the past two decades have prepared us to deal with global environmental threats. They haven't. The current system of international efforts to help the environment simply isn't working. The design makes sure it won't work, and the statistics keep getting worse. We need a new design, and to make that happen, civil society must take the helm.

I set out to write a book that would help people understand what's going on in the world of the global environment by telling the story of how things got the way they are and how we can change them. I have sought, first, to present an accurate account of the seriousness of today's global environmental challenges and point out without exaggeration the implications of letting current trends continue; second, to provide a frank analysis of the failure to date of environmental governance at the international level, including the largely negative role of the United States; and third, to offer a strategy for moving beyond today's stalemate, one that is comprehensive and feasible.

To cover these topics, I have drawn on several branches of science and delved into law, economics, politics, social relationships, international affairs, and more. I certainly cannot claim to be truly expert across this wide field, but my years at the World Resources Institute and more recently at the United Nations Development Programme and the Yale School of Forestry and Environmental Studies have exposed me to a lot of the world. I have drawn on my experience, but I have also turned without hesitation to the writings and suggestions of many experts whose judgment I respect.

As the book took shape I came more and more to focus on the United States. Those of us who live in the United States are fortunate indeed to be here. But the sad fact is that U.S. priorities have strayed badly off the path. There has been one major success in protecting the global environment—the effort to protect and restore the earth's ozone shield in the stratosphere. The United States led that effort, beautifully. But since then the United States has dragged its feet on just about every international environmental treaty that has been suggested. The failure of the United States to give positive leadership on these subsequent efforts has contributed materially to their lack of impact to date.

Throughout, I have tried to follow the advice of the eminent psychologist Robert Jay Lifton: "If one does not look into the abyss, one is being wishful by simply not confronting the truth. . . . On the other hand, it is imperative that one not get stuck in the abyss." I do not think of this book (or myself) as either pessimistic or optimistic; rather, I have tried to be both realistic and hopeful. It is not always a happy marriage. Some may look at the difficulty of reversing current trends and despair; they are stuck in the abyss. Others may blithely assume that things will work out ("they always do"); they are being wishful. The right answer, I believe, lies at neither extreme. However bad the situation looks, remember: *there are solutions*. The chapters that follow are full of them.

I have worked hard to get the facts right. Often the data, for example on deforestation and desertification rates, are not as good as they should be, and in many of the areas covered, large scientific uncertainties remain. There is a lot that scientists do not know about how the world works. The problem is that we are not using what they do know. I believe that the statements in this volume are based on the best science and best evidence we have. Indeed, in a book containing as much bad news as this, one must hope that some of it turns out to be wrong.

My fondest hope is that this will be a book widely read by young people. Those of us who began our careers in the environmental issues of the late 1960s and early 1970s are approaching retirement. I eagerly accepted Yale's offer to be dean of its environment school to make contact with the new generation and to contribute back what I have learned, so that they might benefit from what we got right and not repeat our numerous mistakes. The struggle to put economy and society on an environmentally sustainable path was joined more than three decades ago, and since then there have been periods of advance and periods of retreat. Even the periods of progress have fallen short of achieving a decisive overall victory: an irrevocable commitment to transition to sustainability. So the struggle goes on. It will soon become a new generation's struggle. We must help them get prepared for a difficult assignment. I see this book as part of that effort.

It has been said that people act out of love or fear—to realize a positive vision or to avoid disaster. This volume focuses on the looming disaster and how to avoid it. And the positive vision? You do not need me to provide it. You have seen it at Yellowstone, Yosemite, and the Smokies; when fishing for trout or spotting a bird or hiking the woodlands; in the salt marsh, the blackwater swamp, the grassland prairie, the urban park. You have seen it in the crisp air and clear water, the children playing in the stream, the sunset at the beach, the monarch butterflies on their way to Mexico, the birds newly arrived at the feeder, even the deer eating your sedum. It is part of you, and me, and we are part of it. And it will be there for our children and their children and so on forever if we have the wisdom to protect it.

Although this is not a long book, the list of colleagues who provided helpful advice and information is long, and I am deeply indebted to them. I wish profusely to thank and acknowledge the generous assistance of Tom Lovejoy, Tom Wilbanks, David Hunter, Jane Lubchenco, Raj Pachauri, Norman Myers, Marian Chertow, Hilary French, Simon Levin, Larry Susskind, Michael Teitelbaum, Carol Rosen, David Rejeski, Dan Esty, Kelly Levin, Ben Cashore, Fred Strebeigh, Michael Oppenheimer, Jon Beckmann, Michael Dove, George Woodwell, Steve Kellert, Peter Raven, Barbara Bamberger, Nicole Ardoin, Brenden McEneaney, Alexandra Ponette, Seth Cook, Al Sample, Lester Brown, Monica Araya, Maria Ivanova, Tad Homer-Dixon, John Williamson, Cameron Speth, Richard Sandbrook, Simon Upton, Mats Segnestam, Laura Jones Dooley, Paul Tebo, Bill Ascher, Dean Abrahamson, Peter Haas, Phil Shabecoff, Gordon Smith, Michael Northrop, Jesse Ausubel, Bjorn Stigson, Bob Repetto, Paul Raskin, Paul Ehrlich, Jonathan Lash, Colleen Carey, Vic Edgerton, Nigel Cross, Klaus Toepfer, Paul Harrison, Bill McKibben, Konrad von Moltke, Steve Charnovitz, Sylvia Karlsson, Jeff McNeely,

Herb Bormann, Ernst von Weizsäcker, Heather Creech, Walt Reid, Kilaparti Ramakrishna, Ellen Brennan-Galvin, John Wargo, Brad Gentry, Oran Young, Faye Duchin, Skee Houghton, Carl Safina, Steven Rockefeller, Jean Thomson Black, Douglas Kysar, Joe Spieler, Alan Brewster, Mark Ritchie, Strobe Talbott, Tim Wirth, David Runnalls, John Ashton, Kathy Courrier, Tom Parris, Shimi Anisfeld, and the anonymous readers assembled by the Yale University Press! I am more obviously indebted to all those whose works are cited in the notes. These books and articles contain a treasure trove of compelling information. In the end, of course, despite all this help, any flaws and failings that remain in the manuscript are the responsibility of the author alone. Last, I thank and praise Angela Kühne for her expert assistance in research and manuscript preparation.

Guilford, Connecticut

Prologue: 1980

What did the president know, and when did he know it? Senator Howard Baker, Watergate hearings, 1973

Red Sky at Morning tells a story, and we are its authors. The plot is driven by human propagation and poverty and even more by a vast and growing world economy. There is a beleaguered heroine, Mother Earth. The story's ending has not yet been written. There are two possible outcomes, one tragic and one not. A global crisis has unfolded quickly, and, as in classic Greek tragedy, we have been told what the future may hold, but so far we seem unable to step from the path to disaster that has been mapped out for us. The last act is about to begin.

A quarter century ago, scientists and others sounded the alarm regarding a set of linked threats to the global environment. Governments were put on notice, and, indeed, they acknowledged the issues and the need to address them. An "agenda" of large-scale threats was widely agreed upon and measures were put in place to address them. Yet the rates of environmental deterioration that stirred the international community continue essentially unabated today. The disturbing trends persist, and the problems have become deeper and truly urgent. The steps that governments took over the past two decades represent the first attempt at global environmental governance. It is an experiment that has largely failed.

It would be comforting to think that all the international negotiations, summit and conference agreements, conventions and protocols have at least got us to the point where we are now prepared to act decisively—comforting but wrong. The problems have gone from bad to worse; we are not yet prepared to deal with them; and many countries around the world lack the leadership to get prepared.

My exposure to global-scale environmental concerns began in mid-1977 when President Jimmy Carter asked the Council on Environmental Quality and the Department of State to prepare a report on "probable changes in the world's population, natural resources and environment through the end of the century." I was one of the three members of CEQ at that time and would later become its chair. It was a daunting assignment that took us several years to complete.[1]

While our interagency team was working away, I was approached by Gordon MacDonald, a top environmental scientist, and Rafe Pomerance, then president of Friends of the Earth. They were seeking my help in calling wide attention to an emerging problem that I was just beginning to understand—global climate disruption. I promised to take the matter to the president if they would prepare a reliable, scientifically credible memorandum on the problem. It was not long before the report was on my desk, signed by four distinguished American scientists—David Keeling, Roger Revelle, and George Woodwell, in addition to MacDonald. Its contents were alarming. The report predicted "a warming that will probably be conspicuous within the next twenty years," and it called for early action: "Enlightened policies in the management of fossil fuels and forests can delay or avoid these changes, but the time for implementing the policies is fast passing." The year was 1979.[2]

I soon presented the report to President Carter and others in his administration. The new Department of Energy reacted negatively. It was promoting a massive program of synthetic fuels to be made from coal, tar sands, and oil shale, and these synthetic fuels would produce more climate-altering gases than most other energy technologies. DOE promptly produced a countermemorandum.

The administration responded by asking the National Academy of Sciences to assess the scientific basis for concern about man-made climate change. Massachusetts Institute of Technology scientist Jule Charney led the NAS review, and the "Charney Report" was published in late 1979. Its findings supported those in the report I had received at CEQ. The chair of the NAS's Climate Research Board summarized them: "The conclusions of this brief but intense investigation may be comforting to scientists but disturbing to policymakers. If carbon dioxide continues to increase, the study group finds no reason to doubt that climate changes will result and no reason to believe that these changes will be negligible. The conclusions of prior studies have been generally reaffirmed. However, the study group points out that the ocean, the great and ponderous flywheel of the global climate system, may be expected to slow the course of observable climatic change. A wait-and-see policy may mean waiting until it is too late."[3]

Emboldened, we at CEQ focused our most intense scrutiny on the issue of global climate disruption. In my foreword to our report, prepared in 1980, we sought to explain the climate disruption issue and its seriousness to a large audience:

"In recent decades the concentration of carbon dioxide (CO_2) in the atmosphere has been increasing in a manner that corresponds closely with the increasing global use of fossil fuels. The burning of fossil fuels —oil, natural gas, and coal—releases carbon dioxide, about one-half of which appears to be retained in the atmosphere. The permanent clearing of forests and the decay of soil humus may also be net sources of carbon dioxide.

"Atmospheric carbon dioxide plays a critical role in warming the earth; it absorbs heat radiation from the earth's surface, trapping it and preventing it from dissipating into space. As the concentration of carbon dioxide in the atmosphere increases, more of the earth's radiated heat is trapped. Many scientists now believe that, if global fossil fuel use grows rapidly in the decades ahead, the accompanying carbon dioxide increases will lead to profound and long-term alteration of the earth's climate. These climatic changes, in turn, could have far-reaching adverse consequences, affecting our ability to feed a hungry and increasingly crowded world, the habitability of coastal areas and cities, and the preservation of natural areas as we know them today. . . .

"The carbon dioxide issue may present the ultimate environmental dilemma. Collective judgments of historic and possibly unique importance must be made—by decision or default—largely on the basis of scientific models that have severe limitations and that few can understand. To some, the competing factors will be seen as whether to provide the energy needed for economic and military security or whether to protect humanity from a distant and uncertain threat that currently affects no one. Further, addressing that threat will require a global effort in a world where international cooperation on the scale that may be required is seldom achieved.

"Yet, with atmospheric carbon dioxide already increasing and the pressures here and abroad to expand fossil fuel use, the world economy is well on its way to performing a great planetary experiment. Before the first results are known, our children and future generations may well have been irrevocably committed to an altered world—one that could be better in some respects but that also involves unprecedented risks.

"Clearly, a deeper appreciation of the risks of a carbon dioxide buildup should spread to leaders of government and business and to the general public. The carbon dioxide problem should be taken seriously in new ways: it should become a factor in making energy policy and not simply be the subject of scientific investigation. Every effort should be made to ensure that nations are not compelled to choose between the risks of energy shortages and the risks of carbon dioxide. This goal requires making a priority commitment here and abroad to energy efficiency and to renewable energy resources; it also requires avoiding a commitment to fossil fuels that would preclude holding carbon dioxide to tolerable levels. Steps should also be taken to slow the disturbing global deforestation now under way, particularly in the tropics, and to encourage the regrowth of forests. . . .

"One imperative we share is to protect the integrity of our fragile craft and the security of its passengers for the duration of our voyage. With our limited knowledge of its workings, we should not experiment with its great systems in a way that imposes unknown and potentially large risks on future generations. In particular, we cannot presume that, in order to decide whether to proceed with the carbon dioxide experiment, we can accurately assess the long-term costs and benefits of unprecedented changes in global climate.

"Whatever the consequences of the carbon dioxide experiment for humanity over the long term, our duty to exercise a conserving and protecting restraint extends as well to the community of life—animal and plant—that evolved here with us. There are limits beyond which we should not go in disrupting or changing this community of life, which, after all, we did not create. Although our dominion over the earth may be nearly absolute, our right to exercise it is not."[4]

These observations are more than twenty years old. For more than two decades even nongeniuses like myself have known not only the gravity of the climate challenge but also more or less what to do about it. And, of course, little has been done. We are still struggling to achieve international agreement on the first treaty with any teeth in it—the Kyoto Protocol—and it is only a beginning.

What can one conclude from this? Most obviously, current and past leaders have done a poor job on the climate change issue. We need to understand why. Once that is appreciated, we can figure out how to make the future different. If I were a young person being handed this problem by indulgent predecessors, I would be angry. For twenty years thoughtful people and intelligent leaders should have known that we needed to get busy. Precious time has been wasted. And now a new generation has been given a climate problem that is deeper and more difficult. Climate is already changing—nine of the ten hottest years since record-keeping began have occurred since 1990—and the time to begin responsive action has long passed.

The defenders of business-as-usual on climate change began twenty years ago by telling us that concern about global warming was not scientifically justified. A decade later they said, yes, concern is justified, but we have ample time to solve the problem. Now they are saying it is too late to prevent major climate change, and our best strategy is to adapt to it. Remarkably, the Bush administration moved through this string of evasions in half a presidential term. By contrast, the Clinton administration, which preceded it, acknowledged the problem from the outset but let eight years pass by doing little about it, although in fairness much of the blame must rest with Congress.

But global-scale environmental challenges truly moved into American politics when the broader report that President Carter had requested was released in 1980 as *The Global 2000 Report to the President*. We presented the trends that might unfold between 1980 and 2000 in population and environment if societies continued their business-as-usual approach. Already referred to by some critics as "Bad News Jimmy," President Carter showed courage in supporting this big dollop of gloom and doom in an election year.

From today's perspective, we can look back and see what actually happened. Unfortunately, many of our projections proved correct, at least approximately. *Global 2000* projected that population would grow from 4.5 billion to 6.3 billion by 2000. The actual number was 6.1 billion, so we were more or less on target. The report projected that deforestation in the tropics would occur at rates in excess of an acre a second, and for twenty years, an acre a second is what has happened. It projected that 15 to 20 percent of all species could be extinct by 2000, mostly due to tropical deforestation.[5] Biologists Stuart Pimm and Peter Raven have estimated conservatively that there are about seven million species of plants and animals. Two-thirds of these species are in the tropics, largely in the forests. They have estimated that about half the tropical forests have been lost and, with them, that about 15 percent of tropical forest species have already been doomed.[6] So there is evidence that our species loss estimate was perhaps high but not far off the mark.

Global 2000 projected that about six million hectares a year of dry-lands, an area about the size of Maine, would be rendered nearly barren by the various processes we describe as desertification. And that continues to be a decent estimate today.[7]

We predicted: "Rising CO_2 concentrations are of concern because of their potential for causing a warming of the earth. . . . If the projected rates of increase in fossil fuel combustion . . . were to continue, the doubling of the CO_2 content of the atmosphere could be expected after the middle of the next century . . . The result could be significant alterations of precipitation patterns around the world, and a 2 degree to 3 degree Celsius rise in temperatures in the middle latitudes of the earth."[8] Twenty-three years later, this description still falls neatly within the range of current estimates.[9]

I present these numbers not to pat our *Global 2000* team on the back. Some projections, like those on the prices of food and minerals, *Global 2000* got wrong, and the report had many shortcomings. But on most of the big issues of population and environment, the report pointed to the trends and the consequences. Other reports—from the United Nations Environment Programme, the Worldwatch Institute, the National Academy of Sciences, and elsewhere—were saying much the same around this time.[10] In short, the basics about emerging global-scale environmental concerns were known a quarter-century ago. Political leaders then and since have been on notice that there was a new environmental agenda—more global, more threatening, and more difficult than the predominantly domestic agenda that spurred the environmental awakening of the late 1960s and the first Earth Day in 1970.

Global 2000 also called attention to the important ramifications of environmental decline for human security and social stability, noting that environmental threats "are inextricably linked to some of the most perplexing and persistent problems in the world—poverty, injustice and social conflict." "Vigorous, determined new initiatives are needed if worsening poverty and human suffering, environmental degradation, and international tensions and conflicts are to be prevented," it concluded.[11] The 1980 Report of the Brandt Commission on International Development Issues was prescient in its plea for attention to these linkages: "War is often thought of in terms of military conflict, or even annihilation. But there is a growing awareness that an equal danger might be chaos—as a result of mass hunger, economic disaster, environmental catastrophes, and terrorism, so we should not think only of reducing the traditional threats to peace, but also of the need for change from chaos to order."[12]

President Carter first addressed global-scale environmental issues in February 1980 during the Second Environmental Decade Celebration in the East Room of the White House, noting that they were "long-term threats which just a few years ago were not even considered." He concluded on an optimistic note—"the last decade has demonstrated that we can buck the trends"—and shortly thereafter he requested that I, along with Secretary of State Ed Muskie, prepare a plan of action to do just that.[13] In January 1981 we issued our report, *Global Future: Time to Act*, a 198-page agenda of what the federal government could do to address the challenges identified in *Global 2000*.[14] By this time, of course, President Carter had lost the election, and our report became merely more fuel for the antienvironmental pyre of the early Reagan years.

Looking back over the past two decades, it cannot be said that my generation did nothing in response to *Global 2000* and similar alerts. Progress has been made on some fronts. There are outstanding success stories, but rarely are they on a scale commensurate with the problems. For the most part, we have analyzed, debated, discussed, and negotiated these issues endlessly. My generation is a generation, I fear, of great talkers, overly fond of conferences. On action, however, we have fallen far short. As a result, with the notable exception of international efforts to protect the stratospheric ozone layer, the threatening global trends highlighted a quarter-century ago continue to this day.

With more than two decades of dilatoriness behind us, it is now an understatement to say that we are running out of time. For such crucial issues as deforestation, climate change, and loss of biodiversity, we have already run out of time: appropriate responses are long overdue.

How could this have happened? And where do we go from here? These are the questions I address in the chapters that follow. Major changes are in order, changes that must be driven by a profound sense of urgency. Although time is short, we can build rapidly on hopeful developments that are beginning to appear. These positive signs of change are reported here along with the bad news. President Carter was right when he said, "We can buck the trends," but we had better get on with it.

No president since Carter has given priority to global-scale environmental challenges. The failure has been truly bipartisan. These issues more than most require true political leadership, which we have not yet had. But they also require changes that are far more sweeping and difficult than voting in a new slate of political leaders, as useful as that may sometimes be.

Part One Environmental Challenges
Go Global . . .

The destruction of the environment as a by-product of human enterprise is not new, but for most of our history it remained a localized and limited problem. The many forms of damage to the earth and its creatures increased in severity and scope during the Industrial Revolution. Yet it was not until just after World War II that the fast-forward button was pushed down and held.

Before we can understand why we have failed to act in our own and nature's interest, and what we can do to change, we need to examine what we are doing to the natural world. The degradation of our environment is multifarious and complex. If this phenomenon were personified, we might look to Greek mythology and find the snake-haired Medusa. And now, as then, will the result of the confrontation turn us to stone?

"Abandon all hope you who enter!" Dante placed this notice at the entrance to Hell. Some of the statistics in the following chapters are indeed hellish, but abandoning hope is precisely what we must not do. To despair when confronted with the challenges we have created would only assure a human and natural calamity we still have the power to avoid. There are solutions, but we will not seek them or appreciate their urgency unless we first understand the problems.

I A World of Wounds

I meant no harm. I most truly did not.
But I had to grow bigger. So bigger I got. Dr. Seuss

crisis *1*. Med. *That change in a disease that indicates whether the*
result is to be recovery or death. 2. The decisive moment; turning
point. 3. A crucial time.

We live in the twenty-first century, but we live with the twentieth century. The expansion of the human enterprise in the twentieth century, and especially after World War II, was phenomenal. It was in this century that human society truly left the moorings of its past and launched itself upon the planet in an unprecedented way.

Most familiar is the population explosion. It took all of human history for global population to expand by 1900 to a billion and a half people. But over the past century that many more people were added, on average, every thirty-three years. In the past twenty-five years, global population increased by 50 percent from four to six billion, with virtually all of this growth occurring in the developing world.[1]

Population may have increased fourfold in the past century, but world economic output increased twentyfold. From the dawn of history to 1950 the world economy grew to seven trillion dollars. It now grows by this amount every five to ten years. Since 1960 the size of the world economy has doubled and then doubled again.[2] Energy use moved in close step with economic expansion, rising at least sixteenfold in the twentieth century. One calculation suggests that more energy was consumed in those hundred years than in all of previous history.[3]

The twentieth century was thus a remarkable period of prodigious expansion in human populations and their production and consumption. Four consequences of these developments are important to note. *First,* while twentieth-century growth has brought enormous benefits in terms of health, education, and overall standards of living, these gains have been purchased at a huge cost to the environment. The enormous environmental deterioration is partly due to the greater scale of established insults: traditional pollution like soot, sulfur oxides, and sewage grew from modest quantities to huge ones. What were once strictly local impacts not only intensified locally but became regional and even global in scope.

Many previously unknown environmental risks also surfaced in the twentieth century. After World War II, the chemical and nuclear industries emerged, giving rise to a vast armada of new chemicals and radioactive substances, many highly biocidal in even the most minute quantities and some with the potential to accumulate in biological systems or in the atmosphere. Between 1950 and 1985 the U.S. chemical industry expanded its output tenfold. By 1985 the number of hazardous waste sites in the United States requiring clean-up was estimated to be between two thousand and ten thousand. The use of pesticides also skyrocketed during this period.[4] Today about six hundred pesticides are registered for use around the world, and five to six billion pounds of pesticides are released into the global environment each year.[5]

Turning from pollution to the world's natural resource base we find severe losses. From a third to a half of the world's forests are now gone, as are about half the mangroves and other wetlands.[6] Agricultural productivity of a fourth of all usable land has been significantly degraded due to overuse and mismanagement.[7] In 1960, 5 percent of marine fisheries were either fished to capacity or overfished; today 75 percent of marine fisheries are in this condition.[8] A crisis in the loss of biodiversity is fast upon us. A fourth of bird species are extinct, and another 12 percent are listed as threatened. Also threatened are 24 percent of mammals, 25 percent of reptiles, and 30 percent of fish species.[9] The rate of species extinction today is estimated to be a hundred to a thousand times the normal rate at which species disappear.[10]

Environmentalist Aldo Leopold wrote that "one of the penalties of an ecological education is that one lives alone in a world of wounds."[11] As is clear, there is a lot of bad news in the world of environmental affairs. Since Leopold wrote those words, alas, scientists have begun to study damage that he could not. Our world now suffers wounds beyond imagining at his death in 1948.

That said, in recent decades industrial countries have invested heavily in reducing a variety of well-known pollutants and in banning a number of severely risky substances such as leaded gasoline, DDT, and PCBs. Similarly, advances in agricultural productivity have reduced pressures to expand crop and grazing land into additional natural areas.

Second, the twentieth-century expansion is significant because it has pushed the human enterprise and its effects to planetary scale. This is the globalization of environmental impacts as well as economic activity. Human influences in the environment are everywhere, affecting all natural systems and cycles. Environmental writer Bill McKibben wrote in 1989 about what he called "the end of nature," by which he meant the end of the millennia in which humanity could view nature as a force independent of human beings.[12] Previously it was possible to think of nature as a place free of human control, an external and complex system sustaining life on earth, but the twentieth century brought us across a threshold to a new reality.

There are many measures of this new reality. Human activities have significantly depleted the earth's stratospheric ozone layer, thereby increasing the ultraviolet radiation that reaches the earth's surface and damaging both human health and ecosystems. Our use of fossil fuels —coal, oil, and natural gas—together with deforestation have increased the concentration of atmospheric carbon dioxide, a heat-trapping "greenhouse" gas, by about 32 percent and thus begun the process of manmade climate change.[13] Spring is arriving earlier, and species' ranges are shifting toward the poles.[14] Industrial processes such as the manufacture of fertilizers and other human activities now double the amount of nitrogen transferred from the atmosphere into biologically active forms,[15] with consequences that include the creation of at least fifty dead zones in the oceans, one the size of New Jersey in the Gulf of Mexico.[16] Each year human societies are appropriating, wasting, or destroying about 40 percent of nature's net photosynthetic product.[17] This output is the basic food supply for all organisms, so we are not leaving much for other species. Appropriation of freshwater supplies is similarly extensive, with widespread devastation of freshwater habitats.[18] More than 40 percent of the world's people live in river basins that suffer water stress.[19] By the mid-1990s, eighty countries with 40 percent of the world's population were experiencing serious water shortages.[20]

In terms of humans commandeering natural systems, our impact on the global climate machine is the most risky. In part because of fossil fuel use in the twentieth century, carbon dioxide in the atmosphere is now at its highest level in 420,000 years. While the public in the United States and especially abroad is increasingly aware of this issue, few Americans appreciate how close at hand is the widespread loss of the American landscape. The best current estimate is that, unless there is a major world correction, climate change projected for late this century will make it impossible for about half the American land to sustain the types of plants and animals now on that land.[21] A huge portion of America's protected areas—everything from wooded lands held by community conservancies to our national parks, forests, and wilderness—

is threatened. In one projection, the much-loved maple-beech-birch forests of New England simply disappear off the U.S. map.[22] In another, the Southeast becomes a huge grassland savanna unable to support forests because it is too hot and dry.[23]

Ecologist Jane Lubchenco, in her 1998 address as president of the American Association for the Advancement of Science, made the following observation: "The conclusions . . . are inescapable: during the last few decades, humans have emerged as a new force of nature. We are modifying physical, chemical, and biological systems in new ways, at faster rates, and over larger spatial scales than ever recorded on Earth. Humans have unwittingly embarked upon a grand experiment with our planet. The outcome of this experiment is unknown, but has profound implications for all of life on Earth."[24]

A similar point was made in an eloquent plea released a decade ago by fifteen hundred of the world's top scientists, including a majority of Nobel scientists: "The earth is finite. Its ability to absorb wastes and destructive effluents is finite. Its ability to provide food and energy is finite. Its ability to provide for growing numbers of people is finite. And we are fast approaching many of the earth's limits. Current economic practices which damage the environment, in both developed and underdeveloped nations, cannot be continued without the risk that vital global systems will be damaged beyond repair.

"We must recognize the earth's limited capacity to provide for us. We must recognize its fragility. We must no longer allow it to be ravaged. This ethic must motivate a great movement, convincing reluctant leaders and reluctant governments and reluctant peoples themselves to effect the needed changes."[25]

Third, the world economy's forward momentum is large. Economic growth will continue to expand dramatically in this century. With population poised to grow by 25 percent over the next twenty years, with people everywhere striving to better themselves, and with governments willing to go to extraordinary measures to sustain high levels of economic expansion, there is no reason to think that the world economy will not double and perhaps double again within the lifetimes of today's young people.

The next doubling of world economic activity will surely differ in some respects from the growth of the past. But there are good reasons to believe that that doubling could, from an environmental perspective, look a lot like the last. The pressures to persist with environmentally problematic technologies and practices are enormous. The U.S. Energy Information Agency projects that global emissions of carbon dioxide, the principal climate-altering gas, will increase by 60 percent between 2001 and 2025.[26] The Paris-based Organization for Economic Cooperation and Development estimates that its members' carbon dioxide emissions will go up by roughly a third between 1995 and 2020 if there is not major policy intervention,[27] while OECD motor vehicle use could rise by almost 40 percent.[28] During this same period, emissions of carbon dioxide outside the OECD are projected to go up 100 percent. Growing food demand is expected to increase the area under cultivation in Africa and Latin America, extending agriculture further into once-forested areas and onto fragile lands in semiarid zones. For this reason and others, countries outside the OECD are projected to lose another 15 percent of their forests by 2020.[29]

One area where growing populations and growing demands will come together to challenge us enormously is water—the supply of clean, fresh water. The United Nations' 2003 *World Water Development Report* concludes that twenty-five years of international conferences have yielded few solutions. A fifth of the world's people lack clean drinking water; 40 percent lack sanitary services. Between 1970 and 1990 water supplies per person decreased by a third globally and are likely to drop by a further third over the next twenty years absent a concerted international response.[30] Peter Aldhous, the chief news editor at *Nature*, puts the situation with water in perspective: "The water crisis is real. If action isn't taken, millions of people will be condemned to a premature death. . . . [P]opulation growth, pollution and climate change are conspiring to exacerbate the situation. Over the next two decades, the average supply of water per person will drop by a third. Heightened hunger and disease will follow. Humanity's demands for water also threaten natural ecosystems, and may bring nations into conflicts that—although they may not lead to war—will test diplomats' skills to the limit."[31] The U.N. report notes that to meet internationally agreed water supply and sanitation targets, 342,000 additional people will have to be provided with sanitation every day until 2015.[32]

Of course, economic growth can generate benefits for the environment, and has done so in many contexts. As people become wealthier, public support for a healthy environment and leisure activities based on nature increases. The press of the poor on the resource base can diminish as people live less close to the land. Governments of well-to-do countries tend to be more capable regulators and managers and can have more revenue for environmental, family planning, and other programs. There is no doubt that some important environmental indicators, such as sanitation, improve with rising incomes. But it is extraordinarily misguided to conclude from such considerations, as some do, that the world can simply grow out of its environmental problems. Were that true, the rich countries would have long ago solved their environmental challenges, and we would not have projections such as those just cited from the OECD and the United Nations. In developing countries undergoing rapid industrialization, new environmental problems (such as truly terrible urban air pollution and acid rain and smog over large regions) are replacing old ones. Collectively the environmental impacts of rich and poor have mounted as the world economy has grown, and we have not yet deployed the means to reduce the human footprint on the planet faster than the economy expands.[33]

The *fourth* and final observation about the economic expansion of the twentieth century follows from the preceding three: human society is in a radically new ethical position because it is now at the planetary controls. Scientist Peter Vitousek and his coauthors stated the matter forcefully in a 1997 article in *Science:* "Humanity's dominance of Earth means that we cannot escape responsibility for managing the planet. Our activities are causing rapid, novel, and substantial changes to Earth's ecosystems. Maintaining populations, species, and ecosystems in the face of those changes, and maintaining the flow of goods and services they provide humanity, will require active management for the foreseeable future."[34]

Scientists are a cautious lot, by and large, so when the most respected issue a plea for "active management of the planet," we should take careful notice. I do not think Vitousek and others who call for "planetary management" are suggesting that the uncontrolled planetary experiment we are now running can be made safe through flawless planning, more sophisticated human interventions, or large-scale engineering feats such as seeding the oceans with iron to draw more carbon dioxide out of the air. Rather, our responsibility is to manage ourselves and our impacts on nature in a way that minimizes our interference with the great life-support systems of the planet.

We know what is driving these global trends. The much-used "IPAT equation" sees environmental *Impact* as a product of the size of human *Populations,* our *Affluence* and consumption patterns, and the *Technology* we deploy to meet our perceived needs.[35] Each of these is an important driver of deterioration. However, what this useful IPAT formulation can obscure, in addition to the effects of poverty, is the vast and rapidly growing scale of the human enterprise.

Regarding this growth, here is what happened in just the past twenty years:[36]

Global population	up 35 percent.
World economic output	up 75 percent.
Global energy use	up 40 percent.
Global meat consumption	up 70 percent.
World auto production	up 45 percent.

| Global paper use | up 90 percent. |
| Advertising globally | up 100 percent. |

Today, the world economy is poised to quadruple in size again by midcentury, just as it did in the last half-century, perhaps reaching a staggering $180 trillion in annual global output. We probably could not stop this growth if we wanted to, and most of us would not stop it if we could. Close to half the world's people live on less than two dollars per day. They both need and deserve something better. Economic expansion at least offers the potential for better lives, though its benefits in recent decades have disproportionately favored the already well-to-do. Remember also that while growth is a serious complicating factor, even if we immediately stopped all growth in both population and economic activity, we would still bring about an appalling deterioration of our planetary habitat merely by continuing to do exactly what we are doing today.

The implications of all this are profound. We have entered the endgame in our traditional, historical relationship with the natural world. The current Nature Conservancy campaign has an appropriate name: they are seeking to protect the Last Great Places. We are in a race to the finish. Soon, metaphorically speaking, whatever is not protected will be paved. For biologists Pimm and Raven, the past loss of half the tropical forests will likely cost us 15 percent of the species there. Comparable rates of deforestation in the future would lead to much greater loss.[37] More generally, attacks on the environment of many types will likely be increasingly consequential. Whatever slack nature once cut us is gone.

Humans dominate the planet today as never before. We now live in a full world. An unprecedented responsibility for planetary management is now thrust upon us, whether we like it or not. This huge new burden, for which there is no precedent and little preparation, is the price of our economic success. We brought it upon ourselves, and we must turn to it with urgency and with even greater determination and political attention than has been brought to liberalizing trade and making the world safe for market capitalism. The risks of inaction extend beyond unprecedented environmental deterioration. Following closely in its wake would be widespread loss of livelihoods, social tensions and conflict, and huge economic costs.

2 Lost in Eden

I want to tell what the forests
were like
I will have to speak
in a forgotten language W. S. Merwin

The two megatrends in environmental deterioration are increasing pollution and biological impoverishment. Most of the outpouring of U.S. environmental legislation in the early 1970s was aimed at stopping pollution. But the year after Congress passed the Clean Water Act of 1972, it also passed a piece of legislation exceptional in its scope and audacity: the Endangered Species Act. Among its far-reaching provisions, this act made it unlawful for anyone to collect, kill, or otherwise harm any animal that was in danger of extinction, even on his or her own property. Suddenly, animals had rights, at least the right to survival as a species.

And thus was set in motion a series of fierce struggles—a struggle to get the act properly implemented, with real-estate developers around the country against it; a struggle to get the act reauthorized every few years, since Congress has always kept it on a short string; a struggle to find a lasting rationale for species protection that the American public would buy; and, above all, a struggle to save the country's biological wealth in the face of mounting pressures.

In 1982, testifying before Congress in support of the Endangered Species Act, biologist E. O. Wilson offered his oft-quoted defense: "The worst thing that can happen during the 1980s is not energy depletion, economic collapse, limited nuclear war, or conquest by a totalitarian government. As terrible as these catastrophes would be for us, they can be repaired within a few generations. The one process ongoing in the 1980s that will take millions of years to correct is the loss of genetic and species diversity by the destruction of natural habitats. This is the folly our descendants are least likely to forgive us."[1]

And why will they not forgive us? Many reasons have been offered over the decades for sustaining the earth's biological endowment. The earliest, and the one that seems to animate the Endangered Species Act, is the most challenging to our society and our habits of thought. It is a mere ethical proposition, namely, that we have ethical duties to the communities of plants and animals that evolved here with us. It is to Aldo Leopold that we must turn for this. In his *Sand County Almanac,* he launched what environmental historian Roderick Nash has called "one of the most remarkable ideas of our time: the belief that ethical standing does not begin and end with human beings."[2] Leopold's "land ethic," as he called it, "changes the role of homo sapiens from conqueror of the land-community to plain member and citizen of it. It implies respect for his fellow-members, and also respect for the community as such." "A thing is right," Leopold wrote, "when it tends to preserve the integrity, beauty and stability of the biotic community."[3]

The real revolution in Leopold's thinking was the proposition that we have "obligations to land over and above those dictated by self-interest" and that these obligations stemmed from an appreciation that humans and nature are ecological equals. If we have rights, nature must also. The life that evolved here with us should be allowed to live "as a matter of biotic right," Leopold wrote.[4]

Defending species on a one-at-a-time basis has proven politically treacherous, at least beyond the defense of bald eagles, bison, and other charismatic megafauna. This proved especially true since the first species to become a cause célèbre under the act were not the red wolf or even the ivory-billed woodpecker but a tiny fish called a snail darter and a woodland plant named furbish lousewort.

Nor was it scientifically sound to focus only on the individual species. As Leopold noted, the right focus is on the "community as such." Although individual species—elephants, rhinos, and many others—are indeed threatened by poaching, harvesting and the wildlife trade, it is entire plant and animal communities that are under the most serious assault. The principal cause of individual species loss by far is habitat destruction.

Biodiversity and Ecosystems

For both political and scientific reasons, therefore, the concerned community of scientists, nongovernmental organizations (NGOs), and others advanced a variety of broader concepts throughout the 1980s. They eventually decided on the concept we know and use today, biological diversity or biodiversity. It gathered strength in the 1980s and by the end of the decade had beaten the competition. (The word *biodiversity* does not appear in the *World Conservation Strategy* prepared in 1980 by the World Conservation Union and others, but it is prominent in those organizations' 1991 report, *Caring for the Earth: A Strategy for Sustainable Living.*)[5]

When the World Resources Institute and others issued the *Global Biodiversity Strategy* in 1992, we defined *biodiversity* as having three dimensions: the variety of genetically distinct populations within a given species; the ten million or so species of plants, animals, and microorganisms; and the diversity of ecosystems of which species are functioning parts.[6] This hierarchy had by then become the standard definition. To many, the biodiversity concept is now a shorthand way of referring inclusively to the great variety of plant and animal communities and their interactions.

Biologist Walter Reid, a former colleague at the World Resources Institute who is now leading the international Millennium Ecosystem Assessment, is among those who endorse this broad concept as the focus for both politics and on-the-ground conservation efforts. "The lack of action and the lack of a public constituency stem from the narrow definition of the problem," he has written. "The issue that has dominated public concern and policy response has been species extinction. . . . Although the threat of species extinction may be the best-known aspect of the biodiversity problem, another has far greater practical consequences for human livelihoods and U.S. interests: ecosystem change . . . [and loss in] the ability of these systems to meet human needs."[7]

The ecosystems concept is enormously powerful in explaining what is going on in today's world. The authors of the 2000–2001 *World Resources Report* have described the importance of ecosystems: "Ecosystems are the productive engines of the planet—communities of species that interact with each other and with the physical setting they live in. They surround us as forests, grasslands, rivers, coastal and deep-sea waters, islands, mountains—even cities. . . .

"The fact is, we are utterly dependent on ecosystems to sustain us. From the water we drink to the food we eat, from the sea that gives up its wealth of products, to the land on which we build our homes, ecosystems yield goods and services that we can't do without. Ecosystems make the Earth habitable: purifying air and water, maintaining biodiversity, decomposing and recycling nutrients, and providing myriad other critical functions."[8]

Yet they see the web of life fraying: "At this moment, in all nations —rich and poor—people are experiencing the effects of ecosystem decline in one guise or another: water shortages in the Punjab, India; soil erosion in Tuva, Russia; fish kills off the coast of North Carolina in the United States; landslides on the deforested slopes of Honduras; fires in the disturbed forests of Borneo and Sumatra in Indonesia."[9]

Many now believe that strong back on which to put the case for conserving biodiversity is ecosystem services, by which they mean the valuable goods and services that human societies derive from natural systems. The best way to save biodiversity, they contend, is to convince people that healthy ecosystems provide societies with a huge array of material benefits, some sold on the market but most not. I will discuss momentarily what these ecosystem services are and the efforts that have been made to put a dollar value on them. The point I wish to make here is that we have come a long way: from saving species because they have an independent right to continued existence to saving natural systems because they benefit us materially and economically. The purist might object to the idea that to save nature we must put a big dollar sign on it. Can it be true that the only way to save the marvelous natural world we inherited is to convince people that it is worth more economically alive than dead? To which some advocates of this approach will reply, "Yes, precisely. And the real question is whether even that will work." Stanford University's Gretchen Daily is optimistic. "The overall value of ecosystem services is so gigantic," she writes, "that their maintenance is bound to move toward the top of the international political agenda."[10]

It is indeed quite strange, when one thinks about it, that it should be necessary to convince anyone that nature's services are valuable. Where do some people think we get fresh water, food, forest products, nice climates, the great outdoors, the right kind of air to breathe, protection from ultraviolet radiation? We should just as well have to make the case for factories to purchasers of cars and televisions. Biologists Harold Mooney and Paul Ehrlich correctly observe that "ignorance of the services that natural ecosystems supply to the human enterprise— of the reasons that the economy is a wholly owned subsidiary of those systems—amounts to a condemnation of schools, colleges, universities and the print and electronic media."[11] This area is one of many where we are paying a high price for our neglect of environmental education at all grade levels.

An article by ecological economist Robert Costanza and his colleagues has identified some of the economic benefits of seventeen types of ecosystem services.[12] Interestingly, food production and other products recognized by the market constitute only a modest share of these economic benefits. The biggest of nature's contributions in their estimation is nutrient cycling: the breakdown and recycling of dead plants and animals into materials that enrich soils. Other ecosystem services included in the calculation include pollination, air and water purification, climate control, drought and flood control, and regulation of atmospheric chemical composition. The article is controversial because of the methodology used, and many believe that it understates the true value of nature's services, given their centrality to our lives and welfare. But it does underscore that there are many types of ecosystem services and that their economic contributions are huge, however measured.

I have touched on two reasons for preserving biodiversity: our ethical responsibilities and ecosystem services. There are many others, of course, for example, those related to human psychology and development. Personal encounters with nature yield huge nonmonetary benefits in human development, communication, well-being, and fulfillment. Our literary tradition from the Bible to Shakespeare and down to the present brims over with powerful natural images, settings, and analogies. ("Consider the lilies of the field, how they grow; they toil not, neither do they spin: and yet I say unto you, that even Solomon in all his glory was not arrayed like one of these.") Sociologist Stephen Kellert has written that "living diversity is still an unrivaled context for engaging the human spirit of curiosity, exploration, and discovery, in an almost childlike manner, independent of age."[13]

Along with E. O. Wilson, Kellert has championed the "biophilia hypothesis," which argues that people have a fundamental emotional dependence on nature and living diversity. Kellert notes: "Buried within the human species lies a deep and enduring urge to connect with living diversity. Nature offers an essential medium for our development, both individual and collective, a link that is as vital today as it was in the past. We evolved in the company of other creatures and in a matrix of conditions making this varied existence possible. And we continue to rely—physically, emotionally, intellectually—on the quality and richness of our affiliations with natural diversity.

"Over the millennia, humanity's affiliation with life and natural process conferred distinctive advantages in the human struggle to persist, adapt, and thrive as a species. During the long course of human evolution, we valued nature and living diversity because of the adaptive benefits it offered us physically, emotionally, and intellectually."[14]

The other side of this is the tremendous sense of loss that people feel when a part of nature that has been important in their lives is destroyed. Marine scientist Carl Safina begins his beautiful *Song for the Blue Ocean* with the "unfathomable catastrophe" that occurred when, as a child, he saw the bulldozers arrive on the shore where he and his father fished.[15] Many of us have had similar experiences.

Nature's Economy

Another set of reasons for protecting biodiversity stem from biodiversity's direct economic benefits in the marketplace. The nature-based economy is huge in terms of employment. Agriculture, fishing, and forestry are still responsible for one of every two jobs worldwide. Nature-based tourism and recreation is one of the world's biggest industries. People are less familiar with the many other economic benefits. Many oils, chemicals, rubber, spices, nuts, honey, and fruits are harvested in the wild. A third of all prescription drugs were derived from chemical compounds originally found in nature—digitalis, morphine, quinine, penicillin, and many more—including ten of the twenty-five best-selling drugs. The saliva of the vampire bat is used in treatment to unclog arteries. Ovarian and breast cancer treatments have been derived from the bark of the Pacific yew. A wormwood derivative is being tested on breast cancer with promising results. A tree in Argentina has yielded a compound that appears to attack the AIDS virus. Most plants and coral species have yet to be tested for their medicinal properties.[16]

Ninety percent of the calories we eat come from eighty plant species, domesticated from the wild. The wild relatives of these species are still reservoirs of genetic material that can be useful in disease and pest resistance, in developing more resilient varieties, and in other ways.

And now with the emergence of biotechnology, genetic materials found in nature are essential ingredients. Scientists have spliced spider genes into cows that can now produce spider-web protein in their milk. Fibers as strong as steel can be made from this material. Biomimicry can also lead to new products, like Velcro. Engineers are using the design of the ear of a rare fly, *Ormia*, to design hearing aids and listening devices. *Ormia* has incredibly accurate directional hearing. The economic potential in the genetic material of wild species is sufficient to have sparked a huge debate internationally over the ownership of materials derived from "bioprospecting"—that is, mining the corals and the forests for valuable genes. Glaxo, SmithKline, Aventis, and other pharmaceutical giants are now busily combing the Australian forests and report optimistically on finding compounds that could lead to new antibiotics and pesticides, as well as prostate cancer prevention.[17]

The case for conserving biodiversity would thus seem to be compelling, even overwhelming, since everything from ethics to biophilia to survival of the world as we know it is included. Yet what we have seen in fact is steady, relentless, large-scale biotic impoverishment. Let us turn now to these processes of impoverishment, their consequences, and what is bringing them about.

Threats to Biodiversity and Ecosystems

It is possible to specify at least nine separate but often interacting drivers of biotic impoverishment—nine principal threats to biodiversity and to healthy ecosystems.

Land use conversion. This is the biggest threat of all, and in this category the principal problem is the conversion of tropical forests to agricultural uses and tree plantations. Thirty-six nations lost 10 percent or more of their forest cover in the 1990s. Moreover, short of out-and-out conversion, forest richness is reduced by habitat fragmentation, fires, and other factors. The draining and filling of wetlands of all types is also another type of land conversion that has greatly reduced natural habitats. As noted, the best estimates we have are that at least a third of the earth's original forest cover has been cleared and about half the wetlands have been destroyed.

More than a third of the world's land surface has been converted to human use, and an additional third could be converted to human use in this century. About 12 percent of the earth's land is classified as "protected" in some variety of park or preserve, and much of this area remains threatened by logging and development pressures.[18]

Urbanization is also a major factor in land conversion. The conversion of agricultural lands, wetlands, and forests to urban and suburban uses is occurring rapidly in both industrial and developing countries. Sprawl is not exclusively a problem of the wealthy nations. In 1900, there were sixteen cities with over one million inhabitants. Today, there are around four hundred, nearly a hundred of them in China.

Land degradation. The productivity of crop and grazing land is threatened by water and wind erosion, by the salinization and waterlogging of irrigated lands, and by overgrazing and devegetation. Most severe in arid and semiarid regions, these processes often occur in combination, and their effects referred to as desertification. About three-fourths of the world's drylands are degraded, and about a fourth of all land is degraded to a degree sufficient to reduce its productivity.[19] Replacing depleted agricultural land is one of the drivers behind deforestation.

Freshwater shortages. As freshwater is diverted from watercourses for agricultural, urban, and industrial uses, natural in-stream habitat is lost or diminished, and water supplies that feed forests and other systems decline. An estimated 20 percent of normal river flow globally is now extracted for human use. Water withdrawals climbed sixfold in the twentieth century, twice the rate of population growth, and the trend continues. Freshwater withdrawals for irrigation and other purposes are estimated to grow by 40 percent by 2020. With 40 percent of the world's people already living in countries that suffer from serious water shortages, the prognosis for freshwater habitat is not good. The following rivers no longer reach the sea in the dry season: the Colorado, Yellow, Ganges, Nile, Syr Darya, and Amu Darya.[20] Is California an indication of things to come? Ninety percent of the state's wetlands have disappeared, and 60 percent of the native fish species are extinct or at risk of extinction.[21]

Watercourse modifications. Natural waterways are often dammed, channelized, or diverted, and the swamps and other wetlands associated with them drained or filled, with serious consequences for the biota associated with streams, rivers, and estuaries. Sixty percent of the world's major river basins have been severely or moderately fragmented by dams and other construction.[22]

Invasive species. Non-native, invasive species have emerged as the second most serious threat to biodiversity, after habitat destruction. For example, about 40 percent of all species listed in the United States today as endangered or threatened are so listed primarily because of the threat posed by invasives. Invasives now cover one hundred million acres across the United States and cost the country an estimated $137 billion annually.[23] Thousands of marine species move around the planet every day in the ballast water of cargo ships.

Overharvesting. This is the most serious threat to marine fisheries, including cod, bluefin tuna, Atlantic halibut, and salmon. Current logging rates threaten mahogany. The global market in birds and other wildlife is about ten billion dollars a year, and many species are taken at unsustainable rates. A fourth of the trade in wildlife relies on illegal poaching.[24]

Climate change. Human-caused climate change has not yet been a big factor in the loss of biodiversity, but that could change dramatically in coming decades. One study concludes that climate change could be this century's second most important threat to biodiversity, after land-use changes and habitat destruction.[25] Already, climate change has been linked at least tentatively to the decline of species-rich coral reefs, certain amphibians, polar species, winter flounder in Narragansett Bay, the North Sea cod, white spruce, and others. A major survey of the effects of climate change on ecosystems concluded that the thirty years of warmer temperatures at the end of the twentieth century have already affected the ranges and distributions of many species and that efforts of species to adjust to changing climate will be highly constrained by the rapidity of projected climate changes and the human domination of so much of the landscape.[26] Some researchers are worried that existing warming (about 1° F globally already) has the potential to tear ecosystems apart as different species move in different directions at varying rates, thus disrupting predator-prey and competitor interactions.[27]

Ozone depletion. The weakening of the earth's stratospheric ozone shield caused by CFCs and other chemicals affects biodiversity through the influence of the increased ultraviolet radiation reaching the earth's surface. Ultraviolet-B radiation affects plant growth, form, and biomass allocation; it can change the competition balance in ecosystems; and it can reduce the production of marine phytoplankton.

Pollution. Pollutants of many varieties threaten biodiversity. Toxic substances; oxygen-demanding wastes; nitrogen, carbon dioxide, and phosphorus overfertilization; acidification; and photochemical oxidants (ozone) all degrade the structure and functioning of aquatic and terrestrial ecosystems. I discuss pollution more fully in the next chapter.

Cumulatively, these nine direct, immediate causes of biotic impoverishment are operating on a global scale, stressing natural systems, homogenizing and simplifying them, and reducing biological diversity at a rate and scale not experienced for millions of years.

Data reveal that the global fish catch has shown a strong and consistent downturn every year since 1988 (once the highly volatile Peruvian anchoveta catch is out of the calculation).[28] Overfishing and nutrient pollution of the coastal seas are the main culprits.

Data on freshwater systems tend to be more local and national. One measure of the degree to which we have polluted, fragmented, and otherwise degraded natural waterways is the impact on aquatic life. In the United States aquatic species are the most at risk of all categories of species. In the Southeast 19 percent of the fish are at risk of extinction; in the Southwest the figure is 48 percent. And, as noted, almost 60 percent of California fish species are extinct or on the road to extinction if trends continue.[29]

Natural forests in the tropics disappeared at an annual rate of fourteen million hectares between 1990 and 2000, a rate of loss in excess of an acre a second.[30] (There is some recent evidence that the rate of loss may have been a fourth lower, but these results are preliminary and already the subject of hot debate.)[31] Between 1960 and 1990, about 20 percent of total tropical forest cover was lost.[32] In any case, the data on rates of forest clearing give an unduly rosy picture. The cumulative impacts of fire, El Niño–driven drought, and fragmentation in major forest areas, such as those in Brazil and Borneo, exacerbate the effects of deforestation. And much of what is left is under contract for logging. Eighty percent of Borneo's forest cover is estimated to be slated for future commercial logging and plantations.[33]

Coral reefs and the life on them are now at great risk due to the combined impacts of coastal development and pollution, tourism, global warming, and destructive fishing practices. A recent study found that about 60 percent of coral reefs were at medium to high risk due to a combination of these threats, and a five-year study by scientists and five thousand volunteers around the world found that coral reefs are in terrible shape. The survey found that overfishing has affected 95 percent of the more than one thousand reefs monitored since 1997. Spiny lobster, bumphead parrotfish, Nassau grouper, and other reef species have disappeared from most of the reefs surveyed.[34]

The cumulative consequences of all these forces for species survival are not encouraging. Robert May, president of the Royal Society in Britain, supports those who believe that "we are standing on the breaking tip of the sixth great wave of extinction in the history of life on earth." "It is different from the others," he notes, "in that it is caused not by external events, but by us."[35] The last great extinction episode occurred sixty-five million years ago with the obliteration of the dinosaurs, quite possibly because of a direct hit from a rather large asteroid. And, as ecologist George Woodwell has noted, "Long before extinction becomes important, genetically distinct, local ecotypes are lost and the natural communities in which they were developed become impoverished and dysfunctional."[36]

In this context one should take a deep breath and consider estimates (assembled by the World Wildlife Fund) on what we have done to North America:

Original tallgrass prairie	99 percent transformed
Original primary forests in the contiguous United States	95 percent lost
Old-growth forest of the Pacific Northwest	90 percent cleared
Original U.S. wetland area	50 percent drained or filled
Original U.S. species endowment	500 may be extinct[37]

The World Resources Institute has organized the most thorough global assessment to date on ecosystem health. Researchers there looked at agro-ecosystems, forests, freshwater systems, marine ecosystems, and grasslands. Their conclusion, after examining the status and trends in these five major ecosystem types, is as follows: "Overall, there are numerous signs that the capacity of ecosystems to continue to produce many of the goods and services we depend on is decreasing. In all five ecosystem types [we] analyzed, ecosystem capacity is decreasing over a range of goods and services, not just one or two. This downward trend in global ecosystem capacity is not impeding high production levels of some goods and services today. Food and fiber production have never been higher, and dams have allowed unprecedented control of water supplies. . . . Our use of technology—whether it is artificial fertilizer, more efficient fishing gear, or water-saving drip-irrigation systems

—has also helped mask some of the decrease in biological capacity and has kept production levels of food and fiber high. In sum, [our] findings starkly illustrate the trade-offs we have made between high commodity production and impaired ecosystem services, and indicate the dangers these trade-offs pose to the long-term productivity of ecosystems."[38]

Environmental sustainability requires living off nature's income, not consuming natural capital, at least not without replacing it. What WRI has described is the essence of unsustainability. If current trends continue, there will be large economic, social, and environmental costs to pay in the future. Already, many of the three billion people who live on less than two dollars a day are feeling these costs. They live what used to be called close to the land and have the least capacity to cope with ecosystem change, water shortages, and biological degradation. And, unfortunately, the poor are likely to be hardest hit in the future.

The Amazon

Perhaps the most dramatic setting for today's biodiversity drama is the Brazilian Amazon, home to 40 percent of the remaining tropical rainforests in the world. These forests are in turn home to the planet's greatest storehouse of biodiversity: 2.5 million species of insects, tens of thousands of plants, two thousand bird and mammal species. It is also a storehouse for huge quantities of carbon, safely there and not in the atmosphere contributing to global warming. The Amazon is also rich in cultural diversity: more than two hundred ethnic groups in the Amazon speak over 150 indigenous languages.[39]

For half a century now, this region has been the scene of both ecological and economic disaster. About 15 percent of the Brazilian Amazon, an area the size of France, has been lost to deforestation and today the deforestation in the Amazon dwarfs that of other countries around the globe. On average, about five million acres, an area the size of Connecticut, have been cleared every year, most of it illegally. Yet researchers have concluded that this clearing is only half the picture. They estimate that these deforestation rates capture only half of the Amazon forest area that is impoverished each year by what they call cryptic deforestation—forest loss due to logging and surface fires.[40]

These losses have been brought on by a variety of social and economic forces in Brazil: bad policies including tax breaks and other subsidies that have encouraged ranchers and farmers to develop the Amazon and kept uneconomical enterprises afloat; population pressures as Brazil's poor have moved to the region in search of land and livelihoods; loggers both legal and illegal (an estimated 80 percent of timber taken in the Amazon is illegally felled); and a further influx due to mining, road building, and other infrastructure development.[41] One analysis noted: "Human uses of tropical forests vary greatly in their ecological impacts. Ranchers and farmers 'deforest' land in preparation for cattle pasture and crops by clear-cutting and burning patches of forest. Loggers do not clear-cut and burn, but perforate forests by harvesting or damaging many trees."[42] The Amazon has it all.

Today in Brazil, a battle is under way for the future of the Amazon. On the positive side, a coalition of governments, the World Wildlife Fund, and other NGOs and international agencies have joined with Brazil to launch a new partnership, the Amazon Region Protected Areas Program, that should ensure that 500,000 square miles of the Amazon will be put under federal protection. This extraordinary effort is the largest-ever forest protection initiative, covering an area twice the size of the United Kingdom. Also hopeful, sustainable forestry seems to be taking hold in some of the Amazon, with significant operations shifting to reduced-impact logging and committing to sustainable forest management. In 2002 the Brazilian government announced plans to create a system of national forests in the Amazon, an area the size of Spain, where the focus will be on sustainable forest management. And the Brazilian government has moved to reduce handouts and tax breaks for developers and to suppress illegal logging with a new law.

On the other side of the ledger, illegal felling remains widespread, and the Brazilian government pushed the Advance Brazil program, which proposed to fast-track dozens of major infrastructure projects criss-crossing the Amazon, including new highways, railroads, gas lines, hydroelectric projects, power lines, and river channelization projects, amounting to over forty billion dollars' worth of investment in total. Between 30 and 40 percent of the region could be deforested or heavily degraded because of this development.

Rather than a future of mining, unregulated colonization, logging, land speculation, and soybean agriculture, conservationists suggest that the region's future lies in support for ecodevelopment and indigenous communities, ecotourism, high-value agroforestry and perennial crops, and low-impact forestry in designated areas.

We do not know how these forces will play out or what the outcome will be. This issue is joined, though. Gone are the days, at least in Brazil, where major government and private decisions affecting the Amazon would "just happen" without the public noticing. And it will be a tough, long fight, and a highly political one. For the present, in 2003, both the establishment of protected areas and deforestation have reached new highs.

Drivers of Deterioration

If we look at Brazil and elsewhere, we can ask ourselves: What are the forces and factors leading to deforestation and forest destruction in the tropics?

Historically, the principal reason for the loss of global forests has been clearing for agriculture. Of consequence recently are the pressures generated by large populations of the poor. They should be thought of as victims of economic systems that have not provided alternatives. As a result they are drawn to forested areas for shifting cultivation, farmland, and fuel-wood for use and sale. Extreme concentration of landholdings and lagging employment opportunities leave hundreds of millions in search of land. Governments often encourage these migrations or resettlements to relieve social tensions and population pressures. In some countries settlers can lay claim to land if they "improve" it by clearing the forest.

Serious consequences have followed the decisions of most governments to shift ownership and management of large forest areas to the central government. This has vitiated the traditional right of local communities to exercise customary law over the forests. The shift to the center has not been positive, on balance. Local, traditional controls over forest resources have been weakened, and central governments, even when well-intentioned, have typically been poor stewards. Centralization has opened the forests to heavy political and economic pressures.

Today, governments own almost 80 percent of the remaining intact forests in developing countries. Around the world, it is governments that are deciding what goes on in the forests. Some government giveaways of forest resources are the result of cronyism, corruption, or both. Many countries with high deforestation rates rank high in the international corruption index. Timber concessions in Indonesia, for example, have been awarded to loyal military officers for political reasons, and they have in turn forged partnerships with business groups to exploit their concessions. About three-fourths of Indonesia's timber trade is illegal. Bribes and corruption are rampant. The lowland forests of Sumatra and Kalimantan are projected to disappear within a decade. Asked why, an Indonesian professor of forestry replied simply, "Money, power, and politics."[43]

Deforestation is also the by-product of well-intentioned but misguided policies. Timber concessions—the right to take trees—have been granted at below market rates and without safeguards or requirements for good management. Government subsidization of projects like road building has further fueled both timber booms and large-scale settlement. Another favorite policy of forest-rich countries is to promote agricultural development and ranching in previously forested areas, often with government subsidies so deep that the enterprises would be totally uneconomical without them.

These pressures for forest destruction often have been worsened, not helped, by international factors. International development agencies like the World Bank, though much better today than in 1980, have poured many millions into dams, highways, power development, and transmigration schemes, all to the detriment of forest areas. Critics of globalization charge that economic globalization and the World Trade Organization are magnifying the trend toward expanded logging by encouraging high levels of foreign investment, weaker domestic regulation in the face of international competition, and loss of local community controls.[44]

Looking over this sad history, Roger Stone and Claudia D'Andrea conclude that the only solution, imperfect though it may be, is "the relatively simple act of allocating responsibility for managing and protecting forests to the local groups and communities that depend upon their healthy survival rather than on their destruction."[45] India has done a good job of slowing deforestation. The successes of community-based forest management there lend support to Stone and D'Andrea's recommendation. And the trend is certainly toward decentralization. Over the past fifteen years, the size of the forest area owned and administered by communities and indigenous peoples has more than doubled, to an area about seven times the size of France.[46]

This emphasis on local communities is a needed corrective, but international initiatives are needed as well. A World Wildlife Fund report has concluded that as little as one-fifth of the world's forests, an area twice the size of India, could provide all the commercial wood and fiber needed to meet future demand, if the area were intensively managed using sustainable forest-management principles. They urge the cooperation of ten large multinational companies to help make this happen. If there were agreement from the relevant stakeholders to proceed down this path, tremendous logging pressure could be taken off old-growth forests, fragile ecosystems, and areas of high conservation value.[47]

The U.N. Environment Programme released an important report in 2001 containing findings and recommendations that mesh well with those of WWF. Using a satellite survey of the world's remaining un-broken, mostly old-growth forests—"closed canopy" forests that to-gether comprise about 20 percent of the land area of the world—they found that 80 percent of these forests are located in only fifteen countries and, just as important, that in most of these forest areas there is little development or pressure. (China and India, among the fifteen, are ex-ceptions here.) UNEP called for concentrating significant conservation resources on these areas. In short, with only modest numbers of countries and international companies involved, we should be able to find a way to save the world's ancient, intact forests.[48]

Finally, a series of interesting proposals have been offered for using financial and other incentives to protect forests:

- commercial opportunities for low-income forest-based producers and communities have been identified, including commodity wood for construction and fuel, environmentally certified wood, high-quality timber, and nontimber forest products;[49]
- conservation concessions can be bought, like timber concessions (many forest lands in the developing world are being leased for tim-ber for fifty cents an acre a year!);[50] and
- direct payments have been proposed to "purchase" ecosystem ser-vices conservation easements, like those in widespread use in the United States today, or forest protection.[51]

If we build on these and other ideas, the international development assistance community can, I believe, have a major positive impact on deforestation in the tropics, but its success depends very much on the willingness of national authorities in tropical countries to address the issue with the full participation of the affected communities and groups in each country. Governments in the tropics would be urged to under-take reviews of what would be required to move from net deforestation to net afforestation, and they would be expected to do these reviews "bottom-up" involving local communities and other forest stakeholders. They would then develop a plan of action based on honest assessments of what is needed. Often very difficult and politically costly measures will be required of these leaders. In exchange, the industrial countries would stand ready to make helpful and supportive commitments. Part of each tropical country's plan would be to identify the support required from the international community. That support could take the form of development assistance and economic cooperation designed to take pressure off forest resources, incentives such as debt relief or debt swaps or trade and investment arrangements, agreements to support financially the establishment of parks and other protected areas, political and diplomatic support—indeed, whatever is required within reason to make it possible for the country's plan to succeed. Conservation (rather than timber) concessions could be purchased outright with international support, or donors might pay for conservation services provided by forests such as carbon sequestration, biodiversity and genetic reserves, and watershed protection, or other ideas might be adopted. In short, a North-South compact would be forged between the tropical country and its international partners and would be implemented jointly.

Finally, drawing on the adage that conservation without money is conversation, some calculations have been prepared on what it would cost to buy and manage a broadly representative system of protected nature reserves covering 15 percent of the global land area. The estimate is surprisingly small: about twenty-five billion dollars a year on top of the six and a half billion currently spent.[52] How much is twenty-five billion dollars? It is about what the wealthy OECD countries spend annually on pet food.

3 Pollution and Climate Change in a Full World

The most alarming of all man's assaults upon the environment is the contamination of air, earth, rivers and sea with dangerous and even lethal materials. Rachel Carson

Pollution has been around as long as humans have organized societies and carried out economic activity, though its effects have varied enormously in history. In one of the Star Trek films, Captain Kirk awakes from traveling through time and sees that he and his crew on the starship are, as hoped, orbiting earth. "Earth," he says, "but when?" To which Mr. Spock, checking his instrument panel, replies, "Judging from the pollution content of the atmosphere, I believe we have arrived at the latter half of the twentieth century." And indeed, in the film, they had. In fact, it is possible to use earth's pollution mix and atmospheric condition to determine the date with far greater accuracy than did Mr. Spock.

By definition, pollution is harmful—too much of something in the wrong place. In appropriate quantities, some potential pollutants are beneficial. Phosphates and other plant nutrients are essential to aquatic life; too much of these nutrients, however, and excessive vegetation depletes the water of oxygen needed by fish and other organisms. Carbon dioxide naturally in the atmosphere helps keep the earth warm enough to be habitable, but the buildup of vast quantities of excess carbon dioxide from fossil fuel use and other sources now threatens to alter the planet's climate and disrupt both ecosystems and human communities. Other pollutants, like dioxin and PCBs, are so toxic that even the smallest amounts pose health hazards, such as cancer and reproductive impairment. Still others are acceptable in some parts of the environment but problematic in others. CFCs came into wide use in part because they are so stable and safe to humans, yet because they are stable, they can travel all the way to the stratosphere, where they deplete the ozone layer that protects us from incoming ultraviolet radiation.

Releases of pollutants to the environment are most often the casual by-product of some useful activity, such as generating electricity or raising cows. Pollution of this type is a form of waste disposal. It occurs when it is cheaper for the polluter to pollute than to take alternative measures—a calculation historically skewed in favor of pollution since the atmosphere and waterways have been treated as free disposal sites. But releases of pollutants can also be purposeful, as with pesticides, where biocidal substances are released into the environment to reap economic rewards. Or pollution can be accidental, as in oil spills, where the polluters themselves suffer loss.

Today, pollution is occurring on a vast and unprecedented scale worldwide. It is pervasive, quite literally, affecting in some way virtually everyone and everything. The changes in pollution in the past century are best described in terms of four long-term trends.

From Modest to Huge Quantities

With the twentieth century's increases in population and economic activity came huge changes in the volume of pollutants released. Consider how increased use of fossil fuel influences sulfur dioxide and nitrogen oxide emissions. These two products of fossil fuel combustion are among the principal sources of smog and other urban air pollution; they are also the pollutants that give rise to acid rain. Between 1900 and 2000, annual sulfur dioxide emissions grew sevenfold globally; nitrogen oxide emissions globally grew even more rapidly.[1]

Another gas formed by burning fossil fuels is carbon dioxide, the principal greenhouse gas implicated in global warming and climate change. As a result of human activity, annual global emissions of carbon dioxide increased almost fivefold in the past century, and annual carbon dioxide emissions globally have tripled since 1950.[2]

These examples of sharp increases in the volume of pollution in the twentieth century could be multiplied by many others. The generation of hazardous wastes globally has grown sixtyfold since World War II.[3] In the United States, the mountains of garbage and other solid wastes grew by 50 percent between 1980 and 2000, and now exceeds 230 million tons annually, only about a fourth of which is recovered.[4] About 2.5 billion pounds of toxic wastes are released annually in the United States, according to the federal Toxics Release Inventory.[5] So the twentieth century was a century of vast increases in the quantity of pollutants imposed on a finite environment.

Since 1970, with the new wave of domestic pollution legislation, the volumes of some major pollutants have declined in industrial nations. The discharges of both chemical wastes and sewage into waterways have been reduced in OECD countries, sometimes sharply. The banning of lead in gasoline dramatically reduced human exposure to lead. Emissions of sulfur oxides and particulates, two principal air pollutants, are also down significantly. Between 1980 and 2000, sulfur dioxide emissions declined by 37 percent in the United States and by 56 percent in Europe (but they increased by 250 percent in Asia).[6] Air quality in urban areas in the United States and Europe is much improved.

An important pattern revealing the impact of economic growth is reflected in what has happened to nitrogen oxide emissions in the United States. Regulatory controls under the Clean Air Act have reduced nitrogen oxide emissions greatly from what they would have been, but the over-all increase in fossil fuel use has offset these gains, so that total emissions today are not much below what they were in 1970 when the Clean Air Act was written.[7] There are other reasons for not declaring total victory. The Environmental Protection Agency announced in 2002, thirty years after the Clean Water Act set the goal of "fishable and swimmable waters by 1985," that more than a third of surveyed rivers and half of the lakes and estuaries were too polluted for fishing and swimming.[8]

From Gross Insults to Microtoxicity

Before World War II, concern with air and water pollution focused primarily on smoke and sewers, problems people have grappled with since the dawn of cities. The traditional public health threats—killer fogs like the one that sickened thousands and killed twenty in Donora, Pennsylvania, in 1948 and bacteria-laden water supplies for urban areas —were serious concerns. Buildings coated with soot and grime, and streams thick with algae and pathogens, were typical signs of trouble.

The emergence of the chemical and nuclear industries fundamentally changed the exclusive focus on gross insults. Paralleling the dramatic growth in the volume of older pollutants, such as sulfur dioxide, has been the introduction since World War II of new chemicals and radio-active substances, many of which are highly toxic even in minute quantities and some of which persist and accumulate in biological systems or in the atmosphere.

The synthetic organic chemicals industry is largely a product of the past half-century. The industry hardly existed before World War II, but between 1950 and 1985 its annual U.S. production grew from about 24 billion to 225 billion pounds.[9] Organic compounds (those that contain carbon) occurring in nature are the basis of life, but over the past fifty years, tens of thousands of synthetic organic compounds have been introduced into the environment as pesticides, plastics, industrial chemicals, medical products, detergents, food additives, and other commercially valuable products. Life as we know it would hardly be the same without these products, but the development of the chemical industry has also given rise to a vast and, to many, a frightening array of new products that are harmful to people, nature, or both.

Today several hundred new chemicals are introduced commercially each year.[10] Of roughly eighty thousand chemicals in trade today, about half are thought to be definitely or potentially harmful to human health.[11] This estimate is largely guesswork because, amazing as it may sound, few toxicity data are publicly available for most of these chemicals, almost all of which are synthetic organic chemicals. Former CEQ chair Russell Peterson used to say that chemicals aren't protected by the Bill of Rights; they're guilty until proven innocent. But this application of the precautionary principle (which says that regulatory action need not await full scientific certainty where major potential risks are involved) remains the exception, not the rule. The U.S. Environmental Protection Agency has reviewed the data available on 2,863 commercial-scale synthetic chemicals. For 43 percent there was a complete absence of basic toxicity data; full testing and data were available for only 7 percent.[12] Leadership in dealing with these gaps is now coming from where much of the new century's environmental leadership hails: Europe. In 2003 the European Commission, the executive body of the European Union, announced plans to require extensive testing of thousands of the most commonly used chemicals on the market.[13]

Pesticides, a major product of the modern chemicals industry, are released into the environment precisely because they are toxic. Political scientist John Wargo has described the scale of the pesticide challenge: "In [the last] century, several hundred billion pounds of pesticides have been produced and released into the global environment. Nearly five billion pounds of the insecticide DDT alone have been applied both indoors and out since it was introduced in 1939, and DDT is only one of nearly six hundred pesticides currently registered for use in the world. By 1969, almost sixty thousand different products were sold containing some combination of pesticides along with their inert ingredients. As we [enter] the twenty-first century, an additional 5 to 6 billion pounds of insecticides, herbicides, fungicides, rodenticides, and other biocides are added to the world's environment each year, with roughly one-quarter of this amount released or sold in the United States."[14] It has been estimated that far less than 1 percent of this material may actually reach a pest.[15]

Despite all this pesticide use, we still lose 25 to 50 percent of global crop production due to pests and spoilage. Part of the problem is that five hundred or so species of insects and mites and 150 plant pathogens have become resistant to various pesticides.[16] Another factor is that the international community has focused much more attention on increasing production than on minimizing postharvest losses.

Some recent developments are worth noting. First, the international community finally got around in 2001 to regulating a group of twelve persistent organic pollutants, or POPs.[17] Most, for example DDT and PCBs, were outlawed decades ago in the United States and many other countries. It has been known for a long time that these POPs were showing up everywhere on the globe. In the Arctic, the breast milk of Inuit mothers contains POPs at levels five times those in industrial countries.[18] Most of the substances regulated under the POPs treaty are pesticides like DDT; dioxins are also included. Like many of the most dangerous substances, the twelve POPs addressed in the treaty were mostly chlorinated hydrocarbons.

It is very good to have this agreement, at least if enough countries ratify it so that it goes into effect, but it is a classic case of delayed response. The Children's Health Center of the Mount Sinai School of Medicine has noted that today, using current blood tests, nearly every person on earth can be shown to harbor detectable levels of dozens of POPs. The doctors note that the long-term health consequences of POP mixtures "remain largely a mystery." "We are all involuntary subjects in a vast worldwide experiment in which each day we are exposed to hundreds of chemicals, many of which have been shown to cause harm, and many of which have never been tested."[19]

Inorganic chemicals, notably the heavy metals, are also receiving international attention. An assessment by the U.N. Environment Programme on mercury's threat to human and wildlife has led to an international plan to help reduce mercury releases, most of which come from coal-burning power plants.[20] Mercury is a potent neurotoxin that persists and accumulates in the environment. Though helpful legislation is before the U.S. Congress to reduce mercury emissions, it is doubtful that anything short of international action will suffice. The majority of mercury emissions come from developing countries, and perhaps a third of the atmospheric deposits of mercury in the United States come from sources outside the country.[21]

Public exposure to mercury occurs primarily from consuming contaminated fish. California authorities in 2003 sued twenty national restaurant chains for not warning customers of high levels of mercury in swordfish, tuna, and other fish. The restaurant chains said they had requested the state to sue them to avoid their being sued by environmentalists.[22] Only in America!

Early concern about toxic chemicals centered on cancer, respiratory ailments, and disease-causing pathogens. But recently attention has been called to other categories of more subtle health effects, such as impairment of the reproductive and immune systems. One of these newer concerns is the disruptive impact that plasticizers, pesticides, and other industrial chemicals might be having on hormones in both humans and wildlife. Much recent attention has focused on these "endocrine disrupting substances" (EDSs), sometimes called "gender benders" because many of them act like the female sex hormone estrogen, and exposure in males can lead to feminization, lowered sperm count, and hermaphroditism. There is a hot dispute over how serious the problem actually is outside the laboratory. The Mount Sinai Center reports that EDSs are everywhere, in the tissues of every animal on earth. While acknowledging the large uncertainties that remain, the Mount Sinai researchers believe that "enough evidence has accumulated to justify moving aggressively to limit environmental dispersion of endocrine disruptors."[23] The split in opinions on EDS risks is reflected in two recent reports from the national science academies in the United States and the United Kingdom. The U.S. academy panel left open the verdict on health risks, but the U.K. panel called for worldwide action.[24] In 2003, the U.S. Environmental Protection Agency announced an aggressive program to protect drinking water from atrazine, an EDS that is also one of the most widely used herbicides.[25]

There is also growing concern over developmental and neurological toxins, such as the fire retardant polybrominated diphenylether, that may contribute to learning disabilities, birth defects, attention deficit disorder, retardation, and autism. These problems are increasingly widespread, but large uncertainties regarding their causes remain. Twelve million American children suffer one or more developmental, learning, or behavioral disabilities. Nearly three-fourths of the twenty most-used toxic chemicals are known or suspected developmental neurotoxicants.[26] The journal *Science* reported in 2003 that a Canadian government study of Inuit children found that "for the first time, long-standing villains such as pesticides, PCBs and mercury have been linked to weakened immune systems and developmental deficits."[27]

We know little about the cumulative, long-term consequences of all chemical exposures on people. We know even less about what the Chemical Revolution has done to natural systems. Rachel Carson's *Silent Spring,* published in 1962, concerned both people and natural systems.[28] The book begins by quoting John Keats: "The sedge is withr'd from the lake, / And no birds sing." The peregrine falcon, the bald eagle, and the brown pelican were on their way out before *Silent Spring* ignited a campaign that led to the banning of DDT, aldrin-dieldrin, and other pesticides in the 1970s. We should thank Rachel Carson whenever we see the remarkable pelican hurling itself beak-first into the water just beyond the surf. But we should also acknowledge that the cause to which she summoned us is still at best half-won.

From First World to Third World

A myth still held by some is that pollution is mainly a problem of the highly industrialized countries. Although it is true that the industrial countries create the bulk of the pollutants produced today, pollution is an enormous problem in developing countries, and many of the most dramatic and alarming examples of its consequences are found there. This is true whether we focus on such older problems as sewage, sanitation, and indoor air pollution or on such modern problems as pesticides, heavy metals such as mercury, and other toxic chemicals.

Industrial and energy growth have brought the panoply of traditional air pollutants to the developing world—in spades. Devastating levels of air pollution now recur in many growing developing countries, particularly in megacities. Among the world's most polluted cities are New Delhi, Beijing, Mexico City, Shanghai, Calcutta, and Rio de Janeiro. These cities and many others in the developing world are plagued by gross air pollution levels that greatly exceed recommended limits from the World Health Organization.[29]

The developing world is also the scene of the worst water pollution today. Megacities generate mega-sewage, and the all-too-common pattern is discharge without treatment. Only about 10 percent of India's cities have sewage treatment, and water contaminated by human wastes is one of the biggest killers in the developing world.[30]

Another indication of the growing pollution potential in the developing countries is the rapid expansion of the chemical industry in these countries. Pesticide use in developing countries is accelerating rapidly; developing countries now consume about half of all insecticides.[31] As a result, Third World populations now rank high in their exposure to toxic chemicals. In a sample of ten industrial and developing countries, three of the four countries with the highest blood lead levels of their populations were Mexico, India, and Peru; for the same ten countries, DDT contamination of human milk was highest in China, India, and Mexico. In another comparison of the dietary intake of cadmium, lead, and aldrin-dieldrin, the only developing country in the sample ranked at or near the top for each of the three.[32]

Last, the developing world is now also the scene of many environmental spills and accidents. Perhaps the worst chemical accident in history occurred in Bhopal, India, in 1984: more than two thousand people were killed. The accident occurred when a chemical used in the manufacture of pesticides, methyl isocyanate (MIC), escaped and drifted into crowded, low-income settlements that adjoin the Union Carbide facility. The one positive consequence of this accident was heightened care in the international chemicals industry.

From Local Effects to Global Effects

Nothing better illustrates the broadening perspective of pollution from a local affair to a global one than the evolution of concern about air pollution. Global use of fossil fuels, and the resulting emissions of traditional pollutants such as sulfur and nitrogen oxides that result from it, continue to climb. Acid rain and smog on a regional scale, as well as other consequences of these pollutants, are damaging plant and animal life over significant areas of the globe. Depletion of the stratosphere's ozone layer, despite dramatic reductions in CFC use, continues to reveal itself annually in the Antarctic ozone hole. And, most serious of all, the buildup of greenhouse gases in the atmosphere—largely a consequence of the use of fossil fuels, deforestation, and certain industrial chemicals and agricultural activities—continues, threatening societies with far-reaching climatic changes, rising sea levels, extreme weather events, and other consequences.[33] These interrelated atmospheric issues constitute the most serious pollution threat in history.

Acid Rain

The view of air pollution as primarily an urban problem was first challenged by acid rain. The atmosphere transports many air pollutants hundreds of miles before returning them to the earth's surface. During this long-distance transport, the atmosphere acts as a complex chemical reactor, transforming the pollutants as they interact with other substances, moisture, and solar energy. Under conditions that are common, emissions of sulfur dioxide and nitrogen oxides from fossil fuel combustion are transformed chemically in the atmosphere into sulfuric and nitric acids.

Acid deposition remains a problem in Europe and North America, and it has emerged as a major issue in parts of Asia and Latin America. Many adverse environmental effects have been attributed to it, including damage to buildings and exposed metals. But attention has focused mainly on acid rain damage to the natural environment, particularly the acidification of lakes and streams. Thousands of lakes have "gone acid" and, in effect, died or declined as a result of widespread acid deposition in northern Europe and North America. Despite three decades of efforts to reduce sulfur and nitrogen oxide pollution, data from the United States indicate that little actual recovery of lakes and soils has occurred. Researchers have concluded that deep cuts in these pollutants emissions will be needed if full recovery is to be expected in the next twenty-five years.[34]

Moreover, some dimensions of the problem have expanded. Although acid deposition is still seen as the primary atmospheric agent damaging aquatic ecosystems, other air pollutants, including smog, can join in contributing to crop damage and forest problems. Air pollution has been implicated in large-scale forest die-offs in southwestern China, and the World Bank estimates that the cost of air pollution in China's forests and crops exceeds five billion dollars annually.[35] Japan, India, the Republic of Korea, and Thailand also have regions with serious pollution damages to crops and forests.[36]

Asia is also the scene of another recent example of once-local air pollution becoming a regional or even global threat. Scientists have detected a huge pollution cloud that forms periodically over the Indian Ocean. Its composition resembles suburban air pollution in the United

States and Europe, except that it reflects higher levels of biomass burning, such as the use of wood and dung for energy. The cloud stems from the huge increase in fossil fuel use and biomass burning in South and East Asia. These scientists conclude that further economic growth could make the situation more serious than U.S. air pollution in the bad old days of the 1970s. They have observed that "unless international control measures are taken, air pollution in the Northern Hemisphere will continue to grow into a global plume across the developed and the developing world."[37]

Loss of Protective Ozone

Ozone (O_3), a variant of oxygen, is present throughout the atmosphere but is concentrated in a belt around the earth in the stratosphere. Ozone in the troposphere (nearest the earth's surface) is a component of smog, and it adversely affects human health and plant life. Yet ozone is a valuable component of the upper atmosphere, where it acts as a filter, absorbing harmful wavelengths of ultraviolet radiation (UV-B). Without this radiation shield, more UV-B radiation would reach the surface of the earth, and would damage plant and animal life and increase the risk of skin cancers and eye disease.

In 1974, two University of California scientists, Mario Molina and F. S. Rowland, postulated that the widespread use of CFCs—highly stable compounds used in aerosol propellants, refrigeration, foam-blowing, and industrial solvents—could damage the ozone shield. They hypothesized that CFC gases could add chlorine to the stratosphere and, through complex chemical reactions, reduce the amount of stratospheric ozone, allowing more harmful UV-B radiation to reach the earth's surface.

This hypothesis profoundly affected both the CFC industry and national governments. The United States, Canada, and Sweden first banned inessential uses of CFC propellants, and several other countries followed suit. As a result, world production of the two major chlorofluorocarbons decreased in the late 1970s. They then began climbing again in the early 1980s, renewing international concern.

In 1985, when British scientists reported a dramatic seasonal thinning of the ozone shield over Antarctica—the now famous "hole" in the ozone layer—the debate switched into high gear. At its largest, the hole was roughly the size of Russia and Brazil combined.

I discuss in chapter 4 how the international community has responded to the ozone-depletion problem with precedent-setting international agreements, the 1985 Convention for the Protection of the Ozone Layer and its 1987 Montreal Protocol, which have now required the virtual elimination of CFCs and bromine-containing halons in the industrial countries. The Montreal Protocol now moves to focus on the developing countries, which are responsible for much of the remaining emissions. With the cooperation of the developing nations, scientists estimate that the ozone layer could fully recover by midcentury.[38] The ozone hole should begin closing in the coming decade. We do live in a world of wounds, as Aldo Leopold noted, but this wound is healing.

Global Climate Disruption and Energy Policy

For the past quarter-century, the international scientific community and others have been sounding ever-louder warnings that earth's climate, the climate that has sustained natural and human communities throughout history, is now seriously threatened by atmospheric pollution.

The 1997 Kyoto Protocol to the Convention on Climate Change is the first international treaty with any teeth in it that seeks to address this issue. In its simplest terms the Kyoto Protocol would require that, around 2010, industrial countries reduce their greenhouse gas emissions to a level, on average, at least 5 percent below what those emissions were in 1990. Elaborations of the protocol allow countries to take credit for reductions they accomplish outside their borders and for carbon absorbed by forests and other so-called sinks.

When the Bush administration rejected the Kyoto Protocol, the domestic and international criticism it received prompted the administration to take the same step that the Carter administration took twenty-two years earlier: to refer the matter to the National Academy of Sciences. The answer the administration received from the NAS was not welcomed, I believe, because it supported the scientific consensus that the problem is indeed real.[39] The NAS report concluded that:

- Greenhouse gases are accumulating in earth's atmosphere as a result of human activities, causing temperatures to rise. Global average temperatures warmed by about 1° F in the twentieth century and could increase by 2.5° F to 10.5° F in this century.
- Human-induced warming and sea-level rise are expected to continue throughout this century and into the next.
- This warming is caused by the cumulative effects of several greenhouse gases that have built up steadily in the atmosphere, including carbon dioxide from fossil fuel combustion and deforestation, methane from fossil fuels and agricultural activities, nitrous oxide from agricultural activities and the chemical industry, and specialty chemicals including CFCs.
- Global warming could well have serious adverse societal and ecological impacts by the end of this century, and temperature and sea levels could also continue to rise well into the next century even if societies stabilize the levels of greenhouse gases in the atmosphere.

Let's leave the scientific generalizations for a moment and consider some of the things that are in store if we do not act quickly to halt the buildup of climate-changing gases. Almost all of us will soon face changes in the world we have come to know. I grew up fishing the tidal creeks that ribbon through the salt marshes of coastal South Carolina. An emerging tradition near Charleston, South Carolina, is the Low-country Fishing Tournament, a fund-raising event for the Cystic Fibrosis Foundation that brings fishermen, myself included, to the beautiful coastal marshes of that region in search of spot-tailed bass and sea trout. Sea-level rise, one of the more certain consequences of climate change, would likely lead to the loss of much of these salt marshes. Already, between 1985 and 1995, the southeastern states have lost more than thirty-two thousand acres of coastal salt marsh owing to development, sea-level rise (already up six inches), subsidence, and erosion.[40]

A study by the Pew Center on Global Climate Change describes what could happen: "In salt marsh and mangrove habitats, rapid sea-level rise would submerge land, waterlog soils, and cause plant death from salt stress. If sediment inputs were limited or prevented by the presence of flood-control, navigational, or other anthropogenic structures, marshes and mangroves might be starved for sediment, submerged, and lost. These plant systems can move inland on undeveloped coasts as sea levels rise on sedimentary shores with relatively gentle slopes, but seaside development by humans would prevent inland migration. Marshes and mangroves are critical contributors to the biological productivity of coastal systems and function as nurseries and as refuges from predators for many species. Thus their depletion or loss would affect nutrient flux, energy flow, essential habitat for a multitude or species, and biodiversity."[41]

My wife and I took our SCUBA certification exam in a bar in the British Virgin Islands listening to Jimmy Buffett tapes, and there is not much that we find more moving in nature than the life on a coral reef. Yet coral reefs are another likely coastal casualty of climate change. They are already threatened by abusive fishing and tourism, pollution, and invasive species. Changes in seawater chemistry caused by climate change could decrease coral growth. Modest ocean warming can lead to coral bleaching, the breakdown of the symbiotic relation between the coral animal and the algae that live with coral tissues. Increased coastal erosion could silt up coral habitats. Before 1998, an estimated 11 percent of the world's known reefs had been destroyed by human activities, but the warming associated with the 1997–1998 El Niño event severely damaged another 16 percent, and coral reef scientists are resetting their agendas to focus more on climate change.[42] Indeed, painful to say, some observers believe that most of the world's coral reefs are already doomed. Scientists estimate that sustained global warming in excess of 1° C (about 2° F)—an amount of warming almost certainly already in the pipeline—would cause coral bleaching to become an annual event in most oceans, with severe effects on coral life.[43] The two most serious coral bleaching events ever recorded at the Great Barrier Reef Marine Park, off the Australian coast, occurred recently, in 1998 and 2002.[44]

My hometown, the old colonial town of Guilford, Connecticut, is full of sugar maple trees. Their red and yellow magnificence in the autumn is a small part of the show that draws thousands to this region during that season. Yet the results of ecological modeling show that climate change in the second half of this century, if it is not slowed, will largely eliminate maple trees and the maple sugar industry from New England.[45]

I have a lovely book in my living room about Vermont in wintertime.[46] It was given to me by my daughter, who attended Middlebury College in that beautiful state. The text, written by poet Jay Parini, begins, "'People come here from around the country to see what Christmas ought to look like,' says Marsh Franklin, a farmer near Ludlow. 'They expect snow—lots of snow.'" And, indeed, each of Richard Brown's evocative photographs of outdoor Vermont in winter is a scene of snow. Climate change would alter these scenes. Winters would be milder, and there would be less snowfall. Ski areas are already being warned that maintaining snowpack will be difficult. An increase in winter temperatures of 2° C in the Green Mountains will likely cause large snowpack reductions.[47]

Snow and ice may be the canary in the mine for climate disruption.[48] If so, it would appear that the canary is fast keeling over. Near the ski resort of Saint Moritz in Switzerland, a large dam is being built to hold back not water but the anticipated collapse of a cliff due to melting permafrost.[49] Thawing permafrost is now widespread in northern latitudes and is itself a further source of greenhouse gases as carbon is released from once-frozen soils.[50] Mount Kilimanjaro's famous snowcap is now projected to be gone by 2020: Kilimanjaro's glaciers, measured at five square miles in 1912, have now shrunk to one square mile.[51] A sad joke at Glacier National Park in Montana is: What should the new name of the park be? Melting glaciers high in the Himalayas are creating unstable lakes that threaten to burst and endanger the lives of tens of thousands of people.[52] There and elsewhere, glacial melt could also diminish essential summer water supplies in the valleys and plains below. These water supplies are absolutely critical in many places. In northern Pakistan, for example, glaciers are known to be the source of life and are thought of as spirits and worshipped. Alaska has seen unprecedented winter mudslides. Much of the state is built on permafrost, and its melting could force the state into expensive infrastructure. The Iditarod sled-race in 2003 had to begin in Fairbanks; there was not enough snow in Anchorage.

The Arctic seems to be the epicenter for climate changes. More warming is expected there than anywhere on earth. Since the 1970s, the floating Arctic icecap has thinned by almost half. The area covered year-round by sea ice diminished about 10 percent a decade in the 1980s and 1990s; at that rate, it will disappear altogether in coming decades.[53] But scientists are still trying to sort out natural trends from man-made ones. One of the climate models used in the Arctic Climate Impact Assessment Program wipes out Arctic ice in the summer of 2050; others see sharp declines in Arctic ice (which would open the long-sought Northwest Passage) in the latter half of the century.[54] The consequences for Arctic life would be profound. As researchers reported in *Science:* "If this trend continues, in 50 years the sea ice could disappear entirely during summers—possibly wiping out ice algae and most other organisms farther up the food chain, including polar bears. Whether or not that Arctic nightmare comes true, temperature fluctuations and winds driving the melting are already making many cold-weather creatures uncomfortably warm. And melting is bringing a new threat: people and their machines."[55]

A further risk, at the other end of the earth, is the possible melting of the grounded ice of the giant West Antarctic Ice Sheet (WAIS). British and Norwegian scientists have estimated that there is a 5 percent chance that the WAIS will disintegrate sufficiently because of global warming that sea levels will rise three to six feet over the next two hundred years.[56] That, of course, would be devastating. What if your home and your possessions had a 5 percent chance of being lost in a fire? You would surely take big steps to reduce that risk dramatically.

Perhaps most alarming, a National Academy of Sciences report of 2002 predicts that we are likely to see surprises, sudden shifts, and even drastic upheavals in global climate and its impacts: "Recent scientific evidence shows that major and widespread climate changes have occurred with startling speed. . . . [G]reenhouse warming and other human alterations of the earth system may increase the possibility of large, abrupt, and unwelcome regional or global climatic events."[57] Even though almost all the effects of climate change are estimated, assuming gradual warming, with change unfolding over the twenty-first century, the truth is that climate change may be more like throwing a switch than turning a dimmer.

The scientists with the International Geosphere-Biosphere Program concur: "The evidence is now overwhelming that [rising temperatures] are a consequence of human activities. . . . [W]e are now pushing the planet beyond anything experienced naturally for many thousands of years. The records of the past show that climate shifts can appear abruptly and be global in extent, while archaeological and other data emphasize that such shifts have had devastating consequences for human societies. In the past, therefore, lies a lesson."[58]

Scientists at the Woods Hole Oceanographic Institution believe that the most likely mechanism for abrupt climate change is disruption of ocean currents such as the Gulf Stream.[59] Fossil evidence shows that the Gulf Stream has shut down in the past, quickly, and plunged the North Atlantic region (not just Europe) into a dramatically cooler era. Today's computer models suggest that a shutdown of the Gulf Stream would produce winters twice as cold as the worst winters on record in the eastern United States. What might cause this devastating regional cooling? Global warming and other factors are melting northern ice and causing a dramatic increase in freshwater released into the North Atlantic. This "freshening" is well under way. Indeed, according to the Woods Hole scientists, it is *the largest and most dramatic oceanic change ever measured in the era of modern instruments.*[60] The mechanism by which this extra freshwater could disrupt the Gulf Stream is complicated, but basically the fresher water could both block the Gulf Stream's release of heat and disrupt the ocean currents that pull the warm waters of the stream northward. Scientists reported that rivers were dumping 7 percent more freshwater into the Arctic Ocean in 2002 than in the 1930s, citing global warming as a likely cause.[61]

The impacts of climate change will not, of course, be confined to the northern latitudes. Important asymmetries exist between the countries of the well-to-do North and those of the poorer South. The industrial countries have contributed far more to the buildup of greenhouse gases —the United States alone is responsible for 30 percent—and they have reaped huge economic benefits in the process. The United States now emits the same amount of greenhouse gases as 2.6 billion people living in 151 developing nations. Yet the developing world is more vulnerable to climate change. Its people are more directly dependent on the natural resource base, more exposed to extreme weather events, and less capable economically and technologically to make needed adaptations. If these North-South differences are not addressed with great care, they could easily emerge as an increasing source of international tension. Within societies, the disruption of water supplies or agriculture, as well as rising sea levels and other impacts, could easily contribute to social tensions, violent conflicts, humanitarian emergencies, and the creation of ecological refugees.

Extensive biodiversity loss; extreme weather events such as extraordinary droughts, floods, heat waves, and hurricanes; abrupt regional cooling; sea-level rise; coral bleaching; public health risks; and major new social stresses within and between countries—all are among the many predicted consequences of climate change. Future generations will focus on the following number just as we follow quarterly economic reports today: the amount of carbon dioxide in the atmosphere, measured in parts per million (ppm). Many of the serious environmental consequences—such as those noted in chapter 1 and here—would likely follow if atmospheric carbon dioxide concentration rises from today's 370 ppm to an unacceptable 650–700 ppm in 2100. (The pre-industrial level was about 280 ppm.)[62]

The central goal of the international climate protection treaty signed in 1992 is to prevent this number from rising to a "dangerous" level. Brian O'Neill and Michael Oppenheimer, of Brown and Princeton Universities, respectively, have undertaken an important effort to define "dangerous."[63] In *Science,* they assert that it would indeed be dangerous to risk catastrophic sea-level rise associated with the melting of the West Antarctic Ice Sheet or the disruption of such major ocean currents as the Gulf Stream.

To contain these risks, O'Neill and Oppenheimer conclude that nations should prevent carbon dioxide concentrations from exceeding about 450 ppm. In a business-as-usual scenario, earth is scheduled to reach this level by about 2030, and most observers believe that achieving this goal is impracticable, particularly given the long lead-times involved in changing the energy system. Certainly, this goal cannot be achieved without an early and major international response. The difficulty of the goal does not, however, make missing it less dangerous.

To realize the ambitious goal of halting the buildup of carbon dioxide at 450 ppm or below, O'Neill and Oppenheimer suggest that U.S. compliance with the Kyoto Protocol would be enormously helpful. The Kyoto Protocol, which President George W. Bush rejects but which the nations of Europe, Japan, and Canada now support, would require that U.S. carbon dioxide emissions be reduced to 7 percent below their 1990 level by 2010.

Conventional wisdom holds that complying with Kyoto's goals would be prohibitively costly for Americans, and no doubt full U.S.

compliance would come with a significant price tag at this late date. In an earlier era, the United States did one thing that is now needed. During the years 1973–1986, as a result of oil price shocks and energy efficiency policies, overall energy efficiency in the United States improved by an annual rate of 2.5 percent. It is often thought that these were years of poor economic performance, but between 1970 and 1988, the American economy expanded at a real rate of 3.3 percent per year. Comparable energy efficiency gains, together with switching to natural gas, afforestation, emissions trading, and rapid deployment of available renewable energy technologies, would allow the United States to participate meaningfully in the Kyoto process.

The United States should join the Kyoto process both because America is the largest emitter of climate pollution and because, for all its flaws, the Kyoto Protocol is the best means we have for beginning to reduce climate-altering emissions. The Kyoto Protocol has also forced development of many of the concepts, programs, and procedures that will be needed for the long haul. It is doubtful, moreover, that the developing nations will act on their emissions unless the industrial nations —both richer and the source of most of the climate problems we face —validate the seriousness of the issue and demonstrate their commitment to action by taking the first steps. The Kyoto Protocol, which currently applies only to the industrial countries, follows this approach. If the United States stays out of the Kyoto Protocol, the process could collapse in the next phase, the so-called second commitment period. For all these reasons and others, it is irresponsible for the United States to not ratify the Kyoto Protocol.

That said, there were almost certainly better ways to proceed on climate change than the approach taken in the Kyoto Protocol. More manageable and less susceptible to abuse would have been a simpler scheme that focused first on reducing carbon dioxide emissions from the energy sector in industrial countries and on greatly increasing efficiency of fossil fuel use in the developing countries, leaving international emissions trading and land-use contributions for a subsequent round. (Specialty chemicals like hydrofluorocarbons could be regulated under the Montreal Protocol; tropical forests deserve their own initiatives.)

Looking ahead, it is difficult to exaggerate the scale of the challenge climate change poses to the United States. In the decades ahead the United States and other industrial nations will likely be pressed hard by the developing countries to accept the proposition that the world should move toward equalization of national per capita emissions of carbon dioxide and other greenhouse gases. Today, industrial countries account for about 70 percent of carbon dioxide emissions, about 3.3 tons per capita. By contrast, the developing countries emit the rest at only 0.5 tons per capita. If the idea of eventual equalization among nations becomes an objective, and societies also pursue the climate-friendly goal of preventing carbon dioxide concentrations from exceeding 450 ppm, it follows that industrial countries will have to decrease their carbon emissions per person more than tenfold during this century. Since U.S. emissions are about twice the industrial country average, U.S. per capita emissions would have to decline twentyfold over this century, or by about 95 percent.[64] (Developing nations' carbon emissions per person would also have to be lower in 2100 than they are today, though only slightly.) Even if the far-reaching goals of equalization and stabilization at 450 ppm are not fully adopted, the implications are clear: the Kyoto Protocol goals for the United States represent no more than a modest down payment on what will eventually be required of us.

To achieve this transformation from very high to very low carbon emissions, thus avoiding extraordinary climate risks, two far-reaching shifts in energy technology and policy will be required:

- Societies will have to shift from extraordinarily wasteful use of energy to extraordinarily efficient, precise energy use. Engineer and industrial ecology pioneer Robert Ayres estimates that nineteen of every twenty units of energy generated in the United States go to waste.[65] Not all of it can be captured for useful purposes, but much of it can—and much more than we currently use. Fuel efficiency in transportation can be increased severalfold with such available technology as hybrid cars, fuel cells, light but strong space-age composite materials, and aerospace-related integrated design that reduces the need for heavy steel frames. Heating and air conditioning needs in new buildings can be reduced by as much as 90 percent by modern insulation, triple-glazed windows with tight seals, and passive solar design. In power generation, efficiencies can be greatly increased through combined-cycle (gas and steam turbines) and co-generation (combined heat and power) technologies. And these innovations are only the beginnings of what is possible.

- Societies will also have to move from a mix of fuels that is carbon intensive (relying heavily on coal and oil) to one with very low emissions of carbon for every unit of energy produced. Here, there are several potential paths forward: (1) shift to natural gas—its combustion produces less carbon dioxide per unit of energy than coal or oil; (2) shift to renewable energy sources, including wind, solar thermal, photovoltaic cells, biomass (including organic wastes), and hydropower; and (3) shift to nuclear power, fission and fusion.[66]

Another path forward is beginning to receive considerable attention from scientists and engineers. This option—carbon sequestration—involves extensive capture of carbon far beyond that possible by trees and other vegetation. This approach presumes that a fossil or biomass energy source is used. Chemical processes are then deployed to remove the carbon from coal, from smokestacks, or even from the air. The resulting carbon compounds are then deposited ("sequestered"), presumably safely and permanently, in the oceans, on land, or underground.[67]

My view is that prospective climate change is so risky and carbon dioxide stabilization at safe levels so demanding that virtually all these approaches will be required in some form or other in the decades ahead. We will not find a magic bullet or a simple solution. Nor will all solutions be free of significant environmental costs. The best one can say for some is that they will be better than climate disruption.

The public policies needed to move impressively in these directions have been developed and, indeed, have been presented repeatedly over the past two decades. One review of the large potential for renewable energy in the United States advocated targeted R&D funding, tax incentives, vehicle fuel economy standards, energy efficiency standards for buildings and equipment, renewable energy goals for electric utilities, regulatory reform, and removal of subsidies supporting the fossil and nuclear power industries.[68] Drawing on a Department of Energy study, this survey indicated that a wide array of renewable power technologies should be competitive with coal by the decade 2010–2020, even without policy measures to change their economic competitiveness.[69]

The potential for renewable energy to meet U.S. energy needs is widely underappreciated. Wind power is becoming competitive with coal-fired electricity generation today. Stanford engineers Mark Jacobson and Gilbert Masters have calculated that deploying about 250,000 new wind energy turbines in the United States could eliminate the need for almost two-thirds of U.S. coal-fired electricity generation. To provide a sense of the significance of such a shift from coal to wind, they estimate that it would reduce U.S. carbon dioxide emissions to the Kyoto Protocol goal of 7 percent below 1990 levels. They further calculate that the space required for this deployment would only be a square 120 miles on a side of open farmland or ocean.[70]

Wind energy has already emerged as a significant and rapidly growing component of energy systems in Europe, and the United States is beginning to catch up. In 2001 Denmark was halfway to meeting its goal of generating 30 percent of its energy from wind. Germany is the world's largest wind-power nation. Its wind machines produce electricity equivalent to about ten large (1,000 megawatt) nuclear power plants.[71] Modern wind machines are safer for birds and less noisy than early versions. Investors take notice: a power company controlled by Warren Buffett announced in March 2003 that it plans to build in Iowa the largest land-based wind-power farm in the world.[72]

Another renewable power technology with great promise for the future is photovoltaic (PV) energy. Not yet competitive, its potential is enormous. John Turner of the U.S. National Renewable Energy laboratory in Colorado puts it this way: "A square 100 miles on a side would, during one year, produce the energy equivalent to that used annually in the entire United States. Although 10,000 square miles is a large area, it is less than one-quarter of the area that this country has covered with roads and streets. If wind is added to the energy mix, this area for PV is reduced (in fact, the United States also contains enough usable wind resources to produce all of the electricity used by the nation); if geothermal energy is added, the PV area is even smaller, and if hydroelectric energy is added, the area is again smaller. The point is clear—we can gather more than enough renewable energy to power our society."[73]

The other area where new energy technology can contribute enormously to meeting climate change and other environmental challenges is in transportation. Already gasoline-electric hybrids are on the market, getting better than 45 miles per gallon (mpg). Over fifty years, a fuel economy standard of 40 mpg in the United States would save fifteen times more oil than the Arctic National Wildlife Refuge in Alaska is likely to produce. Unfortunately, in 2001 U.S. fuel economy fell to 20 mpg, its lowest level in two decades.[74]

Auto manufacturers in Japan, Europe, and the United States are among the many who are betting that one day we will be driving automobiles with electric motors powered by hydrogen-consuming fuel cells. Producing the hydrogen, containing it, getting it to vehicles, and using fuel cells (or, alternatively, modified internal combustion engines) to consume it all remain significant challenges, but the potential benefits are enormous. If design features that allow a vehicle to get 45 mpg are combined with fuel cells, the vehicles should be able to exceed the equivalent of 80 mpg while producing water as the only tailpipe emission. Many observers believe that the next energy carrier will be hydrogen and that the "hydrogen economy" may be only decades away. Fuel-cell vehicles are expected to enter mass production within a decade or two, and renewable energy sources of hydrogen should be also competitive within that time frame.[75] But many questions, economic and environmental, remain unanswered, and fuel cells in the future are no substitute for increased fuel economy today.

The United States has about a hundred thousand gas stations. The shift from what we have to a new system will not be easy. Another big challenge will be "leapfrogging" these new technologies into the developing world, where growth rates in the number of vehicles and of vehicle miles traveled will continue to be high. By 2015, greenhouse gas emissions from transport in the developing world are likely to exceed those in the industrial countries, unless special steps are taken.

Finally, coal is still in the race and is likely to stay there. In early 2003, the Bush administration announced an initiative (called Future-Gen) with the coal and power industries to build an advanced power generation facility that begins with coal gasification, produces electricity with a fuel cell, and sequesters at least 90 percent of carbon emissions. This initiative, if successful, would not solve environmental problems associated with coal mining and transport, but improvements on it could conceivably open the door to continued use of coal as a low-pollution fuel. Given America's huge coal reserves and the political power of the "coal states" in American politics, this initiative is not a bad idea if sufficient attention is given to the challenges of permanently sequestering the carbon dioxide generated by the coal gasification process. Some caveats must go with this endorsement: federal energy R&D spending should be fairly distributed among all solution-oriented technologies, renewable and nonrenewable; energy should not be subsidized at all, but, if it is, the subsidies should favor those energy technologies with the lowest environmental impacts; and we should not sit around waiting on this new coal technology—wind energy, efficiency improvements, and other green measures are already available.

There are rays of hope that things are beginning to change on the energy policy front. Perhaps the brightest of these rays is that more than half the U.S. states are pursuing initiatives that reduce greenhouse gas emissions. New Hampshire and Massachusetts have legislation to

cut power plant emissions of carbon dioxide; California has moved to regulate carbon dioxide emissions from auto exhausts; New Jersey has committed to reducing its greenhouse gas emissions to several percent below 1990 levels by 2005; Oregon has established carbon dioxide emission standards for new power plants. On the renewable energy front, Iowa plans to get 10 percent of its energy from renewable resources by 2015, and Texas has a renewable energy portfolio requirement of 2,000 megawatts of renewable power capacity in this decade, among others.[76]

If more states head in these directions, congressional action should not be far behind, and indeed action in Congress is beginning. Early in 2003, Senators Joe Lieberman and John McCain introduced legislation to curb global warming by establishing a market-based emissions credit trading system that will reduce greenhouse gas emissions. The legislation, which is modeled after the successful acid rain trading program of the 1990 Clean Air Act, would require a reduction in carbon dioxide emissions to the 2000 level by the year 2010, and a reduction to 1990 levels by the year 2016. In other words, U.S. emissions in 2016 would be "capped" at the level that existed in 1990. The bill would apply to emissions from key sectors—electricity generation, transportation, industry, and commercial, which together account for 85 percent of overall U.S. greenhouse gas emissions. These goals are much weaker than those in the Kyoto Protocol, but, if enacted, they would put the United States on the right track. The "cap and trade" approach is an excellent way to proceed. We must hope that this legislation or something like it passes the Congress soon. Another source of pressure for climate action is likely to come from the courts. Citizens, states, and other parties injured by climate disruption could seek redress in court. In 2003 several northeastern states sued the Environmental Protection Agency under the Clean Air Act for failing to regulate carbon dioxide as a pollutant.

One factor that should drive renewed interest in energy policy in the United States is our continuing dependence on foreign oil, now up

to 55 percent of U.S. consumption. A 2002 Department of Energy report forecast increased dependence on oil from Saudi Arabia and other Middle Eastern producers over the coming two decades.[77] Phil Clapp, president of the National Environmental Trust, summed up our vulnerability in a wonderful bit of overstatement: "The entire world economy is built on a bet of how long the House of Saud can continue."[78] Interestingly, *Business Week* broke with many of its advertisers in February 2003 with its cover story "Getting Smart About Oil." The magazine powerfully advocated a farsighted energy policy for the United States. On its agenda:

- Boost industrial energy efficiency. A leader in this area, 3M Corporation has cut its energy use per unit of output by 40 percent since the OPEC oil embargo and is still improving it at 4 percent a year;
- Raise car and truck fuel efficiency. Require new SUVs and pickup trucks to achieve forty miles per gallon, and oil savings will be over two million barrels a day within ten years, about 10 percent of current use;
- Nurture renewable energy. The United States should catch up with northern Europe, where wind already provides almost 20 percent of power needs, and we should set a renewable energy goal of 15 percent of total U.S. energy, up from the current 6 percent, with a deadline;
- Phase in fuel taxes. The cover story also advocates a gradually increasing tax on oil and gasoline consumption so that their prices to businesses and consumers reflect their true costs—including security and environmental costs.[79]

It is encouraging to see *Business Week* recommending this "soft" energy agenda. Amory Lovins urged us in the same direction long ago, in 1976, in a farsighted *Foreign Affairs* article, "Energy Strategy: The Road Not Taken?"[80] His letter to *Business Week* in response to the cover story did not gloat. It said simply, "Your sensible energy prescription becomes even easier and more profitable with four additions: 1) More than

200 uncounted 'distributed benefits' make decentralized power sources about tenfold more valuable (www.smallisprofitable.org). 2) Tripled-to quintupled-efficiency cars, like the uncompromised 99-mpg midsize SUV developed in 2000, needn't cost more: Ultralight materials and integrative design can make big savings cheaper than incremental ones (www.hypercar.com). 3) Such vehicles' lower propulsive load makes fuel cells small enough to afford even at early prices, permitting a rapid, profitable hydrogen transition using existing technology (www.rmi.org/images/other/HC-StrategyHCTrans.pdf). 4) Win-win policies such as revenue-neutral car 'feebates' and rewards for scrapping inefficient cars can command broad bipartisan consensus (www.nepinitiative .org)."[81] Lovins has persisted with these themes for a quarter-century, and slowly but surely he is gathering important converts.

An Addition to the Environmental Agenda

What could be the next big global-scale pollution issue? Earth's atmosphere is mostly nitrogen, bound together as N_2 and not reactive. Bacteria such as those associated with legumes "fix" nitrogen, changing it to a biologically active form. But here is the problem: we humans have started fixing nitrogen, too, industrially, and today humans are fixing more nitrogen than nature does. Once fixed, nitrogen remains active for a very long time, cascading through the biosphere.[82]

Basically, the anthropogenic nitrogen is coming from two sources: 75 percent from fertilizers and 25 percent from fossil fuel combustion. Nitrogen fertilizers are often ammonia-based; their use is a huge global enterprise. Ninety percent of this fertilizer is wasted, though, ending up in waterways and in the air and soil. High-temperature combustion in power plants oxidizes the nitrogen to produce a variety of nitrogen oxides.

Nitrogen in waterways leads to overfertilization and, when heavy, to algal blooms and eutrophication—aquatic life simply dies from lack of oxygen. Nitrate in ground and surface waters is also a threat to

human health. And there is another pathway. Forty percent of the world's grain goes to feed livestock, which produce vast volumes of nitrogen-rich manure, much of which ends up in the water. All this extra nitrogen is also having effects on biodiversity and natural systems —shifting the species composition of ecosystems by favoring those that respond most. Absent corrective action, nitrogen added to waterways is projected to increase 25 percent in the OECD and 100 percent in the developing world between 1995 and 2020.[83]

In the air, nitrogen oxide from fossil fuel combustion reacts with volatile hydrocarbons and sunlight to produce smog, a nasty mix of photochemical oxidants, one of which is ozone. It can also become nitric acid and contribute to acid deposition. Ozone (from smog) and nitrous oxide (from fertilized soils) are greenhouse gases, so nitrogen fixation also contributes to global warming. As the 2001 Statement of the International Nitrogen Conference notes, biologically active nitrogen can "contribute to smog, fine particle formation, visibility impairment, acid deposition, excess nutrient inputs to estuaries and near-coastal waters, global warming, and stratospheric ozone depletion."[84] Essential to life and necessary in our gardens and agricultural fields, nitrogen is the classic case of too much of a good thing.

The problem is truly global. Asia now contributes 35 percent of the world's synthetic nitrogen. Serious though this problem is, it has yet to attract the attention that CFCs or carbon dioxide have received. Physicist Robert Socolow at Princeton is among those calling for some type of international nitrogen management agreement: "As the agriculture and food system evolves to contain its impacts on the nitrogen cycle, several lessons can be extracted from energy and carbon: one, set the goal of ecosystem stabilization; two, search the entire production and consumption system (grain, livestock, food distribution, and diet) for opportunities to improve efficiency; three, implement cap-and-trade systems for fixed nitrogen; four, expand research at the intersection of agriculture and ecology, and five, focus on the food choices of the prosperous."[85] Once again, scientists are calling attention to a ma-

jor global-scale issue and are taking the lead in calling for remedial action.[86]

Americans began the war on pollution in 1970 with the Clean Air Act. It is hard to know what happened to the commitment that was so evident then, but I suspect it has something to do with our having addressed with some success the acute, obvious, and local pollution insults, thereby creating the illusion that the problem is solved. Yet we merely created a fool's paradise for ourselves, for the more serious pollution problems are chronic, insidious, and global.

Part Two   . . . And the World Responds

The elephant in the room is our seriously deteriorating global environment, but few want to acknowledge it. In chapters 4 and 5, I review
the current effort to respond to global-scale challenges and chart the
lack of progress. What is especially troubling is the contrast between
the successful confrontation of many domestic environmental issues
and the failure on the global front. An analysis of the differences between
the responses to each challenge yields some answers why attempts so
far at solving planetary environmental ills have fallen short. Given the
magnitude of the challenges, the responses mounted by the international
community appear pitifully weak.

4 First Attempt at Global Environmental Governance

We travel together, passengers in a little spaceship, ... preserved from annihilation only by the care, the work, and, I will say, the love we give our fragile craft. Adlai Stevenson, in his last speech, 1965

The good news is that, starting in the 1980s, governments and others did take notice of large-scale environmental deterioration and did begin the process of assuming responsibility for planetary management. What has emerged since is the international community's first attempt at global environmental governance. All is not well in this new arena, to say the least, but it is important to acknowledge what has been accomplished.

Before examining these accomplishments, I should comment on vocabulary. "Global governance" does not imply a global government; nor does it include only the actions of governments. Many nongovernmental communities, for-profit and not-for-profit, are already playing large roles in the governance of the global environment as we know it today.

Also, it is interesting to contrast the environmental field with the economic one. The phrase "managing the global economy" comes easily; it is frequently heard because it is a priority enterprise of governments, multilateral financial institutions, and many others. But "managing the global environment"? It still sounds a bit strange, perhaps futuristic. Yet it should not. The global environment is more of an integrated system than the global economy. It is even more fundamental to human well-being. And, as we have just seen, it is powerfully affected by human activities and requires management.

So what has been accomplished to date in the area of global environmental governance?

An agenda of the principal large-scale environmental concerns of the international community has been defined, and it is widely understood that addressing these concerns requires international agreement and cooperation. In response to this agenda, there has been a huge upsurge of international conferences, negotiations, action plans, treaties, and other initiatives. New fields of international environmental law and diplomacy have been born. There are fat law casebooks on international environmental law now, a far cry from the situation when I attended law school in the late 1960s and there were no courses in environmental law, domestic or international. These casebooks are huge because there are now about 250 international environmental treaties, two-thirds of them signed in recent decades. Most of these agreements are bilateral or regional agreements; about 15 to 20 have broad international sponsorship and significance.

There has been a vast outpouring of impressive and relevant scientific research and policy analysis as well as a flourishing of sophisticated action by an ever-stronger international community of environmental and other nongovernmental organizations. Initiatives have ranged from global to local, from civil disobedience to the publication of countless reports by analytical think tanks.

Both national governments and multilateral institutions, such as the United Nations and the World Bank, have recognized these concerns. Although many multinational corporations are still in denial, others have become highly innovative and have moved ahead with impressive steps, often before their governments. In the academy, international environmental affairs have become a major subject of scholarly inquiry and teaching in environmental studies, political science, economics, and other departments. A large body of relevant scholarship now exists.

Let us turn now to the agenda of large-scale environmental concerns to which governments and others have paid attention. How did this agenda emerge? How were the issues identified and framed? By whom? How did they gain recognition and political traction?

To put these issues in perspective, it is useful to begin at the beginning with the emergence of the modern era of environmental concern. This emergence occurred first in the United States, though others like Canada and Japan were in this early wave. It was driven by concerns that were domestic; indeed they were mostly local issues: local air and water pollution, strip-mining, highway construction, noise pollution, dams and stream channelization, clear-cutting, hazardous waste dumps, the local nuclear power plant, exposures to toxic chemicals, oil spills, suburban sprawl. Concern about these issues gathered strength throughout the 1960s, culminating in the passage of the National Environmental Policy Act in December 1969 and in the first Earth Day a few months later. Within the short span of a few years in the early 1970s, EPA and CEQ were established, the Clean Air and Water Acts and other major federal legislation were passed, and the federal courts were deluged with lawsuits brought by a new generation of environmental advocacy organizations, often funded by major U.S. foundations. It was during this period that groups like the Natural Resources Defense Council and Environmental Defense were launched, NRDC and Environmental Defense with major support from the Ford Foundation.

The new environmental movement handed the business community and foot-dragging government agencies a long string of defeats; it often left scientists anxious in their efforts to keep up. Large majorities of the public were strongly pro-environment, and the public was fully aroused. Congress responded with far-reaching, expensive requirements

Timeline: Some U.S. and International Developments Relating to the Global Environment

1962	Rachel Carson publishes *Silent Spring*
1967–69	Environmental Defense Fund, Natural Resources Defense Council, and Friends of the Earth are formed
1969	Oil spill in Santa Barbara, California
	National Environmental Policy Act passes Congress
	U.S. Environmental Protection Agency and Council on Environmental Quality are created
1970	First Earth Day
1972	U.N. Conference on the Human Environment is held in Stockholm
	U.N. Environment Programme is launched
1973	Endangered Species Act is enacted
1974	Rowland and Molina release chlorofluorocarbon/ozone depletion research
1975	Worldwatch Institute is established
	Convention on International Trade in Endangered Species of Flora and Fauna comes into effect
1977	U.N. Conference on Desertification is held
1979	Convention on Long-Range Transboundary Air Pollution is adopted
	National Academy of Sciences releases report on climate change ("Charney Report")
1980	IUCN releases its World Conservation Strategy
	Global 2000 Report to the President is released
1982	World Resources Institute is launched
	U.N. Convention on the Law of the Sea is adopted
	U.N. World Charter for Nature is published
1985	Austria meeting of World Meteorological Society, United Nations Environment Programme, and International

	Council of Scientific Unions reports on the buildup of CO_2 and other "greenhouse gases" in the atmosphere
	Antarctic ozone hole is discovered
1987	Report of the World Commission on Environment and Development (Brundtland Commission) is released
	Montreal Protocol on ozone depletion is adopted
1989	Basel Convention on the Control of Transboundary Movement of Hazardous Wastes is signed
	Center for International Environmental Law established
1992	Earth Summit is held in Rio de Janeiro
	Agenda 21 is adopted
	Framework Convention on Climate Change is signed
	Convention on Biological Diversity is signed
1994	Global Environment Facility is created
	U.N. Conference on Population and Development is held in Cairo
	U.N. Convention to Combat Desertification is signed
1995	World Trade Organization is established
1997	Kyoto Protocol is signed
1998	Rotterdam Convention for the Application of Prior Informed Consent for Trade in Hazardous Chemicals and Pesticides is signed
2000	Stockholm Convention on Persistent Organic Pollutants (POPs) is signed
2002	World Summit on Sustainable Development held in Johannesburg
2003	Kyoto Protocol enters into force?

Source: Adapted from "Sustainable Development Timeline," International Institute for Sustainable Development, http://sdgateway.net/introsd/timeline.htm

and tough deadlines for industry. A tipping point—a phase change—was reached: government action that once seemed impossible became inevitable.

How did this happen? A number of factors came together. First, there was the rising demand for environmental amenity in an increasingly affluent postwar population. Between 1950 and 1970 U.S. per capita income rose by 52 percent. People sought the amenities of the suburbs: by 1970 there were more Americans in the suburbs than the cities or rural areas. National park visitation doubled between 1954 and 1962 and doubled again by 1971.[1]

Second, pollution and blight were blatant and obvious to all. Smog, soot, smarting eyes, coughs from air pollution; streams and beaches closed to fishing and swimming; plastic trash and toxic chemicals that would not go away; birds, even our national symbol the bald eagle, threatened by DDT; pesticide poisoning; fish kills; power plants and highways through neighborhoods; marshes filled for new tract houses and streams channelized for navigation and drainage.

Third, the social and antiwar movements of the 1960s had given rise to a new questioning and politically active generation. These movements showed that political activism could work. Our young group at the Yale Law School who helped found the Natural Resources Defense Council, for example, was inspired by the work of the NAACP Legal Defense Fund. And some were not so young. Senator Gaylord Nelson, aware of the teach-ins to protest the Vietnam War, had the idea for a national teach-in for the environment and thus launched what became the first Earth Day in 1970.

Fourth, there was a widespread view that major corporations were getting away with murder. Rachel Carson published *Silent Spring* in 1962, first in the *New Yorker*.[2] Ralph Nader wrote *Unsafe at Any Speed* in 1965.[3] The play had to have a villain, and corporate America was it. In 1968, I was the research assistant to Yale professor Charles Reich. He was working on a best-seller he would release in 1970, *The Greening of America*, again first in the *New Yorker*. In it, Reich would write: "In the second half of the twentieth century [the] combination of an anachronistic consciousness characterized by myth, and an inhuman consciousness dominated by the machine-rationality of the Corporate State, have, between them, proved utterly unable to manage, guide, or control the immense apparatus of technology and organization that America has built. In consequence, this apparatus of power has become a mindless juggernaut, destroying the environment, obliterating human values, and assuming domination over the lives and minds of its subjects."[4] Reich saw in the new generation the force that could change all this.

Fifth, the likely opposition—the business community—was caught off guard, without time to marshal its troops or gather its ammunition. Interestingly, even the Sierra Club was surprised. The club's executive director was later to note that they "were taken aback by the speed or suddenness with which the new forces exploded. . . .We were severely disoriented."[5]

Last, there were the precipitating events: the Cuyahoga River in Cleveland bursting into flames; the Interior Department proposing to flood the Grand Canyon. Most significant, there was the Santa Barbara oil spill in 1969. The rest, as they say, is history.

Several points about these seminal developments are notable. The global-scale challenges that concern us today were largely absent from discussion. Second, science and scientists aided but did not drive the Earth Day agenda. Some individual scientists played major roles— Paul Ehrlich, John Holdren, Barry Commoner, and George Woodwell among them. But the issues were advanced mainly by key events and by the realities of people's experiences. Similarly, there was little need to try to define and promote "an agenda." The agenda was defined by everyday insults and the cumulation of actions in response. To illustrate the degree to which this was true, we who were responsible for environment in the Carter White House, and indeed the environmental community generally, were largely unaware of thousands of abandoned hazardous waste sites scattered across the United States. Housewife Lois Gibbs and her efforts at Love Canal put this topic on the agenda, not the scientists or the government, and it happened after much of the early environmental legislation had been passed.

So if this was the domestic scene, where were the global-scale issues of primary concern to us here? Much as the domestic agenda of 1970 was forming in the 1960s, the global change agenda was quietly taking shape in the 1970s. Throughout the 1970s, a steady stream of publications emerged with a planetary perspective, calling attention to global-scale concerns. Most were written by scientists with the goal of taking their findings and those of other scientists to a larger audience. I would call particular attention to the following path-breaking publications, not all of which met with universal acclaim:

1970   *Man's Impact on the Global Environment,* the Report of the Study of Critical Environmental Problems (a scientific group assembled at MIT)[6]

1971   *This Endangered Planet* by Richard Falk[7]

1972   *Exploring New Ethics for Survival* by Garrett Hardin[8]

1972   *The Limits to Growth* by Dennis and Dana Meadows and colleagues[9]

1972   *Only One Earth* by Barbara Ward and Rene Dubos[10]

1978   *The Human Future Revisited* by Harrison Brown[11]

1978   *The Twenty-Ninth Day* by Lester Brown[12]

There were also numerous reports from scientific groups, especially panels and committees organized by the International Council of Scientific Unions, the U.S. National Academy of Sciences, the International Union for the Conservation of Nature and Natural Resources, and the United Nations Environment Programme. These reports included the now-famous 1974 study of Sherwood Rowland and Mario Molina explaining the potential of CFCs to deplete the ozone layer.[13] (This remains the only environmental research to date to win the Nobel Prize.) And they also included the first effort of the National Academy of Sciences on the problem of global climate change, the "Charney Report" in 1979, which said most of what we needed to know about climate change to take action.[14] These reports and the steady stream of publications from Lester Brown and his team at the Worldwatch Institute collectively laid out the key issues.

Then, around 1980, a series of reports began to pull together these issues into a coherent agenda for international action. These included the *World Conservation Strategy* by IUCN and UNEP;[15] "Environmental Research and Management Priorities for the 1980s" published in *Ambio* by an international group of scientists organized by the Royal Swedish Academy of Sciences;[16] *The World Environment: 1972–1982* by a UNEP scientific team;[17] and the two that I helped lead, *The Global 2000 Report to the President* and its follow-up report *Global Future: Time to Act,* by U.S. government teams organized by President Carter's Council on Environmental Quality.[18] These syntheses were predominantly scientific efforts designed to bring global-scale challenges forcefully to the attention of governments.

Collectively, these reports stressed ten principal concerns:

1. Depletion of the stratospheric ozone layer by CFCs and other gases
2. Climate change due to the increase in "greenhouse gases" in the atmosphere
3. Loss of crop and grazing land due to desertification, erosion, conversion of land to nonfarm uses, and other factors
4. Depletion of the world's tropical forests, leading to loss of forest resources, serious watershed damage (erosion, flooding, and siltation), and other adverse consequences
5. Mass extinction of species, principally from the global loss of wildlife habitat, and the associated loss of genetic resources
6. Rapid population growth, burgeoning Third World cities, and ecological refugees
7. Mismanagement and shortages of freshwater resources

8. Overfishing, habitat destruction, and pollution in the marine environment
9. Threats to human health from mismanagement of pesticides and persistent organic pollutants
10. Acid rain and, more generally, the effects of a complex mix of air pollutants on fisheries, forests, and crops

Clearly, this was a new agenda, very different from the one that sparked Earth Day in 1970.[19]

Parallel with these efforts of the scientific community to influence the agenda were a series of stage-setting developments that opened the door to their influence. Political scientist Keith Caldwell has noted that before the international environmental movement could be born, two events had to occur: environmental policy had to be legitimized at the national level, and the life-sustaining processes of the biosphere had to be perceived as a common concern of all peoples. Caldwell sees the 1972 U.N. Conference on the Human Environment, the Stockholm Conference, as crucial in both respects.[20] It forced many national governments to develop domestic environmental programs (even those in Europe, which were clearly lagging behind the United States at this point), and it legitimized the biosphere as an object of national and international policy and collective management.

The Stockholm Conference also had a further major consequence: the creation of UNEP, which had a major impact in the 1970s in framing the global agenda. UNEP made estimates of deforestation and promoted strategies of action; it convened the 1977 international conference on desertification; it promoted international agreements on the protection of migratory species; it promoted the World Climate Program of the International Meteorological Organization, all in the 1970s.

Also of consequence in setting the stage were the international agreements of the early 1970s. This period saw the beginnings of some of the most successful, if narrowly focused, environmental treaties, including those regulating marine pollution from ships and the international trade in endangered species. The United States provided strong international leadership in this period. As the first chairs of the Council on Environmental Quality, Nixon administration appointees Russell Train and Russell Peterson were vigorous and visible advocates. The deliberations on these treaties as well as those on World Heritage Sites and protected wetland areas helped move international environmental concern into the spotlight.

By the mid-1980s, the intellectual and policy leadership of the scientific community, of the environmental community (with groups such as IUCN, Worldwatch, and the World Resources Institute) and UNEP had paid off: a new and international environmental agenda had been established—one that governments would have to address collectively in some way to be credible. The case for major action on these ten issues was too strong to ignore, and the intellectuals in the scientific and environmental communities could get excellent media access to keep the pressure on and the issues before the public. All of this was advanced and reinforced by the influential report of the Brundtland Commission, *Our Common Future*, in 1986.[21]

In other words, the global agenda emerged and moved forward thanks primarily to a relatively small international leadership community in science, government, the United Nations, and civil society. They took available opportunities to put these issues forward—indeed, they created such opportunities—so that governments had little choice but to respond. The game that many governments played, as we shall see, was to respond but not with force.

With this as a background, comparing the politics of the global agenda with that of the original, predominantly domestic, agenda of a decade earlier is instructive. The differences have proven consequential. Consider these contrasts:

- The issues on the domestic agenda were acute, immediate, and understandable by the public. Those on the global agenda tend to be more chronic, more remote (at least from the well-to-do North), and technically complicated and thus difficult to understand and relate to.

- The global agenda mostly did not spring bottom-up from actual impacts on people; it was forged top-down at the international level by science, often disputed science; by environmental groups, often with circumscribed credibility; and by UNEP, a peanut-sized U.N. agency tucked away in Nairobi.
- The domestic agenda was translated into legislation before corporate and other opposition was aroused. Action on the global agenda has been pursued in the context of alerted, prepared, and powerful opposition when perceived corporate interests are viewed as threatened.
- The world's most powerful country led in the fight for national-level action in the 1970s, but it has largely failed to give international leadership on the global agenda. Indeed, following its leadership on ozone depletion, the United States has typically been the principal holdout on international environmental agreements.
- The villainy of the global agenda is ambiguous. Global-scale environmental problems can't be blamed only on big corporations when our own lifestyle, mismanagement by governments North and South, and other factors are so clearly implicated. Increasingly, pollution comes not from something going wrong but from normal life.

Collectively, these contrasts underscore the weak political base on which our concern for the global environment has rested. In light of these barriers to progress, it is a wonder that any was made. Yet by the mid-1990s each of the ten challenges mentioned previously had become the subject of international treaties, plans of action, or other initiatives. Several of the issues received major attention at the Earth Summit in Rio de Janeiro in 1992.

Let's return to the list of the ten global-scale concerns—the global change agenda that emerged around 1980—and ask in each case what has been the primary international response.[22]

1. *Ozone layer depletion.* The 1985 Vienna Convention (or treaty) on the Protection of the Ozone Layer and its 1987 Montreal Protocol and its subsequent revisions are by far the most consequential of all the international agreements mentioned here. The Montreal Protocol has effectively banned almost all the ozone-depleting chemicals around the world. The Montreal Protocol established a special fund that helped to ensure almost universal participation by developing countries.

2. *Climate change.* The Earth Summit at Rio was the site of the signing of the Framework Convention on Climate Change of 1992, and funding to assist the developing world is available under the Global Environment Facility (GEF). The GEF was created following the Earth Summit to provide financial support to developing countries for the efforts to address global-scale environmental concerns. The now-famous Kyoto Protocol is an agreement within the framework of this convention. At this writing it appears that the Kyoto Protocol will soon enter into force even without U.S. participation. The Kyoto Protocol sets specific targets and timetables for the reduction of climate-altering gases in industrial countries.

3. *Desertification.* Here, principally two things have happened: following a commitment at the Rio Earth Summit, the international community agreed in 1994 to the Convention to Combat Desertification, and efforts have since been made to increase the volume of development aid targeted to this problem. This convention, like those for biodiversity and climate, contains requirements that participating governments develop their own plans of action focused on the issue.

4. *Deforestation.* No convention has yet been adopted addressing deforestation, but nonbinding principles to guide the sustainable management of forests were agreed to at the Rio Earth Summit. They were followed by an impressive international effort led by environmental organizations and private foundations to promote

the certification and ecolabeling of forest products when those products are derived from sustainable forest management based on these principles. The certification process is beginning to gather steam: half the wooden doors sold today by Home Depot are so certified. Also, there has been a substantial increase in development assistance and NGO activity to protect tropical forests.

5. *Biodiversity loss.* The Convention on Biological Diversity was also signed at the Rio Earth Summit in 1992. Funding to support bio-diversity conservation is provided under the GEF. As with forest protection, NGOs and the development assistance community have increased cooperation to protect biodiversity, as we noted with regard to the Amazon. Many other conventions address narrower issues of wildlife and habitat protection.

6. *Population growth.* There is no population convention, but a major international plan of action was forged under U.N. auspices in Cairo in 1994. Funding of international population programs has increased, but not by the amount agreed at Cairo.

7. *Freshwater resources.* The Convention on the Non-Navigable Uses of International Watercourses has been negotiated but has not gone into effect, and it may never succeed unless political support picks up. A number of regional agreements now address the environmental aspects of watershed management. Funding for protection of international waterways is one of the funding windows under the GEF.

8. *Marine environment deterioration.* A host of international agreements, led by the U.N. Convention on the Law of the Sea, now cover ocean pollution, overfishing, whaling, and other issues. International environmental law is arguably more developed in the oceans area than any other.

9. *Toxification.* The Basel Convention now regulates the international toxic wastes trade, and the Stockholm Convention on Persistent Organic Pollutants (POPs) promoting the phaseout of twelve highly dangerous chemicals was signed in 2001. The POPs convention

provides a framework for the regulation of other chemicals in the future.

10. *Acid rain*. The Convention on Long-Range Transboundary Air Pollution, a regional agreement involving Europe, regulates emissions of both sulfur and nitrogen oxides. Some countries, including the United States, have their own domestic regulations, and the United States and Canada have an important bilateral air quality agreement.

How can we characterize this international response? One pattern that has emerged is what can now be called the "standard model"— that of first negotiating a general framework convention that defines the problem and provides for agreement on broad policy issues. The framework convention is then implemented over time with more specific and stronger protocols, as science and politics allow. Making technical and financial assistance available to developing countries facilitates their participation. The evolving system of norms and rules specified in the convention and its protocols are referred to as a "regime." Not all multilateral environmental agreements follow this standard model, but many do, especially the more recent.

It is very important to note that these regimes for climate, for biodiversity, and so on are legal regimes. The principal response of the international community to global-scale environmental challenges to date has been a legal one. Other avenues have been pursued, such as somewhat increased government spending on these issues, but the primary focus of the international community has been international environmental law, including so-called soft law, the nonbinding international policy declarations. This area is where most people concerned about the global environment, whether in or out of government, have placed their bets; this is where the solutions have principally been sought. This is where most of the intergovernmental effort has been expended.

The 1985 Vienna Convention for the Protection of the Ozone Layer and its 1987 Montreal Protocol show how the process is supposed to work.[23] Let's trace the ozone-layer protection process through its various stages. Numerous analysts have taken their hands to outlining the stages in the life of an international environmental regime. I break the process down into four stages here.

The first stage precedes actual international negotiations. It is the stage of problem identification, fact finding, and agenda setting. In many cases, scientists have brought the issue forward to the attention of the public and policymakers. Sometimes "focusing events" dramatize that the problem is real, not just scientific speculation. Coalitions of environmental groups, concerned scientists, and government staffs typically form in this stage. Through their policy entrepreneurship and advocacy, they get the issue on the agenda that governments feel obligated to address. And typically the first thing governments do is to commission more research and fact-finding.

In the case of ozone depletion, scientific concern first focused on the risk that exhausts from the proposed super-sonic transport (SST) aircraft—now represented by the Concorde—could deplete the earth's protective ozone shield. Then in 1974 Molina and Rowland published their research showing that CFCs, though highly stable compounds in the troposphere, could release chlorine in the hostile environment of the stratosphere. The chlorine would in turn set off a chain reaction that would deplete the ozone there. CFCs and similar chemicals were in widespread use at the time as aerosol propellants (spray cans), refrigerants, and solvents, so the Molina-Rowland hypothesis led to intensive research efforts by scientists in and out of government. The media, environmental groups, and others raised the issue's visibility. Then, in 1977, the United States, Canada, and Nordic countries called upon UNEP to undertake a major fact-finding and issue definition exercise. So, between 1974 and 1977 the ozone depletion issue moved beyond a question of science and made it onto the intergovernmental agenda.

The second stage in the convention/protocol process is the stage of negotiation, bargaining, and agreement on what actions to take. The typical framework convention provides only general findings and policies, statements of broad goals, and institutional and governance arrangements. The more difficult negotiations are reserved for the more specific and action-oriented protocols that follow. In the case of ozone depletion, there was still much uncertainty about the seriousness of the problem when UNEP, showing leadership here as it would later, called for international negotiations in 1981. (This eagerness to start negotiations in the face of scientific uncertainty contrasts with the later reluctance to act in the face of uncertainty that has characterized the issue of climate change.) In 1984 and 1985, NASA coordinated a major international scientific review, and a powerful case for international action was made. The study pointed out that CFCs in the atmosphere had doubled between 1975 and 1985, and it projected a 9 percent depletion of stratospheric ozone by 2150 if 1980 use rates of CFCs continued. Additional skin cancers were estimated. The framework convention on protecting the ozone layer followed promptly in 1985.

The framework convention itself merely called on governments to take "appropriate measures" to protect the ozone layer. It also did two things that are now standard. It established a Conference of the Parties to the convention consisting of all countries that have ratified the convention. And it established a U.N. secretariat to service the Conference on the Parties. These secretariats are of great importance. They can commission studies, consolidate research results, develop ideas for protocols and early drafts of them, and generally provide ongoing expertise and frame the agenda for the Conference of the Parties.

Moving beyond the framework convention, the real action in this second stage began in the effort to agree on what became known as the 1987 Montreal Protocol. Before the beginnings of the Montreal Protocol negotiations in 1986, two big stumbling blocks prevented action. The United States and others in the "lead states group" advocated, first, a freeze on CFC production and, second, a 95 percent phaseout of their production over ten to fourteen years. These measures were resisted strongly by the chemical manufacturers, represented in the United

States by the fifty-member Alliance for a Responsible CFC Policy. (As late as 1988 the CFC Alliance was claiming that CFCs present no significant risk.) That was the first stumbling block. The other was Europe. Europe seems ahead of the United States today on climate protection and other issues, but that was not true in the mid-1980s. Most major European governments tended to adopt the position advocated by their national companies 100 percent.

But all this was about to change, and it is useful to understand why. First, the U.S. government made the ozone issue a true priority and turned the State Department loose to lobby more than sixty governments intensively. Second, the industry coalition began to collapse when the single biggest manufacturer, DuPont, announced in 1986 that it could develop CFC substitutes within five years. But DuPont was reluctant to initiate production of these substitutes unless strong international regulation created a market for them by phasing out CFCs. Others in industry understood that they would be better off with international action than with further unilateral U.S. action, which was also a strong possibility. Third, UNEP's executive director, Mostafa Tolba, came out swinging, as he would do often thereafter, putting both his and the United Nations' weight and credibility behind action. Strong personal leadership from outstanding individuals has proven essential in forging many global-scale agreements. Fourth, a major "focusing event" occurred when the ozone hole was discovered over Antarctica. And, finally, the United States and other governments showed a willingness to compromise. In the end the Montreal Protocol required that the industrial countries reduce their CFC production by 50 percent below 1986 levels by 1999, a formulation that would later influence those negotiating the Kyoto Protocol.[24]

The third stage in the treaty-making process is the formal adoption stage. Conventions and protocols are first signed but do not "enter into force" until they are ratified by a specified number of countries or, sometimes, countries representing a specified share of the problem or its solution.

The final stage of the convention/protocol process is that of implementation, monitoring, assessment, and strengthening. Here again, the ozone convention process is instructive. Driven by further science and by "focusing events" like the ozone hole over Antarctica, the Ozone Layer Conference of the Parties has responded repeatedly to strengthen the regime. It also acted to create the so-called Multilateral Fund to support the ability of developing countries to shift to safe substitutes. As political scientist Gareth Porter and his colleagues note, "The Montreal Protocol is the best example so far of a regime that has been continually strengthened in response to new scientific evidence and technological innovations."[25] As a result, if developing nations reduce their emissions as expected, scientists are now forecasting the recovery of the ozone layer by 2050.

The Montreal Protocol is the crowning achievement of global environmental governance. Diplomats, corporations, scientists, and environmental leaders have succeeded in sharply reducing the release of ozone-depleting substances, to the point that it is possible to envision recovery of the earth's ozone shield, a remarkable accomplishment. But what of the other nine challenges on the global environmental agenda, and what can we say about the overall international response to date?

Clearly, progress on ozone depletion gets an Honors, but what of the other issues? I am not a very tough grader, but I'm afraid my grades would be low. I'd give a Low Pass to our progress on population control and acid rain but, I'm afraid, Fails to the other seven, for two reasons. First, as discussed in the prologue and part I, the threatening environmental trends highlighted a quarter-century ago have continued, so that today the problems are deeper and more urgent. But if we have not actually done much, perhaps we have in these twenty-plus years laid a good foundation for rapid and effective action. Perhaps the international treaties and action plans have given us the policies and programs we now need, and we can at last get on with it. Here, unfortunately, we arrive at a second set of distressing conclusions.

The results of two decades of international environmental negotiations are disappointing. It is not that what has been agreed upon, for example, in the framework conventions on climate, desertification, biodiversity, or in the Law of the Sea is wrong or useless. Those conventions have raised awareness among governments, provided frameworks for action, stimulated some useful national planning exercises, and generally had some modestly beneficial effects. The process of negotiating these agreements has both advanced basic principles of international environmental law and instilled in governments a deeper appreciation of such key values as sustainability, reciprocity, and commonality.[26] But the bottom line is that these treaties and their associated agreements and protocols do not drive the changes that are needed.

Thus far, the climate convention is not protecting climate, the biodiversity convention is not protecting biodiversity, the desertification convention is not preventing desertification, and even the older and stronger Convention on the Law of the Sea is not protecting fisheries. Nor are they poised to do so in the immediate future. The same can be said for the extensive international discussions on world forests, which never have reached the point of a convention. International environmental law has had its successes; I would cite the Convention on Trade in Endangered Species and the Ocean Dumping Convention as among them. These successes have tended to be narrow in focus or regional in scope. No blanket condemnation of international environmental law is appropriate.[27] But the bottom line is that on the big issues the trends of deterioration continue. With few exceptions, our instrument of choice, international environmental law, is not yet changing them, and the hour is late.

A special word must be said about the Kyoto Protocol, which is beginning to drive important corporate decisions in Europe and Japan. The problem is that progress under the protocol as it now stands will likely be too little and too slow. As we saw in chapter 3, the Kyoto Protocol mandates only a small fraction of the greenhouse gas emission reductions that are needed to protect climate, and even so, a decade was required to move to the point where it could be adopted. And, alas, if its goals for the period 2010 are met, that will likely be because of the extensive use of "flexibility mechanisms" and carbon sinks—some would say loopholes—that reduce its impact. One must give credit to the serious efforts being made to breathe life into the Kyoto Protocol, but it is also important to appreciate, as discussed in chapter 3, how far we are from a program to address the challenge of climate change.

In general, the issue with the major treaties is not weak enforcement or weak compliance; the issue is weak treaties. These agreements are easy for governments to slight because their impressive goals are not followed by clear requirements, targets, and timetables. Underlying these shortcomings are debilitating procedures and an unwillingness to commit financial resources needed for real incentives. We still have a long, long way to go to make our major environmental treaties effective.[28]

In chapter 5, I explore a deeper question: whether we are even on the right track with the current emphasis on the treaty approach. Dissatisfaction with the current approach can be seen in the changing attitude among many environmental leaders regarding the desirability of a convention on global forests. They worry that at the end of protracted and all-consuming negotiations, the result could be nearly worthless or even a setback on some issues. Some would prefer forest compacts, which I presented in chapter 2.

Right track or wrong track, it is a frightening thought to conclude that either way we have wasted much of the twenty years we could have spent preparing for action. It would be comforting to think that all of the international negotiations, summit meetings, conference agreements, conventions, and protocols at least have taken the international community to the point where it is prepared to act decisively —comforting but wrong. Global environmental problems have gone from bad to worse, governments are not yet prepared to deal with them, and, at present, many governments, including some of the most important, lack the leadership to get prepared.

5 Anatomy of Failure

"But the Emperor has on nothing at all!" cried a little child.
Hans Christian Andersen

If our first attempt at global environmental governance has yielded so little, it is important to ask why. Our second attempt may be our last chance to get it right before we reap an appalling deterioration of our natural assets, so we should learn quickly from past mistakes.

Here is the way I would characterize the response to global threats to date: a highly threatening disease is attacking our patient, Mother Earth, and, to cure it, we have brought medicine that is pitifully weak. This is not to say that the medicine has done nothing—it helped a bit —but it also compounded the problem by making some people think, mistakenly, that an effective response was being administered.

Let us explore the disease first and then turn to the medicine. Three factors make the disease—global environmental deterioration—extraordinarily difficult to reverse: it is driven by powerful underlying forces; it requires far-reaching international responses; and the political base to support these measures tends to be weak and scattered. These are all inherent problems stemming from the very nature of most global-scale environmental challenges.

The underlying drivers of deterioration were mentioned briefly in chapter 1; they merit detailed consideration and are therefore the subject of chapters 6 and 7. The point to note here is that these forces—notably the steady expansion of human populations, the routine deployment of inappropriate technologies, the near universal aspiration for affluence and high levels of consumption, and the widespread unwillingness to correct the failures of the unaided market—are indeed powerful and will not yield to half-measures.

The second factor making the global agenda inherently difficult is the far-reaching, complex responses required. Consider some of the measures needed to address global climate change: new energy policies, new transportation strategies, changes in agriculture and the management of forests around the world, and so on. Consumers willingly abandoned CFC-based aerosol sprays, but will we so easily abandon our profligate energy habits? Moreover, the global-scale issues demand international cooperation on a scale seldom achieved. Some of the required actions will intrude on domestic affairs and challenge sovereignty much as the international trade regime and the WTO have. Thus far, governments have been willing to concede much in the area of sovereign autonomy to achieve economic expansion but not to protect the environment. The asymmetry between economic initiative and environmental neglect surfaces here and elsewhere.

The final inherent difficulty of the global agenda is difficult politics. One way to bring out the political problem of grappling with the global-scale challenges is to stress the contrasts between the global issues that emerged around 1980 and the predominantly domestic ones that led to the first Earth Day in 1970, as I did in chapter 4. Consider the following contrasts in the way the issues tend to be seen from the developed world, somewhat overstated to make the point:

1970 Domestic Agenda	*1980 Global Agenda*
understandable scientifically	complex, difficult to understand
highly visible impacts	remote or difficult to perceive impacts
current problem	future problem
us/here	them/there
acute problem	chronic problem

These contrasts do not apply equally to all global-scale concerns—ozone depletion raised the specter of skin cancer—but they do underscore the technical complexity of the global-scale issues and the political vulnerability of efforts mounted to respond. Ecologist Simon Levin puts the problem this way: "The familiar acronym NIMBY ('not in my back yard') expresses the principle that people can best be motivated to take action when the problems and rewards hit closest to home. The nature of the process of addressing local issues makes for tighter *feedback loops,* a key element in maintaining resiliency in any system.

"Increasingly, however, we are being challenged by a new class of problems, including global climate change and biodiversity loss, in which the feedback loops are weaker and less specific. Change is slower, and signals less clear (hence the delay in recognizing them)."[1]

Interestingly, this picture may be about to change somewhat. Global warming is now bringing a series of highly visible and unwanted consequences. As these mount, public perceptions of the threat could shift.

Now, the medicine. To confront such difficult challenges, what did we do? Instead of acting with a seriousness commensurate with the threats, the international community framed and implemented an inadequate, flawed response—weak medicine for a very ill patient. First, it opted for international environmental law as the primary means of attack while badly neglecting measures that would more directly address the underlying drivers of deterioration. And, second, having selected international environmental law as the chosen instrument, it never gave that approach a chance to succeed. International agreements are essential in confronting global environmental challenges, but rarely will they solve major problems by themselves, and even less rarely will they succeed if their requirements are not clear and meaningful.

Why was the environmental law approach adopted so thoroughly and quickly? Why did the international community slide easily into negotiating conventions and protocols? There were, first of all, plenty of precedents. The legal-regulatory approach was the approach most often taken domestically with environmental protection. And it was taken internationally in the regulation of trade, aviation, and other areas. So the model was readily available. It is used so frequently because it seems a sensible way to frame agreements and monitor compliance. Also, words and even regulation are cheap, at least for governments. The principal alternatives to regulation are spending and taxing, both politically difficult. For many governments, their comfort level with these approaches was also improved by two considerations: first, the knowledge that in international negotiations the legal principle of state sovereignty would ensure that they could protect their interests, and, second, the fact that in developing international law, environmental or otherwise, the public and public interest groups have very limited opportunities to participate. Another factor not to be discounted, lawyers are hustlers and, of course, lawyers prefer these legal-policy approaches. Finally, there does seem to have been a failure of imagination. The world fell easily into the treaty-protocol approach without much thinking either about alternatives or about how to make legal regimes succeed.

Heavy reliance on the convention-protocol model—the standard model—got off to a good start with acid rain, successfully flowered in the protection of the ozone layer through the regulation of CFCs and halons, but then fared less well when applied to bigger problems like desertification, biodiversity, and climate change that are much more complicated and deep-rooted socially and economically. Perhaps this is the Peter Principle at work in global environmental governance?

Another significant feature of the international response to the global change agenda is that the responses have followed closely what we can call the "problem-defined approach." A biodiversity problem led to a biodiversity convention. The challenge of climate change yielded a climate change convention. The real problem may be poverty, weak and corrupt governments, or fossil fuels, or transportation, or chlorine-based organic chemistry, but the conventions were framed to address the surface worry rather than the deeper problems. They did not go after the underlying causes or drivers of deterioration.

Again, one should ask why. I think there were basically three reasons. First, those of us promoting these agreements found it easy to adopt the "problem-defined approach" because that was the approach typically taken in environmental management domestically. For good or ill, we have air pollution laws to address air pollution, and so on with water pollution and all the others. This model was in everyone's mind. Second, by defining the solution in terms of the publicly perceived problem, treaty advocates maximized the chance of ongoing public support. And third, imagine the disaster that would have happened if the solutions had been defined more in terms of underlying drivers and forces. The environmental community in and out of government quickly would have lost control of the process, which would have moved to the agriculture community or the energy industry. Thus, the relatively weak environmental community pursued a defensible strategy to keep control of the process. Better to keep the issue under environmental control on environmental turf, and let the implications for these powerful interests emerge more indirectly.

There are costs associated with this problem-defined approach. Most important, of course, is the fact that we are directly addressing not the real, underlying problems but only the symptoms. Another cost is that we end up with many conventions because there are many problems. This gives rise to coordination problems, limits on participation especially from capacity-short developing countries, and various inefficiencies.

Further, we have accepted, or at least lived with, procedures for reaching global agreements that could not be slower, more cumbersome, and more inclined to weak results. A revealing exercise is to contrast national legislating, say, in the Congress, with international legislating, say, in climate negotiations.

- In international negotiations, sovereign nations are represented at the table, and sovereignty means that no country is required to accept the will of the majority or be obligated without its consent. Whereas most congressional decisions require agreement by a majority (51 percent), international agreements, to the degree that they are to be effective, must secure the agreement of essentially every country that is important to the outcome (100 percent). Getting such a consensus almost always requires more compromise than securing a simple majority. Although powerful legislators can sometimes block legislation they do not like, that power pales by the power of a country that is essential to the agreement's success simply to walk away.

- Diplomats and other executive branch employees are normally the negotiators in international fora, rarely elected politicians or professional legislators. There is little shared political culture at the international level, and there are few shared political institutions, certainly nothing comparable to political parties, legislative committees, their professional staffs, and opportunities for public participation.

- The interests represented in international negotiations are far more diverse than those represented on the floor of a national legislature; the world is a far more diverse place. However challenging it is for a national politician to represent the various interests within his or her constituency, representing an entire country is a more complex matter. Typically an interplay occurs between the international negotiation process and domestic politics.

- When Congress acts, that is the end of the matter, unless the president decides to veto the legislation. But the negotiators of international legislation rarely have the last word. In the United States, treaties and amendments to them signed by the executive branch must be consented to by two-thirds of the U.S. Senate before they become effective. National legislatures must often approve international agreements, and unless enough countries ratify the agreement, the treaty does not become effective or, as the phrase goes, it does not enter into force. Even when enough countries ratify the treaty for it to enter into force, they may not be the right countries. Environmental treaties are in force where countries critical to their success have not ratified them. The Senate is a virtual graveyard full of unapproved environmental treaties.[2] Also, domestic legislation is usually necessary to implement the agreement within the country in question, and that, too, can derail action.

- Although independent U.N. secretariats serve the overall negotiating process internationally, the vast majority of countries rarely have adequate staff. Negotiators are often more or less on their own in a sea of complex issues. The average level of genuine expertise in the negotiations is often low. Compounding this expertise deficit is poor communication between the capital and the on-the-site negotiators. The negotiators' brief or instructions from capitals often turn out to be inadequate.

- The legislative process in Congress is, generally speaking, very open to the public, and public interest groups are present and active. Although this is changing, the negotiation of international agreements tends to be a closed discussion among governments—and one that is distant and opaque to most people. Thus, just as international environmental issues tend to be more remote from people's everyday lives, the process through which these issues are addressed is also remote. A big gap exists between the process and the people.

All these weaknesses make international legislating much more difficult than the normal national legislative process. The weakness of current international environmental treaties should thus come as no surprise. They were forged in cumbersome negotiating processes that give maximum leverage to any country with an interest in protecting the status quo. The United States successfully weakened the Kyoto Protocol, Brazil worked to keep a forest convention at bay, and Japan and other major fishing countries watered down the international marine fisheries agreement.

Relatedly, the international institutions created in the United Nations to address global environmental issues—the United Nations Environment Programme, ECOSOC's Commission on Sustainable Development, and the secretariats of the various convention bodies—are among the weakest multilateral organizations. UNEP's budget, for example, is quite small—the World Wildlife Fund's and the Nature Conservancy's are many times larger—and its role is partially undermined by the proliferation of independent treaty secretariats outside UNEP.

International negotiating procedures differ radically from both national legislative processes and even more radically from the rule-making processes of independent regulatory agencies. Imagine two ends of a spectrum. At one end we have U.S. regulatory agencies like the Federal Trade Commission and the Food and Drug Administration, which, operating under broad "public interest" mandates from Congress, set rules and norms in their areas. A small group of appointed officials is, in effect, writing laws for the country, subject, to be sure, to congressional oversight and reversal. One could imagine a world environment agency like these federal regulatory agencies. It is a wild idea, you might think, but it anchors one end of the spectrum. The processes we have been examining for regime formation and so on are at the other end of this spectrum. These processes are full of opportunities for delay, indecision, unsatisfactory resolution of issues, and weak results. One interesting step back toward the middle of this spectrum was the intergovernmental decision to allow the Montreal Protocol negotiators to set targets for ozone-depleting substance reductions without nation-by-nation ratification and to do so by a two-thirds vote, thus breaking with consensus decision-making. In other words, the ozone convention Conference of the Parties functions a bit like an international regulatory agency. Several environmental agreements now adopt an approach similar to the Montreal Protocol.

If governments wanted a strong, effective process in the international environmental area, there are ample models from which to choose. Those governing international air transportation, trade, intellectual property rights, and other subjects offer useful ideas. That a tougher approach is not used to protect the global environment is a conscious decision of governments to stick with a weak international process. Much as states in the United States have not wanted to cede certain issues to the federal level, such as land use controls, nations have not wanted to cede their sovereign control in this area to an international body.

Beyond their shortcomings, the potential success of international environmental law in these areas has been undermined by the unfortunate tendency to neglect the social and political context in which international agreements are arrived at and then implemented. Consider, for example, the conditions within individual countries that would favor treaty success:

- peace and stability, certainly;
- favorable economic conditions and the absence of financial or other economic crises;
- an open, democratic society and an independent, effective media presence;
- a high level of public concern and active NGOs;
- the presence of rule of law and a culture of compliance with international law; and
- the human and institutional capacities in government to participate meaningfully at all stages.

Of course, no one should expect nirvana on all these fronts, but the truth is that we are far from achieving these conditions in much of the world, and, as discussed in chapter 6, the wealthy countries of the OECD are investing only miserly amounts in assisting the developing world in these areas.

Finally, the international community has also dealt poorly with the inevitable political opposition and conflicts that war against effective agreements. Three political fault lines surface repeatedly in international negotiations on the environment, and we have not been very forceful or creative about closing these gaps.

The environment versus the economy. Here as elsewhere, economic interests are typically pitted against environmental ones. There is often a seamless link between economic interests and the positions governments take in negotiations. An excellent analysis by David Levy and Peter Newell compares corporate approaches to global environmental issues in Europe and the United States. The comparisons are interesting, but their bottom line is that "government negotiating positions in Europe and the United States have tended to track the stances of major industries active on key issues, such that the achievement of global environmental accords is impossible if important economic sectors are unified in opposition.

"Moreover, the effective implementation of international environmental agreements requires the active cooperation of large multinational companies that possess adequate financial, technological, and organizational resources to innovate and commercialize new technologies. . . . [T]hese large companies are the 'street level bureaucrats' on whom policy makers rely, like it or not, for successful implementation."[3]

Economic pressures can lead to political decisions that undermine even well-crafted treaties. This happened, for example, with the Convention on the Law of the Sea, which created for each coastal country a two-hundred-mile exclusive economic zone designed to overcome open-access fishing on what were once the high seas. In response, rather than protecting their new fishing grounds, governments responded by subsidizing new fishing fleets and neglecting needed regulation. Widespread overfishing has resulted.[4] The new Stockholm Convention on Persistent Organic Pollutants has been blocked in the United States due primarily to concern with its provisions facilitating the regulation of additional dangerous chemicals beyond the dozen in the original agreement.[5]

The North versus the South. To generalize, the poorer countries of the global South have perceived the global environmental agenda as an agenda of the wealthy North, and, indeed, international environmental regimes have typically been pushed by the richer countries. The poorer countries have not only given these concerns a lower priority, they have feared that agreement would undermine their growth potential or impose high costs of compliance. For this reason both the Montreal Protocol (protecting the ozone layer) and the Kyoto Protocol (protecting climate) have taken the approach of regulating the industrial countries first.

There have been exceptions where developing countries have taken the lead. They took the initiative in calling for control of hazardous wastes exports from rich to poor, and they were the principal advocates of the Convention to Combat Desertification. But, in general, the developing world often feels more than a little put upon by the many international processes under way and worries that its priorities are not reflected there. Many developing countries are struggling to exist as viable entities and to be heard, and these factors can intensify assertions of sovereignty.

Whenever we have a global challenge with a major South dimension, we should pay special attention to the points made by Anil Agarwal, who for decades was one of India's leading environmental advocates: "The issue of equity has become a very contentious one in environmental diplomacy. Equity is a prerequisite for global agreement, and environmental cooperation can only be possible through solutions that are both equitable and 'ecologically effective.' These negotiations throw up major political challenges for the people of the world. . . . Enhancing sustainability is the ultimate purpose of these negotiations but without an equitable framework, they are unlikely to generate sufficient confidence and willingness to participate across the world."[6]

As Agarwal indicates, we are unlikely to get effective international agreements engaging the South unless the developing countries are dealt with fairly in a way that recognizes their aspirations and special challenges. Doing so will require, among other things, increased development assistance. This was recognized at the Rio Earth Summit, where commitments were made to roughly double official development assistance to support the summit's ambitious Agenda 21, a compilation of far-sighted policies and goals covering many sectors and issues. Unfortunately for the credibility of the North and much else, development assistance after Rio declined significantly, not increased, dropping more than 15 percent in the 1990s. For this reason (and for others discussed in chapter 7 on the impacts of economic globalization), Agenda 21 was never seriously implemented. Had it been, the possibility of greater international cooperation on the North's treaty agenda would have been enhanced. Agenda 21 is a good example of a compilation of measures that, if fully supported, would have both complemented the treaty processes since Rio and more directly tackled some of the underlying forces leading to today's large-scale environmental challenges. In short, Agenda 21 was just what was needed, and the failure to pursue it is central to understanding the lack of progress over the past decade. Despite the Bush administration's recent increase in U.S. development assistance—an additional five billion dollars a year into the new Millennium Development Account—the United States still remains dead last among OECD countries in development assistance as a percentage of GDP. Worse, on a more sophisticated ranking that takes into account not only aid but also trade, foreign investment, and peacekeeping, the United States is still at the bottom (next-to-last, just ahead of Japan) in the effort it makes to help poor countries.[7]

The United States versus the world. Legal scholar David Hunter has noted that "more than any other country, the United States is responsible for the existing gulf between Rio's rhetoric . . . and the post-Rio environmental reality."[8] If there is one country that bears most responsibility for the lack of progress on international environmental issues, it is the United States.

Of course it is true, as my Yale colleague Ben Cashore has said, that just because the "environmental coalition" is "winning" today in Europe, that does not mean they will win in the future, just as they have not in the past. And just because the environmental coalition is losing today in the United States, that does not mean it will continue to lose in the future, any more than it always lost in the past. Unfortunately, the problem for the United States is not this simple.

At the root of America's negative role is what can only be described as a persistent American exceptionalism, at times tinged with arrogance. It appears in many guises, including not feeling it necessary to participate in international treaties. Consider the following. At last check, 192 countries have ratified the Convention on the Rights of the Child. There must be at least 193 countries today, for the United States is not among the 192. Most countries have ratified the Convention on the Elimination of All Forms of Discrimination Against Women, 173 at last count, but the United States has not. Our company in opposing the Land Mine Convention includes Cuba, Democratic People's Republic of Korea, and Libya. We join Libya again in being among the few that have not ratified the Convention on Biological Diversity, and believe it or not, we have not yet ratified the Law of the Sea Treaty. It is well known that the Bush administration has rejected the Kyoto Protocol, but the list of important international environmental treaties not ratified by the United States is long. The list goes on, and the pattern is clear —a pattern of unilateralism and of staying outside the multilateral system unless we need it—à la carte multilateralism.

The Bush administration was in the process of pushing this approach to new heights before 11 September 2001. In January 2001 it announced that it could not support the new treaty establishing an International Criminal Court; in March it abandoned the climate treaty's Kyoto Protocol; in May it said it would pull out of the 1972 Anti-Ballistic Missile treaty; it then threatened to withdraw from international conferences on racism and illegal trafficking in small arms; and in July it rejected a proposed enforcement measure for the Biological Weapons Convention. All of which prompted *The Economist* to note that "after five treaties have been shot down in seven months, it is hard to avoid the suspicion that it is the very idea of multilateral cooperation that Mr. Bush objects to."[9]

As elaborated in chapter 7 on globalization, the United States has also been a leader in the business of pursuing trade, financial liberalization, and promarket adjustment at the expense of the partnership compact for sustainable development forged at Rio. With "trade, not aid" as their motto, many U.S. policymakers have seen the globalization (market) paradigm as supplanting the need for the Earth Summit's sustainable development (partnership) paradigm.

The Beacon on the Hill is shrouded today. Political philosopher Benjamin Barber, commenting on the U.S. corporate scandals of 2001 and 2002, puts the failure of U.S. leadership on global environmental issues in a larger context: "Business malfeasance is the consequence neither of systemic capitalist contradictions nor private sin, which are endemic to capitalism and, indeed, to humanity. It arises from a failure of the instruments of democracy, which have been weakened by three decades of market fundamentalism, privatization ideology and resentment of government. . . . The corrosive effects of this trend are visible not only on Wall Street. The Bush administration, which favors energy production over energy conservation, has engineered a reversal of a generation of progress on environmentalism that threatens to leave the [hazardous wastes clean-up] Superfund program underfunded, air-quality standards compromised and global warming unchecked. These policies can be traced directly to that proud disdain for the public realm that is common to all market fundamentalists, Republican and Democratic alike. . . . The United States fails to see that the international treaties it won't sign, the criminal court it will not acknowledge and the United Nations system it does not adequately support are all efforts, however compromised, at developing a new global contract to contain the chaos. . . . The ascendant market ideology claims to free us, but it actually robs us of the civic freedom by which we control the social consequences of our private choices."[10]

The Environmental Law Institute is a middle-of-the-road organization that serves as our country's principal watering hole for mainstream environmental lawyers. Its president in 2002, William Futrell, was driven, however, to sound an extraordinary alarm: "America's legacy of robust environmental law and policy is now in serious jeopardy. Anti-government ideologues of the bar and the bench are resurrecting the pre-modern dogmas of radical federalism and unfettered economic liberty to attack not just environmental laws themselves but the constitutional substructure on which those laws are erected. According to some advocates and judges, the Constitution demands massive deregulation, special rights for corporations and developers, and the curtailment of citizens' access to justice. If left unanswered, this reinterpretation of constitutional principles could lead to a judicial dismantling of environmental protection in the United States. . . . These developments in the courtroom are not accidental, but the result of a well-financed effort to reshape the judiciary (as well as the political branches of government) along strict ideological lines. . . . Today, a handful of right-wing foundations provide generous funding for organizations . . . hostile to environmental regulation."[11] Those who attack long-settled domestic environmental protections are, of course, even more dead-set against international ones.

In early August 2002, shortly before the World Summit on Sustainable Development at Johannesburg, twenty-five conservative think tanks and other organizations wrote President Bush to "applaud [his] decision not to attend the Summit in person." They continued: "We also strongly support your opposition to signing new international environmental treaties or creating new international environmental organizations at the Johannesburg Summit. In our view, the worst possible outcome at Johannesburg would be taking any steps towards creating a World Environment Organization, as the European Union has suggested. . . . [T]he least important global environmental issue is potential global warming, and we hope that your negotiators at Johannesburg can keep it off the table and out of the spotlight."[12]

In the end, not only was President George W. Bush not among the 104 heads of state in attendance, but the United States fought with considerable success against tough targets and timetables, including helping to defeat the European proposal to set a goal of having 15 percent of countries' energy provided by renewable sources by 2015. Joining the United States in this opposition were Iraq, Iran, and most of OPEC. The United States also succeeded in blocking an endorsement of the Kyoto Protocol, and the possibility of a favorable review of the World Environment Organization idea was so remote in this setting that it hardly surfaced.[13]

I often ask myself why more American conservatives do not more actively seek to conserve America. Part of the answer, I suspect, lies in the point made by Benjamin Barber. Environmental challenges threaten the ascendant promarket, antigovernment ideology. They require major governmental responses, including action at the international level. They require "interference" with the market to ensure that social and environmental goals are served. And they require rethinking the utopian materialism that puts a premium only on unlimited economic expansion.

To escape this dilemma many people opt for denial: environmental challenges, they must conclude, are not that serious and are routinely exaggerated by environmental advocates. A group of environmental Dr. Panglosses—from Julian Simon in the early 1980s down to today's Bjorn Lomborg—have intentionally or unintentionally lent a semblance of credibility to this denial, but it is still a condition of denial, of not facing reality. Although there are certainly exaggerations and also honest mistakes in environmental advocacy, national academies of science, Nobel laureates, intergovernmental scientific panels, and countless others have for two decades repeatedly affirmed the reality and seriousness of global-scale environmental challenges.

Bjorn Lomborg's efforts to make the case that "things are getting better" have recently attracted wide attention. In his book *The Skeptical Environmentalist,* published in 2001, the Danish statistician notes that "we are all familiar with the Litany: the environment is in poor shape here on Earth. . . . There is just one problem: it does not seem to be backed up by the available evidence."[14] Lomborg then addresses many of the environmental issues and finds that the "real state of the world" is on the whole very positive.

Legal scholar Douglas Kysar has offered a sober assessment of Lomborg's claims: "What Lomborg and other environmental optimists fail to acknowledge is that . . . with its tap at the bottom, a keg simultaneously can be flowing steadily and nearing empty. Lomborg's approach to environmental policy, which focuses upon measuring flows of material inputs to drive production, may not perceive an end to the total stock of such inputs nor, consequently, an end to the economic party. The environmental pessimist's contention in contrast is that nature, like the keg, has a finite capacity that limits human development in ways both far more varied and subtle than revealed by Lomborg's study. This debate, of course, is an empirical one, and *The Skeptical Environmentalist* does little to resolve it, despite the promise to deliver a comprehensive scientific assessment of the human condition. Rather, what Lomborg offers is simply a particular view as to how humanity should govern itself in the face of uncertainty (namely, do nothing, for regulatory cures are generally worse than environmental disease). Good for him. He does not, however, offer a true description of the 'real state of the world,' any more than environmentalists have offered a false one. Put differently, Lomborg provides his reader with heavily-footnoted, yet eminently familiar political argument, *not* scientific description."[15]

Water expert Peter Gleick has reached much the same conclusion. In a recent review of *The Skeptical Environmentalist*, Gleick concludes that "Lomborg does precisely what he criticizes the environmental community for doing: He misinterprets the scientific literature, simplifies and generalizes about environmental problems, misunderstands environmental science, misuses data, misinterprets the work of others, and draws conclusions based on hidden value judgments."[16]

On water supply issues, Gleick notes that Lomborg's assessment is "fairly simple, half true and wholly deceptive." He characterizes Lomborg's assessment that "basically we have enough water" as particularly dangerous because it is "basically true but completely misleading. . . . The global supply of water is irrelevant given the gross disparities in local water availability and—more important—use. . . . He notes that global average per-capita freshwater availability is very large and concludes that there is plenty of water for all. However, the global average is irrelevant to severe and complex regional and local problems. Hundreds of millions of Indian and Chinese citizens lack basic water services, but they are excluded from his estimates of people without enough water because, on average, both countries appear to have adequate supplies."[17]

Lomborg's attack on biologists' estimates of species loss is also off the mark. One of the best procedures we have today for estimating species loss—and the one used by biologists E. O. Wilson, Peter Raven, Thomas Lovejoy, and many others—is to project losses from known and anticipated habitat destruction. Lomborg challenges this approach with two pieces of claimed evidence. First, he asserts that there is little documented species loss associated with the 98–99 percent loss of forests in the eastern United States, but as Lovejoy and others have pointed out, simultaneous reforestation ensured that total forest cover in the eastern United States never dropped below 50 percent. Lomborg's other claim is that "only" seven out of sixty species of birds went extinct in a well-studied deforestation episode in Puerto Rico, when in fact the seven were all from a group of only twenty bird species unique to the island.[18]

My Yale colleague Michael Dove has observed that important parts of our society have, in effect, been "preconfigured" to accept Lomborg's analysis. I believe it would be a big mistake for thoughtful people, conservatives included, to take comfort from *The Skeptical Environmentalist.* I devoutly wish that I could accept his reassurances, much as I hope that some credible body of scientists will tell us convincingly that we need not worry about global climate change. Yet to do that, we would have to disregard the best science and the wisest counsel that is available to us.

The upshot of all these factors is that the international legislating process is slow, hugely difficult, and prone to weak results. Why, then, has it worked at all? Different governments at different times have shown true leadership and pushed hard for agreement. There is some honest recognition within at least parts of most governments that genuine problems requiring multilateral action do exist. While there is as yet no strong popular groundswell calling for action, environmental and other NGOs are able to generate considerable public scrutiny and pressure. Finally, some international institutions are "bridging institutions," working at scales larger than single nations. Included here are environmental groups and other civil society organizations, multinational corporations, international science with its great credibility, the United Nations, the multilateral development banks, and other multilateral institutions. These bridging institutions have facilitated dialogue and information sharing and have often sought to assert broad interests, regardless of nationality. And last, but not least, the system holds together because tough issues and tough measures are avoided.

In sum, the failure of green governance at the international level is a compound of many elements. The issues on the global environmental agenda are inherently difficult: as I discuss in chapters 6 and 7, powerful underlying forces drive deterioration and require complex and far-reaching responses, while the inherently weak political base for international action is typically overrun by economic opposition and protection of sovereignty. Meanwhile, the response that the international community has mounted has been flawed: the root causes of deterioration have not been addressed seriously, weak multilateral institutions have been created, consensus-based negotiating procedures have ensured mostly toothless treaties, and the economic and political context in which treaties must be prepared and implemented has been largely ignored. To some degree these results can be attributed to accidents, errors, and miscalculations, but the lion's share of the blame must go to the wealthy, industrial countries and especially to the United States, which, since the Montreal Protocol, has not accorded global-scale environmental challenges the priority needed to elicit determined, effective responses.

Part Three   Facing Up to Underlying Causes

We have seen that scientists alerted us to the spread of global environmental degradation during the past several decades. We have also seen that, with few exceptions, attempts to eliminate or even slow the destructive patterns have largely failed. The failure stems in part from having focused too much on symptoms while neglecting the underlying causes. When we look closely at the underlying causes, they are greater in number and more complicated than one would ordinarily conclude. A clearer view of the way these factors feed one another suggests a process of deterioration analogous to metastasis, which makes the need to develop remedial action especially urgent. Chapters 6 and 7 examine the driving forces that are endangering the health of the planet, including one that accelerates the others, globalization.

6 Ten Drivers of Environmental Deterioration

We who prayed and wept
for liberty from kings
and the yoke of liberty
accept the tyranny of things Wendell Berry

I got this bank of bad habits
In a corner of my soul
One by one they'll do you in
They're bound to take their toll Jimmy Buffett

If the first attempt at global environmental governance was aimed primarily at symptoms, future efforts must attack the disease itself. Powerful forces drive the overlapping and interacting processes of biotic impoverishment, toxification, and atmospheric change. We know that these processes are caused, first, by human appropriation and consumption of natural resources and, second, by pollution. Our economic activity, in the largest sense, is consuming nature and pouring out products and pollution. What James Carville famously said about what was important politically in 1992—"It's the economy, stupid"—applies equally when we ask what is important in causing environmental deterioration.

But this answer is obviously not very satisfactory. So let's look deeper and ask ourselves, What are the proximate or immediate drivers of large-scale environmental deterioration, and what is behind these drivers? What gives these forces for ecosystem and atmospheric change such extraordinary power and forward momentum?

In the widely used IPAT equation, environmental impact is seen as the product of population size, the affluence of the population, and the technology deployed in the economy.[1] The relationship is a mathematical identity; it is true by definition. Environmental *Impact* equals *Population* times GDP per capita (that is, *Affluence*) times environmental impact per dollar of GDP (that is, *Technology*). The fact that it must be true and the fact that it is handy and revealing, have led some analysts to rely on it to excess. So as we use it we want to ask what it obscures as well as what it reveals. It tells a part of the story, but not the whole story.

Let us begin with the three IPAT drivers: (1) population, (2) affluence, and (3) technology. We will round out the picture by adding to this list: (4) poverty, (5) market failure, (6) policy and political failure, and (7) the scale and rate of economic growth. And at an even deeper level we will look at (8) the nature of our economic system and (9) our culture and its values. In chapter 7 we will examine (10) the forces loosed upon the world by the globalization of the economy.

Population. The fourfold expansion in human numbers in the twentieth century, from one and a half billion to six billion, has been a huge driver of environmental decline.[2] And the story is far from over. Global population went up 35 percent in the last twenty years and is projected to go up another 25 percent in the next twenty years. Virtually all of the current growth is in the developing world, but this has not always been the case. The billion or so souls in the rich countries had their population explosion earlier, and these countries have now completed what is called the demographic transition. The transition begins when improvements in health and nutrition lead to reduced infant mortality and longer lives. Fertility rates do not immediately decline, so population grows rapidly. Later, fertility rates decline and population size tends again toward stability. The transition is thus one from high births and high deaths to low births and low deaths. Indeed, in some industrial countries birth rates are now well below replacement levels.

It is possible that the demographic transition will be completed in the developing world around midcentury and that global population growth may level off at about eight to nine billion and then perhaps begin to decline.

Once upon a time, I thought only uninformed people could believe that population growth was the principal cause of our environmental ills. Then, in 1980, after we released the *Global 2000 Report to the President,* I received the following letter from the senior editor of a leading scientific journal: "At the heart of the somber projections outlined in the *Global 2000 Report* are problems that are really not the responsibility of the United States. For example, the peoples of many of the LDCs insist on breeding like rabbits. They are not so stupid that they don't know how babies are made. . . . We have enough problems of our own without asking to share those of people who refuse to be responsible." I was shocked by this crude letter—still am—but it does underscore how many people, including highly educated ones, can have uninformed opinions.

If sex is too simple, to what can we attribute the high fertility rates that drive rapid population growth? Economist Partha Dasgupta begins his analysis with the great burden and severe risk of life that childbearing has on women in developing societies. Women in sub-Saharan Africa are four hundred times more likely to die of childbearing complications than those in Sweden. He argues that if women had a choice, they would opt for fewer children. He points out that birthrates are higher where women have the least power and control and notes that: "Data on the status of women from 79 so-called Third World countries display an unmistakable pattern: high fertility, high rates of illiteracy, low share of paid employment and a high percentage working at home for no pay—they all hang together." He points out that raising the earnings of women would also raise the implicit costs of procreation to men, since childbearing keeps women from bringing in cash income.[3]

A second factor is that children are needed as productive assets. The daily work of living off the land is labor intensive. Over two billion people lack access to modern energy supply. Little hands are needed for this work, and children also provide security in old age. High infant mortality rates and a variety of traditions, customs, and attitudes also push toward high fertility. Customs become locked in.

All of this is obviously linked to low incomes and resource depletion in a mutually reinforcing way. As populations expand they place additional pressures on the resource base because other resources and options are not available to them. As the resource base declines—and, for example, as women and children have to walk farther each year in search of water and fuelwood—the need for even more children to do the work increases.

Global population is a gross abstraction. Population pressures become reality at the local level. Virtually all population growth in the next thirty years will be in urban areas. The urban poor often establish informal settlements in ecologically fragile areas; without sewers and garbage collection, wastes accumulate and degrade both land and water supplies. Ecological migrants and refugees are commonplace today. At the extreme, population pressures can contribute to the violent conflicts. Shortly after I joined UNDP in 1993, the genocide occurred in Rwanda, with hundreds of thousands of people slaughtered. I traveled twice to Rwanda after the genocide to support the U.N. program there. We came to believe that the Rwandan situation was in part the result of a true Malthusian situation. James Gasana was the Rwandan minister of agriculture and later defense in the early 1990s, before the crisis of April 1994. Here is his description of the causes: "Environmental scarcities became acute in the 80s as an effect of complex interactions between high population pressure, land shortage and its inequitable distribution, and soil degradation. The effect of these interactions was a socio-economic crisis that converged with the elites' power rivalry and with a high rate of rural unemployment. This caused dissatisfaction amongst the poor peasantry, mostly in the southern region, and strengthened the opportunity for internal opposition to threaten the regime's legitimacy. Environmental scarcities not only influenced the strategies and tactics of political and military actors but also they amplified the political violence."[4]

The good news is that the population issue has not escaped international attention. There have been a series of major international conferences and plans of action on population and advancement of women, and population programs have been attractive parts of the aid budgets of the OECD countries.

At one of these conferences—the Mexico City Population Conference during the Reagan years—the United States parted company with the other OECD countries and announced the now-famous Mexico City Policy. Under this policy, the United States would withhold family-planning assistance from any family-planning provider that supported abortions even if U.S. funds were not used for that purpose. The Clinton administration rescinded the policy, but the George W. Bush administration reinstated it in its first month in office. With the Bush administration's support, the Congress withheld support for the U.N.'s excellent population work in 2002, claiming that the U.N. funding went to groups that support abortions. In these and other ways U.S. abortion politics have been injected into international family-planning efforts.[5]

The latest and most successful U.N. conference on population was in Cairo in 1994. I was there representing UNDP when the donor community agreed to put up six billion dollars for population programs by 2000, the external funding required to meet the plan's objectives. The developing countries were to put up twelve billion dollars by 2000, for a total of about eighteen billion dollars. Eighteen billion dollars is less than what the world spends every week on armaments. But even these modest sums were not forthcoming. Only about half of the promised money had been delivered by 2000—a major disappointment.

Consumption. The level of consumption or affluence can be defined in many ways. In the original IPAT formulation developed by John Holdren and Paul Ehrlich in the early 1970s, consumption was per capita goods and services, or GDP per capita. But for our purposes we will focus on the twentieth century's pattern of rapidly rising household demand for goods and services, particularly those that place a heavy burden on the environment.

In the twentieth century, population went up fourfold and affluence increased fivefold, so that the world economy as a whole grew twentyfold. A fivefold increase in individual consumption is substantial, but increases were even higher in the richer countries and much higher for many environmentally risky goods and services. For example, per capita fossil fuel consumption went up sevenfold globally in the twentieth century, while per capita industrial activity grew twelvefold.

Major world religions have inveighed against material desires and pointed out the perils of wealth:

Judaism: "Riches profit not in the day of wrath: but righteousness delivereth from death."

Christianity: "It is easier for a camel to go through a needle's eye, than for a rich man to enter into the kingdom of God."

Islam: "Those that desire the life of this world with all its finery shall be rewarded for their deeds in their own lifetime: nothing shall be denied them. These are the men who in the world to come shall have nothing but Hell-fire. Fruitless are their deeds, and vain are all their works."

Hinduism: "When you have the golden gift of contentment, you have everything."

Buddhism: "A man who chases after fame and wealth and love affairs is like a man who carries a torch against a strong wind; the flame will surely burn his hands and face."

Despite these teachings, we live in a global consumer society, a material world, with seemingly endless consumer demands. Why should it be so?

Clearly, there are many answers. One is that beyond meeting basic needs, consumption brings us pleasure and helps us to avoid pain and, worst of all, boredom and monotony. Consumption is stimulating, diverting, absorbing, defining, empowering, relaxing, fulfilling, educational, rewarding. If pressed, I would have to confess that I truly enjoy most of the things on which I spend money.

Consumption also responds to artificially created needs. John Kenneth Galbraith, the Harvard economist, highlighted this issue in 1958 in his book *The Affluent Society:* "The central argument in the book [he noted forty years later] was that in the economically advanced countries, and especially in the United States, there has been a highly uneven rate of social development. Privately produced goods and services for use and consumption are abundantly available. So available are they, indeed, that a large expenditure on talented advertising and salesmanship is needed to persuade people to want what is produced. Consumer sovereignty, once governed by the need for food and shelter, is now the highly contrived consumption of an infinite variety of goods and services.

"That, however, is in what has come to be called the private sector. There is no such abundance in the services available from the state. Social services, health care, education—especially education—public housing for the needful, even food, along with action to protect life and the environment, are all in short supply."[6]

It is not only advertising that works to create needs. "Keeping up with the Joneses" is one thing, but keeping up with the lifestyles of the rich and famous is quite another. Economic inequality—large and growing disparities between the top and the rest—contributes to ever-new consumer demand.

Private consumption that damages the environment is also maintained at artificially high levels because of massive market and policy failure. The free market price of various goods and services typically does not incorporate the full environmental costs of production, use, and disposal. The more an environmentally destructive product or service is underpriced, the more it will be consumed. Policy failure perpetuates and often exacerbates market failure. It comes into the picture in part because governments typically fail to require producers to pay for all their environmental damage. And governments have also often made a bad situation worse by subsidizing many environment-destroying activities. Our energy and water prices not only do not include the environmental damage economists call negative externalities, but these prices also are artificially low because government subsidizes their production.

In their book *Perverse Subsidies* of 2001, Norman Myers and Jennifer Kent have analyzed the hundreds of studies that quantify subsidies in agriculture, energy, transportation, water, fisheries, and forestry. They have classified as "perverse" those subsidies that have demonstrable negative effects both economically and environmentally. Their conclusion is that, at the behest of powerful interests, governments intervene in the marketplace to create each year $860 billion in perverse subsidies worldwide. Admittedly a rough estimate, that is about 2.5 percent of a $35 trillion global economy, creating a huge economic incentive for environmental destruction.[7]

Another aspect of these market failures is that even green consumers rarely have convenient, reliable information on which to base purchasing decisions. The business of ecolabeling is still in its infancy.

Last, despite the religious teachings mentioned earlier, our values are proconsumerist, and there is little by way of an anticonsumerist message. We Americans were even told in the wake of 11 September 2001, that the patriotic thing to do was quickly to resume consumer spending.

Biologist Paul Ehrlich wonders if the consumer culture might have its roots in human cultural or even biological evolution: "It seems certain that acquisitiveness was favored by cultural evolution, especially if an ability to provide goods (especially food) to others or simply to possess them had a payoff in prestige. It probably also would have had a payoff in reproductive success, as seen in several pre-industrial groups —and could thus have a genetic evolutionary element. Control of resources by males, at least, certainly often appears to have had that effect historically."[8]

In their book *Mean Genes,* biologist Jay Phelan and economist Terry Burnham are sure that there is a genetic component: "Fast-food pushers did not create our taste for fatty, salty, calorie-laden foods, they simply exploit our existing desire by producing a product with exaggerated features. Our taste buds go crazy for a meal that has more, more, and finally even more of the ingredients that kept our ancestors going. . . . What all products—both helpful and destructive—have in common is that they tap into our instinctual desires. It is precisely these desires that so frequently get us into trouble." But they are hopeful: "As tough as our self-control battles are, we at least have a fighting chance. Most animals, even intelligent chimpanzees, have no ability whatsoever to override their passions."[9]

Paul Ekins has argued that our natural acquisitiveness has been pushed to the extreme by deliberate decisions such as those taken after World War II to stimulate consumer purchases. He quotes U.S. retailing analyst Victor Lebow from that period: "Our enormously productive economy . . . demands that we make consumption our way of life, that we convert the buying and selling of goods into rituals. . . . We need things consumed, burned up, worn out, replaced and discarded at an ever increasing rate."[10] World advertising spending has doubled over the past twenty years, growing at a rate three times faster than world population.

Technology. Turning to technology, one can ask why societies have unleashed so many environmentally harmful technologies on the world and done so little to control their market penetration. Of course, societies have also unleashed many technologies of enormous benefit. The issue here is not that technology is bad for environmental and social goals per se, but that, for reasons we need to understand, societies have been largely unable to assess new technologies and direct technological change in ways that avoid huge environmental costs.

To take up this question, I would like to take you back to 1971. On 26 September of that year, President Nixon made a brief visit to the Atomic Energy Commission's reservation at Hanford, Washington.

The speech he delivered that afternoon is instructive in understanding why technology is so often in the saddle, riding us.[11]

The president took the occasion of his Hanford speech to announce his support for the construction of a fast-breeder nuclear reactor demonstration plant. According to Atomic Energy Commission plans, the breeder reactor, so called because it "breeds" new nuclear fuel, plutonium, at the same time as it produces power, was to be introduced commercially in the mid-1980s and become our predominant source of electricity early in the twenty-first century. AEC's program to commercialize the breeder was extremely controversial; it aimed to have two hundred breeder reactors operating commercially in the United States by 2000. In a lawsuit I filed against AEC a few months before the president's speech, the Scientists' Institute for Public Information alleged that "plutonium is one of the most explosive and toxic substances known to man" and that the breeder program "poses the risk and hazard of an explosion in a reactor core causing the release into the biosphere of dangerous quantities of plutonium or radioactive wastes or both" as well as the possibility of a "black market" in weapons-grade plutonium, since "the technology and nonexplosive materials for construction of an atomic bomb are readily available." SIPI further stated that "there are alternatives to the present [breeder] development program which deserve the most serious national study, attention and debate."

Nixon was keenly aware of the nuclear power controversy when he spoke at Hanford. "Many people in this country, because nuclear power is so destructive, are afraid of it," he noted. The president then justified his decision to support the breeder:

"Well, don't ask me what a breeder reactor is; ask Dr. Schlesinger [then-chairman of the AEC]. But tell him not to tell you, because unless you are one of those Ph.D.s you wouldn't understand it either; but I do know that here we have the potentiality of a whole new breakthrough in the development of power for peace. That means jobs—jobs for this area, and jobs and power for hundreds of millions of people all over the world. . . .

"One final thought before we go in for the tour. I mentioned a moment ago how all of this business about breeder reactors and nuclear energy is over my head. . . . But it always has been fascinating to me because it seems to me that if a people are to be a great people, we must always explore the unknown. We must never be afraid of it. That is why we have to go to space. That is why, as far as that particular matter is concerned, in terms of nuclear power we must not be afraid. We must explore it.

"We can't be sure what it is going to produce, but on the other hand, we know that by exploring the unknown, we are going to grow and progress and progress in a way that will be good for all Americans and for other people in the world." [12]

Nixon's defense of the breeder reactor is a classic invocation of the tenets that have traditionally guided technological development in our society. His implicit themes—the trustworthiness of experts, the beneficence of technology, the inevitability of progress—are the very habits of thought that have traditionally made it easy for new technology to escape rigorous public scrutiny and penetrate easily into the economy.

In the end, the breeder reactor story had a happy ending, at least for its critics. The SIPI lawsuit led to an intensive public review of the breeder program under the National Environmental Policy Act, and because of its risks and shaky economics, it was ultimately halted by President Carter and the Congress. The breeder reactor and the SST are good examples of environmental and other factors combining to block commercialization of major technologies, but it is unusual for environmental considerations to exert such influence.

An openness to technological change has been a principal ingredient of Western ideology since the eighteenth century. Our society has encouraged technological virtuosity, equating it with progress. Although the social costs of industrial innovation have often been considerable, the material benefits have been irresistible. From an early point, the fact of these tangible benefits reinforced the positive, permissive attitude toward technology. As J. B. Bury observed in 1932 in his classic study

The Idea of Progress: "The spectacular results of the advance of science and mechanical technique brought home to the mind of the average man the conception of an indefinite increase of man's power over nature as his brain penetrated her secrets. The evident material progress which has continued incessantly ever since has been a mainstay of the general belief in progress which is prevalent today."[13]

But by the early 1970s, a new pessimism regarding technology was on the rise. It was driven primarily by concerns about nuclear power, environmental deterioration, and invasion of privacy. Then and since, many perceptive critics have found technology and its organization at the core of social and environmental problems. With some consistency, they liken present society to a corporate conglomerate dominated by technological imperatives and divorced from real human needs and aspirations. John Kenneth Galbraith has described "the new industrial state" dominated by a "techno-structure" that has succeeded in making its goals those of the society at large.[14]

A new movement for technology assessment and choice grew out of these concerns. One result of efforts to harness technology—to put people in the saddle—was the creation of the Congressional Office of Technology Assessment in 1973. For two decades it did excellent studies until Congress lopped it off in a budget-cutting spree. It is badly needed now, when technological innovation is driving so many public issues and concerns.

In the mid-1980s the picture on technology took another turn. Some of us noticed the obvious—namely, that if you examine the IPAT equation, the only one of the three drivers that can reduce environmental impacts is technological change. Affluence and population would surely continue to climb. Our World Resources Institute study from this period put the matter this way: "If [the predicted] doubling and redoubling of economic activity is accomplished with the technologies now dominant in energy production, transportation, manufacturing, agriculture, and other sectors, truly catastrophic impacts are likely on global climate, human health, and the productivity of natural systems. Seen this way, reconciling the economic and environmental goals societies have set for themselves will be possible only through a transformation in technology—a shift, perhaps unprecedented in scope and pace, to new technologies that dramatically reduce environmental impact per unit of prosperity."[15]

The WRI study concluded: "Environmental regulation needs to be overhauled to promote long-term innovation and pollution prevention; more effective economic incentives for investments in clean technologies are long overdue; current measures of industrial productivity need to be reconceptualized so they recognize environmental costs; and altogether more attention needs to be paid to how clean technologies can be transferred successfully from country to country."[16] I regret to say that not much was done in response to our policy prescriptions.

So the bottom line on technology is much like that for consumption. Public attitudes toward technology have generally been supportive, welcoming, and trustful. This receptivity continues today with information technology, robotics, nanotechnologies, and even genetic engineering despite the controversy about the health and ecological impacts of genetically modified organisms. The control of technologies has been largely in the hands of large corporations that benefit from their deployment and are clearly in no position to be impartial judges of the public's best interests. The current market fails to guide technology toward good environmental choices, and governments have failed to correct poor market signals. And once a technology has reached a certain level of deployment, it gains an often unwelcome lifespan, something one could say with equal truth about both the inefficient QWERTY keyboard on which we type and the internal combustion engine that has powered our cars for a century.

Poverty. The environmental impacts of this fourth driver are not well captured in the IPAT formulation. Half the world's people get by on less than two dollars per day. Many live close to the land, putting great pressure on the resource base because good alternatives are not open to them. The 1980 *World Conservation Strategy* issued by the U.N.

Environment Programme and the International Union for the Conservation of Nature put the matter as follows: "Human activities are progressively reducing the planet's life-supporting capacity at a time when rising human numbers and consumption are making increasingly heavy demands on it. The combined destructive impacts of a poor majority struggling to stay alive and an affluent minority consuming most of the world's resources are undermining the very means by which all people can survive and flourish."[17] In my six years as administrator of the U.N. Development Programme, I visited scores of developing countries, most of them desperately poor. (In the 1990s the forty or so "least developed countries" had an average per capita income of about a dollar a day.) On many occasions I saw excessive harvesting of fuelwood, overgrazing, and wildlife poaching, so much so that we made the alternative—sustainable livelihoods for the poor—one of our principal development assistance themes.[18]

The World Bank's *World Development Report 2003* describes the vicious circle in which a quarter of the developing world's people living on fragile lands—some 1.3 billion in all—find themselves.[19] Many of the things they are forced to do merely to survive degrade the environment: the search for fuelwood de-vegetates the land, making it more susceptible to erosion and fertility loss; the effort to produce more food depletes soil nutrients and leads to overgrazing and clearing of forests and woody areas; and reducing fallow periods compounds these problems.

It is important to stress that environmental destruction is not a pathology of the poor. Deprived of both access to better resources and the power to get that access, they are often forced "to eat their own seed corn," metaphorically and sometimes actually.

In addressing poverty, development projects have often failed because they neglected the environment, just as environmental projects have often failed because they neglected development.

The fifth and sixth forces driving deterioration—*market failure* and *policy and political failure*—taken together reflect our badly flawed political economy. Basically, our economic system does not work when it comes to protecting environmental resources, and, second, the political system does not work when it comes to correcting the economic system.

Economist Wallace Oates has provided a clear description of "market failure"—the core reason the market does not work for the environment: "Markets generate and make use of a set of prices that serve as signals to indicate the value (or cost) of resources to potential users. Any activity that imposes a cost on society by using up some of its scarce resources must come with a price, where that price equals the social cost. For most goods and services ('private goods' as economists call them), the market forces of supply and demand generate a market price that directs the use of resources into their most highly valued employment.

"There are, however, circumstances where a market price may not emerge to guide individual decisions. This is often the case for various forms of environmentally damaging activities. In the first half of the last century at Cambridge University, A. C. Pigou set forth the basic economic perspective on unpriced goods (encompassing pollution) in his famous book, *The Economics of Welfare*. Since Pigou, many later economists have developed Pigou's insights with greater care and rigor. But the basic idea is straightforward and compelling: the absence of an appropriate price for certain scarce resources (such as clean air and water) leads to their excessive use and results in what is called 'market failure.'

"The source of this failure is what economists term an externality. A good example is the classic case of the producer whose factory spreads smoke over an adjacent neighborhood. The producer imposes a real cost in the form of dirty air, but this cost is 'external' to the firm. The producer does not bear the cost of the pollution it creates as it does for the labor, capital, and raw materials that it employs. The price of labor and such materials induces the firm to economize on their use, but there is no such incentive to control smoke emissions and thereby conserve clean air. The point is simply that whenever a scarce resource comes free of charge (as is typically the case with our limited stocks of clean air and water), it is virtually certain to be used to excess.

"Many of our environmental resources are unprotected by the appropriate prices that would constrain their use. From this perspective, it is hardly surprising to find that the environment is overused and abused. A market system simply doesn't allocate the use of these resources properly. In sum, economics makes a clear and powerful argument for public intervention to correct market failure with respect to many kinds of environmental resources. Markets may work well in guiding the production of private goods, but they cannot be relied upon to provide the proper levels of 'social goods' (like environmental services)."[20]

Oates says that Pigou's book is famous, but I fear it is famous mostly among economists. When Pigou is as well known as Adam Smith, John Maynard Keynes, or Paul Samuelson, we will know that times are changing. And when they have truly changed, power plants emitting sulfur oxides, nitrogen oxides, and mercury will be required to contribute to a fund to pay the estimated cost of their damage to human health, crops, and natural areas. A carpet manufacturer that sells a carpet that cannot, when old, be composted for use as garden fertilizer, will need to provide the carpet buyer with guaranteed, prepaid fees to ship the nonbiodegradable carpet to the factory for disposal or recycling. There is much to be done if we take Pigou seriously.

We have seen that market failure is central to both environmentally bad consumption and environmentally bad technology. We could say more about the failure of economic signals and indicators, especially the way gross domestic product is calculated. Economist Robert Repetto has noted that a country could cut all its forests, drain all its aquifers, and pollute all its waterways, and GDP would only go up, up, up. Yet governments worship at its altar. The problem here is that we are counting consumption of nature's capital as income—in effect, consuming our assets in addition to the income they generate and thus robbing our children of part of their natural heritage.

Political failure perpetuates, indeed magnifies, market failure. Government policies could be implemented to correct market failure and make the market work for the environment rather than against it. But, typically, powerful economic and political interests stand to gain by not making those corrections, so they are not made or the correction is only partial. Water could be conserved and used efficiently if it were sold at its full cost, including the estimated cost of environmental damage, but both politicians and farmers have a stake in keeping water prices subsidized and low. Polluters could be made to pay the full costs of their actions, but typically they do not. Earlier, in chapter 2, we saw that natural ecosystems provide societies with economic services of tremendous value. A developer's destruction of wetlands, for example, reduces these services to society, but rarely does the developer pay for those lost services. Also, as the earlier discussion of perverse subsidies reveals, it is not just that governments often shy away from correcting market failure; governments also exacerbate the problem by creating subsidies and other practices that make a bad situation worse.

Economist Theo Panayotou has described the basic situation: "A combination of institutional, market and policy failures results in underpricing of scarce natural resources and environmental assets, which is then translated into underpricing of resource-based and environment-intensive goods and services. Institutional failures such as absence of secure property rights, market failures such as environmental externalities and policy failures such as distortionary subsidies, drive a wedge between the private and social costs of production and consumption activities. As a direct result producers and consumers of products and services do not receive correct signals about the true scarcity of resources they use up or the cost of environmental damage they cause. This leads to the socially wrong mix of economic output: overproduction and over-consumption of commodities that are resource-depleting and environment-polluting, and underproduction and underconsumption of commodities that are resource-saving and environment-friendly. Thus, the emerging pattern of economic growth and structure of the economy is one that undermines its own resource base, and is ultimately unsustainable, since relative scarcities are not respected."[21]

The seventh factor in global environmental decline is *the scale of the global economic enterprise and its phenomenally rapid expansion.* Scale is important in relationship to the earth's carrying capacity. Imagine a world that had the same number of people as ours doing the same things with the same technologies. But what if that planet were twenty times larger than ours? We would not be quite as worried as we are now. Indeed the situation there would be like earth in 1900 in some respects. It would not be a full world.[22]

The rapid pace of change is another factor. Social and political institutions can be slow to respond, as can science. The development of international environmental law is painfully slow. But the world economy and urbanization surge ahead, faster than societies can respond. There were decades of CFC production before scientists raised concerns. Then it took a decade to agree on a phaseout, which took another decade. And this response was fast by international standards. Today's global economy is even more efficient at spreading a new technology, but our capacity to anticipate and respond effectively has not greatly improved. By the time today's students reach leadership positions twenty-five years from now, the world economy will likely be twice its current size.

Political analyst David Rejeski has pointed to a related reason for political failure. He believes that some developments unfold rapidly enough to warrant policy action but not fast enough to catch politicians' attention. Take tropical deforestation. These forests are being cleared at a slow rate compared to many other phenomena—about 1 percent a year. But even at this pace, they could virtually disappear in one lifespan. "There seems to be some threshold of concern (estimated here at approximately four percent per year) where important social, economic, technological, or demographic phenomena can change and remain under the political and public radar screen," Rejeski notes. "In some cases, the public has become socially conditioned to pay attention to small change—in areas such as unemployment, inflation, and GDP—but in most areas small increases fail to catch our attention. Such changes, if they remain persistent, can degrade systems, stress the government's capacity to respond, and trigger threshold effects where change becomes difficult to reverse or systems fail catastrophically."[23]

At the root of this failure is lack of understanding that even slow rates of change compound rapidly. An economy growing at 3 percent a year will be twice as big in a short twenty-three years. Carbon dioxide emissions in the United States have been growing at about 3 percent a year. Here is a handy rule that everyone should know. If something is growing at a steady rate, and you want to know how long before it will double, divide the growth rate into sixty-nine. If college tuition grows by 5 percent a year, it will double in fourteen years.

Probing for still deeper driving forces, let us return to James Carville's 1992 presidential campaign theme, "It's the economy, stupid." So much in our society, economy, and polity is geared to rapid, continued economic growth. Historian J. R. McNeill has noted that the "growth fetish" solidified its hold on imaginations and institutions in the twentieth century. He writes:

"Communism aspired to become the universal creed of the twentieth century, but a more flexible and seductive religion succeeded where communism failed: the quest for economic growth. Capitalists, nationalists—indeed almost everyone, communists included—worshiped at this same altar because economic growth disguised a multitude of sins. Indonesians and Japanese tolerated endless corruption as long as economic growth lasted. Russians and eastern Europeans put up with clumsy surveillance states. Americans and Brazilians accepted vast social inequalities. Social, moral, and ecological ills were sustained in the interest of economic growth; indeed, adherents to the faith proposed that only more growth could resolve such ills. Economic growth became the indispensable ideology of the state nearly everywhere.

"The growth fetish, while on balance quite useful in a world with empty land, shoals of undisturbed fish, vast forests, and a robust ozone shield, helped create a more crowded and stressed one. Despite the disappearance of ecological buffers and mounting real costs, ideological lock-in reigned in both capitalist and communist circles. No reputable sect among economists could account for depreciating natural assets. The true heretics, economists who challenged the fundamental goal of growth and sought to recognize value in ecosystem services, remained outside the pale to the end of the century. Economic thought did not adjust to the changed conditions it helped to create; thereby it continued to legitimate, and indeed indirectly to cause, massive and rapid ecological change. *The overarching priority of economic growth was easily the most important idea of the twentieth century."*[24]

McNeill has captured well the eighth of the driving forces—*the growth-at-all-costs imperative.* Is it possible that, in the end, it will prove impossible to control? Political scientist J. A. Scholte has put the question forcefully: "Students of globalization must surely take seriously the possibility that underlying structures of the modern (now globalized) world order—capitalism, the state, industrialism, nationality, rationalism— . . . may be in important respects irreparably destructive."[25] Scholte's possibility offers an extraordinarily bleak prognosis if true. As I hope to make clear in part IV, I am certainly not ready to concede that we are confronting a system that is irreparably destructive, but it is a possibility we should keep in mind in part because it reminds us of the seriousness of the changes that are now required.

Our culture is full of *values and habits of thought* that war against effective environmental protection—driver number nine. Two very basic ones are captured in the awkward words anthropocentrism and contempocentrism. Regarding the former, Lamont Hempel has noted that the decline of theocracy and the rise of science in Europe gave Western civilization a self-confident belief in the human ability to dominate nature. "No longer merely caretakers of God's creations," he notes, "people began to imagine themselves, in René Descartes's words, as the 'lords and possessors of nature.'"[26] This view of the world—that nature belongs to us rather than we to nature—is powerful and pervasive, and it has led to much mischief.

Contempocentrism is the habit of thought that discounts the future in favor of the present. Like anthropocentrism, it is another form of self-centeredness. As one wit said in a public hearing we held in the Carter administration, "Future generations? What have they done for us?" Joking aside, contempocentrism is at war with one of the two central principles of environmental ethics—the proposition that we have duties to future generations (the other is Aldo Leopold's proposition that we have duties to other species). It is significant that the first principle in the first statute of the modern environmental era, the National Environmental Policy Act of 1969, calls upon the federal government and "the Nation" generally to "fulfill the responsibilities of each generation as trustee of the environment for succeeding generations." It is a sacred trust—our duty to our children, our neighbor's children, and their children—and it is a trust at which we are failing.[27]

We incline to other pernicious habits of thought, some deeply embedded in our culture such as trying to satisfy needs by buying things, the easy acceptance of technological change, the primacy of money and economic values in measuring success and gauging relevance, and seeing the natural world as a resource for the economy rather than seeing the economy as nested in the natural world.

Americans may have a particularly difficult time shedding outdated habits of thought. We are a country whose very national character has been shaped by economic abundance.[28] We have pursued it and preached it and are now having the utmost difficulty coming to terms with its consequences.

7 Globalization and the Environment

There are more things in heaven and earth, Horatio,
Than are dreamt of in your philosophy. William
Shakespeare

Globalization, columnist Thomas Friedman says, "shrinks the world from a size medium to a size small."[1] It is a process of integrating not just distant economies but also remote cultures, environments, and governments.[2]

To its proponents, globalization is seen as helping to cure a multitude of the world's ills. To its critics, it is seen as a "false dawn" driven by the "manic logic of global capitalism."[3] But all agree that it is happening, and most believe that it is unstoppable.

Perhaps the only concept as heavily laden with multiple agendas as globalization is "sustainable development." Former President Clinton, a recent convert to sustainable development, has remarked that the phrase is "Aramaic to most people."[4] But within environment and development circles, it has become *mots d'ordre* since being popularized by the World Commission on Environment and Development in 1987. The commission offered this now-famous definition: sustainable development is development that "seeks to meet the needs and aspirations of the present without compromising the ability to meet those of the future."[5] Most analysts now agree that, from an environmental perspective, sustainable development requires living off nature's income rather than consuming natural capital. In the terminology of the economists, it implies nondeclining natural assets, at a minimum.

The call for sustainable development was born of conflicting realities. On one hand, economic expansion will surely occur on a grand scale in the decades ahead. In most countries, rapid economic growth is essential to attack the problem of widespread poverty. On the other, environmental quality has been everywhere deteriorating as economic activity has expanded. Conscientious observers have little choice but to seek a development path that simultaneously alleviates poverty and sustains environmental resources.

Today, the transition to a globalized world is progressing rapidly, but the transition to a sustainable one is not. Some believe that globalization is a prime reason for the failure to realize sustainable development. Others argue that globalization can and should advance the transition to sustainability.

Has economic globalization been an important driving force in the large-scale environmental deterioration that has occurred in recent decades? A broader question is whether economic globalization has been undermining the prospects for sustainable development. If so, must it continue to do so in the future?

These questions address a reality of immense complexity and will not yield to simple answers. Arthur Mol in his *Globalization and Environmental Reform* sets out to show "that it is not globalization that the [Seattle demonstrators] attack and reject, and that it should not be. Globalization . . . is a multifaceted phenomenon with potentially devastating but also potentially beneficial consequences. The environmental

NGOs were particularly afraid—and not without reason—of global-ization in its one-sided neo-liberal, economic aspect."[6]

Mol goes on to point out that rigorous analyses of the links between globalization and the environment are scarce. But he notes that those writers who have addressed the subject have typically come to the same conclusions: "The common view put forward by most scholars was a rather negative one: globalization processes and trends add to environ-mental deterioration, to diminishing control of environmental problems by modern institutions, and to the unequal distribution of environmental consequences and risks between different groups and societies. The dominance of economic (that is, capitalist) globalization processes is often believed to be the root cause of these detrimental environmental effects. Global political institutions, arrangements, and organizations and a global civil society are believed to be lagging behind."[7] This last point is one to which I shall return here and again in chapter 9.

Martin Khor, director of the Third World Network, is a leading critic of current globalization processes. I agree with him sometimes but not always. He asks why the implementation of Agenda 21 and other agreements reached at the Rio Earth Summit, U.N. Conference on Environment and Development, in 1992 has "largely failed." His answer is clear: "The reason for failure is not to be found in the sustain-able development paradigm [forged at Rio]; rather, the paradigm was not given the chance to be implemented. Instead, intense competition came from a rival—the countervailing paradigm of globalisation, driven by the industrialised North and its corporations, that has swept the world in recent years. This is perhaps the most basic factor causing the failure to realise the [Rio] objectives."[8]

Khor believes the main factor in the ascendancy of the market para-digm and the marginalization of the sustainable development paradigm has been "the strong support and aggressive advocacy of the powerful countries" for *both* results. He sees the governments of these countries serving their private commercial interests, downgrading the United Nations in favor of the World Bank and the World Trade Organization, promoting the competitiveness of their economies by minimizing environmental and other standards, and generally giving an increasingly global corporate sector nearly free rein.[9]

Khor is undoubtedly right that the governments of the large-economy, G-7 countries have vigorously pursued the market globalization agenda while badly neglecting the Earth Summit agenda and its efforts to realize sustainable development. What is more interesting is his assertion that market-based globalization has been seen by its advocates as eliminating the need to take the Rio agenda seriously. My own view is that Khor is basically correct on this point, at least with regard to the United States. Many U.S. policymakers have seen the globalization (market) paradigm as supplanting the need for the sustainable development (partnership) paradigm. "Trade not aid" has become a Washington mantra. Writing in *The Economist,* economist Jeffrey Sachs offered a stinging critique of U.S. policy: "America has wanted global leadership on the cheap. It was desperate for the developing world and post-communist economies to buy into its vision, in which globalization, private capital flows and Washington advice would overcome the obstacles to shared prosperity, so that pressures on the rich countries to do more for the poorer countries could be contained by the dream of universal economic growth. In this way, the United States would not have to shell out real money to help the peaceful reconstruction of Russia, or to ameliorate the desperate impoverishment and illness in Africa. . . . Washington became skittish at anything or anybody that challenged this vision."[10]

This said, the eclipse of the Rio Earth Summit commitments has surely been brought about by more than the ascendancy of the globalization paradigm. Many of us hoped that the post–Cold War period would bring a peace dividend of financial and political resources that could be applied to promoting environmental and development objectives. Instead, the United States and others have been enmeshed in a series of military and peacekeeping engagements, now embracing the war on terrorism, that have consumed much of the available time, energy, and money. Shortly after I joined the United Nations Development

Programme in 1993, we began to focus on a disturbing trend—U.N. spending in peacekeeping and humanitarian emergencies was skyrocketing while resources for long-term development assistance focused on poverty and the environment were declining. I and others repeatedly spoke out against cuts in funding for our programs, pointing out that with so many fires starting we should not neglect fire prevention—but the pattern persisted.

Interestingly, even defenders of globalization do not have much to say for themselves on the environment issue. In their *Foreign Policy* article "The Globalization Backlash," John Micklethwait and Adrian Wooldridge ask, "Is globalization destroying the environment?" and answer, "Not really." They point out, correctly, that there are other powerful anti-environmental forces at work beyond globalization (they cite the large annual subsidies for environmentally destructive activities globally) and that multinational corporations are often better environmental performers than local counterparts. But they concede that, in the short term, increased international trade harms the environment by increasing business activity generally because "business of all sorts tends to despoil the environment." Twice they ask, "How much is greenery worth?" implicitly acknowledging that economic benefits exact environmental costs—even while they try to demean the environment as mere "greenery."[11]

Maurice Strong, who led both the Stockholm Conference on the Human Environment in 1972 and the Earth Summit in 1992, has been a successful businessman, diplomat, and environmental leader. He has also become a critic of today's globalization. In his 2001 book *Where on Earth Are We Going?* he writes: "The 'environment' isn't just an issue, something to be fixed while everything else remains the same. Ecological destruction is a sign of the imbalance in the way our industrial civilization sets its priorities and governs itself. The phenomenon we now commonly refer to as 'Globalization' is creating new wealth at an unprecedented scale while increasing the dichotomy between industrial capitalism's victors and victims."[12]

One can identify at least nine reasons to suppose that globalization can exacerbate environmental problems. In this critique, economic globalization leads to (1) an expansion of environmentally destructive growth, (2) a decrease in the ability of national governments to regulate and otherwise cope with environmental challenges, (3) an increase in corporate power and reach, (4) the stimulation of particular sectors like transportation and energy that have largely negative environmental side effects, (5) the increased likelihood of economic crises, (6) the commodification of resources such as water and the decline of traditional local controls on resource use, (7) the spatial separation of action and impact from responsibility, (8) the further ascendancy of the growth imperative, and (9) the rapid spread of invasive species and the resulting biological homogenization.

A contrary list of forces can be developed—factors that suggest that globalization may help environmental quality. (1) Global corporations can help spread the most advanced environmental management technology and techniques. (2) The strengthening of capacities in government to manage economic affairs can have spillover effects, strengthening environmental management. (3) Globalization can lead to increased incomes, which in turn can lead to governmental revenues for environmental and social programs and to increased public demand for environmental amenity. (4) And increasing international trade in such resources as timber could lead to higher prices, more secure property rights, and larger investments in sustaining forest resources. Although something can be said for each of these forces, their effects are certainly farther down the road than most of the negative effects mentioned earlier. Nor on balance do they seem as powerful. The result, as Nobel economist Joseph Stiglitz has noted, is that "globalization today . . . is not working for much of the environment." Nor, in his view, is it "working for many of the world's poor" or "for the stability of the global economy."[13]

Research carried out by political scientists Ben Cashore and Steven Bernstein concluded that globalization does indeed have negative environmental consequences but that these downward pressures can be countered by international pressure coupled with demands that make international investment conditional on a demonstrated commitment to environmental protection.[14]

Whatever the severity of globalization's environmental consequences in the past, the future offers much room for improvement. There are a great many things that can and should be done to promote the greening of globalization and to give it a human face. Indeed, observers have known for many years some of the steps that are required. More than a decade ago, the World Resources Institute convened a distinguished group of thirty Western Hemisphere leaders for a "New World Dialogue on Environment and Development in the Western Hemisphere." Two members of the group were members of their respective senates, Fernando Henrique Cardoso of Brazil and Al Gore, Jr., of the United States, and would later become the president and vice president, respectively, of their countries. In its Open Letter to the Heads of State and Government of the Americas in October 1991, our group said the following: "Realizing this brighter future will require heightened international cooperation, particularly between industrial and developing countries, but also among developing countries. We therefore welcome current initiatives to liberalize trade and to revive growth in our region and more broadly. But these proposals are too limited. They will succeed only in expanding unsustainable and inequitable patterns of growth unless they are complemented by powerful initiatives to promote social equity and to protect the environment. Indeed, there is much reason to believe, based on past experience and current trends, that unless major complementary initiatives are undertaken to bring environmental, economic, and social objectives together in the new synthesis called *sustainable development,* liberalizing trade and reviving growth could lead to short-term gains and long-term disaster. More than anything else, the Compact for a New World must be a compact for sustainable development."[15] The group proposed a North-South compact with eight initiatives, including initiatives for hemispheric cooperation on deforestation, sustainable energy, pollution prevention, poverty, population, science and technology, and additional finance for sustainable development. Liberalization of trade and investment regimes was only *one* of the eight.

Globalization should hold great promise, but that promise is not being realized today, nor will it be unless globalization is consciously managed for people and for the environment. If the world wishes to evolve toward an international economy, and it certainly seems to, it will need to develop an international polity equal to the challenge of governing its newly global economy.

Part Four   The Transition to Sustainability

Despite the repeated alarms rung over the past quarter century, the earth's ills have deepened and widened. Our initial effort at global environmental governance has fallen short, and we must turn with urgency to new approaches and to a new generation of environmental leaders. The focus of the job has to be widened to include economic, political, and social dimensions that are not usually thought of as belonging to environmentalism's purview. The leadership of civil society and of the private sector will be especially important. Technology will play an important part, as will the market—but a market operating with prices and other signals that are honest environmentally. And, at the heart that drives the flow of these many actions, there must be a deeper change, a different way of seeing ourselves in relation to the planet on which we live.

8 Attacking the Root Causes

As never before in history, common destiny beckons us to seek a new beginning. The Earth Charter

Though much is taken, much abides. Alfred, Lord Tennyson

Global environmental challenges are closely interlinked. They cut across economic sectors and geographical regions. They cannot be addressed issue by issue or by one nation or even by a small group of nations acting alone. They are driven by powerful forces and will not yield to the modest efforts we have been mounting.

Against this backdrop, what the world community does in the decades immediately ahead is crucial. Environmental decay will inevitably continue during this period: today's trends pack such enormous momentum that halting them will take many years. But this period can also become the watershed during which nations and peoples everywhere come together finally to deal with the problems massing on the environmental front. If we can make that happen, our legacy from these early decades of the new century will be a world sustained, not a world of wounds.

The Eightfold Way

The principal way to a sustainable world is to apply major resources of time and money to the promotion of eight broad, linked transitions that seek to redefine and redirect growth. These transitions will move us from where we are today to where we need to be for a sustainable future. These transitions require genuine partnership between countries of the North and South, as well as actions far outside the traditional areas of environmental policy. Collectively, they will do three things of immense importance. They will directly attack the underlying drivers of deterioration. They will greatly enhance the prospects for success of treaties and other agreements by altering the context in which the agreements are operating. And they will facilitate a very different, more hopeful and powerful way of doing the business of environmental governance. Political leadership should be measured by whether it promotes this "eightfold way"—the megatrends we need for global environmental protection and sustainability.[1]

In each of these eight areas, there are encouraging and hopeful developments on which to build. And these transitions interact strongly, supporting each other and forming a whole that will one day define a qualitatively new epoch.

Transition 1: A Stable or Smaller World Population

The first of these transitions to sustainability is the most familiar. It is the need for an early demographic transition to a stable or smaller world population. How are we progressing on this front? I would say much better than we expected. The midrange projection of global population for 2050 was 10 billion people; now it is below 9 billion.[2] One projection of developing country population in 2100 was 10.2 billion. Analyses suggest that an escalation of proven approaches could reduce this number to 7.3 billion, with global population leveling off at 8.5 billion and perhaps beginning to decline thereafter.[3]

What are these proven approaches? The prescriptions that have emerged from many studies and observations have been widely applied, and they are remarkably successful. They include empowering women socially and politically, making contraceptives and other noncoercive family planning services available, providing maternal and child health care, education for girls, and employment for women. Declining fertility rates and the demographic transition will be hastened by actions that further these measures, including fully funding the United Nations' Cairo program of action, which embodies these approaches.[4]

I noted earlier Partha Dasgupta's view that if women had control over reproduction, they would choose fewer children. This is proving to be a powerful force. The *New York Times* on 10 March 2002 reported: "For decades, experts assumed that the world's biggest developing nations, the home of hundreds of millions in big families, would push the global population to a precarious 10 billion people by the end of this century. Now, evidence is coming in that women in rural villages and the teeming megacities of Brazil, Egypt, India and Mexico are unexpectedly proving those predictions wrong. In India alone, by 2100 there may be 600 million fewer people than predicted. The declining birthrates in nations where poverty and illiteracy are still widespread defy almost all conventional wisdom. Women are taking charge of their lives— not waiting for the slow processes of education and cultural change."[5] These developments are exciting and suggest that rapid "bottom-up" change by individuals and households is possible.

Of the eight transitions, the demographic transition is the most advanced by far. But a note of caution: the hopeful trends discussed here are not inevitable. If fertility rates were to remain constant in all countries at current levels, global population would double to 12.8 billion people by 2050. The hopeful population projections reported earlier are based in part on past funding of international population programs, which could get either stronger or weaker depending on political decisions. For starters, the United States should work with others to ensure that the Cairo funding and other goals are met.

Transition 2: Free of Mass Poverty

Second, human development must transition to a world that is free of mass poverty, where the prospects for widely shared prosperity are good. Over much of the world, poverty contributes to environmental decline—the poor often have no choice but to lean too heavily on an eroding resource base. (Environmental decline also contributes to poverty.) Enhanced development prospects will also promote peace, amelioration of social and ethnic tensions, and good governance, all of which are necessary for the transition to sustainability.

There is good news to report on the human development front. Since 1960 life expectancy in developing regions has increased from forty-six years to sixty-four. Child death rates have fallen by more than half. Adult literacy rose from 48 percent in 1970 to 74 percent in 2000. Yet the bleak realities of poverty remain. Among the 4.5 billion people who live in developing countries, half live in communities without basic sanitation; a quarter are without safe drinking water and adequate housing; and a fifth are undernourished. Almost 2 billion people lack modern energy services. For the 1.2 billion people who live on less than a dollar a day, there can be no doubt that poverty is a brutal denial of their human rights.[6]

On the policy front, an impressive consensus has emerged around objectives. The international development assistance community has coalesced around the goal of halving the incidence of absolute poverty by 2015, and this goal and others dealing with health and education were endorsed by all governments in the Millennium Assembly of the United Nations.[7] Eliminating large-scale poverty is not a crazy dream. It could be accomplished in the lifetimes of today's young people. But, as with population, a serious threat to achieving these goals is near-miserly development assistance. Low levels of international aid are compounded by unfair trade regimes that restrict developing countries' trade access to the markets of rich nations and subsidize industrial agriculture against competition from developing countries, by the continuing burden of international debt, and by restrictions on access to technology. Sustainable development requires that aid, debt management, trade, private foreign investment and capital flows, and access to technology all work together, not in conflict with one another, as they often do today.

The countries that have reduced poverty greatly have been studied. We know what it takes.[8] I wish to suggest a progression in terms of the means needed to realize the Millennium Development Goal of halving world poverty by 2015. I will start at what I believe is a very naive and incomplete strategy and move toward a full, more integrated, and potentially successful strategy.

At the naive end of the spectrum, some observers merely stress overall economic growth as the solution. We do indeed have to stress economic growth and all the things that are necessary to achieve high levels of it in the poorer countries. Peace, the rule of law, minimum corruption, and a macroeconomic framework that encourages savings and attracts investments are all vital. Liberia, for example, was once a country making steady progress, but the violent conflicts raging there when I visited in 1994 and still occurring today have set the country back by several decades.

Yet growth alone will never suffice. Unaided, it tends to benefit those least in need of it, further dividing societies socially and geographically. The next step is to add social safety nets like welfare and unemployment payments or other supports. Unfortunately, many people think that growth plus social safety nets is an adequate strategy against poverty. I would put many U.S. policymakers in this camp.

The next level of sophistication would add the need for investments in small-scale infrastructure reaching to the poor, such as the farm-to-market roads I saw in Uganda and the small-scale irrigation works I visited in Vietnam. The fourth level would add very large investments in basic social services for the poor—in health, in education, particularly for girls, and in family planning services. Here, bias against the poor must be overcome, including subsidizing higher education to the neglect of primary education, and spending on urban hospitals instead of clean water, sanitation, and control of communicable diseases, which must include a major effort on HIV/AIDS.

The fifth level would add a concerted effort on sustainable livelihoods for the poor, empowering the poor with access to productive assets such as credit (including the microcredit programs that have been successful in Bangladesh and elsewhere), land and clear title to it, training and upgrading skills, appropriate technology, and energy services. Too often, credit rationing favors large borrowers, agricultural programs favor large farmers and ranchers, and the poor lack access to modern energy services. Empowerment of the poor works best when it builds on the traditional knowledge of local communities.

The sixth level would add the need to sustain and regenerate the environmental resource base on which the poor depend. Fully half of the world's jobs still depend on fisheries, forests, and small-scale agriculture. Analysts have long stressed the need to avoid environmentally destructive development projects; more recently the focus has been on environmental restoration.

The final level is the social and political empowerment of the poor, particularly women. Political empowerment means integrating human rights with sustainable development, and it often means empowerment of local communities, which requires decentralization of much decision-making to the local level.

If one works up these levels of increasing sophistication, one finally gets to the proper development model. It includes all the elements. Given all that is required, a successful national antipoverty strategy is not going to fall into place accidentally or easily. It must be the product of conscious political decisions taken at the highest levels, backed by substantial resources, carried forward with full participation of affected communities, and pursued with commitment for a sustained period. To mount a successful national strategy to reduce poverty dramatically, a country must make that strategy one of its highest priorities and keep it there. The international community has a tremendous responsibility to create the external environment (for example, regarding fair trade, generous but tough-minded aid, and debt relief) that promotes such national strategies and helps them to succeed. The OECD aid donors should open their markets to developing country exports, honor the goal set at the Rio Earth Summit of doubling their development assistance, and go much further with debt relief. A responsible level of development assistance from the United States—initially one that put us in the top half of the OECD as a percentage of GDP—would move impressively in this direction.

Transition 3: Environmentally Benign Technologies

The third transition is one in technology. We urgently need a worldwide environmental revolution in technology—a rapid ecological modernization of industry and agriculture. The prescription is straightforward but challenging: the principal way to reduce pollution and resource consumption while achieving expected economic growth is to bring about a wholesale transformation in the technologies that today dominate manufacturing, energy, transportation, and agriculture. Applying knowledge gained in the rapidly developing field of industrial ecology, we should phase out the twentieth-century technologies that have contributed so abundantly to today's problems and invest in twenty-first-century technologies designed with eco-efficiency in mind. The focus should be on "dematerializing" the economy through a new generation of environmentally benign technologies that sharply reduce the consumption of natural resources and the generation of residual products per unit of economic output. Capital investment will shape the future, and investment is all about technology choice.[9]

The good news here is that across a wide front, technologies that would bring about a vast improvement are either available or soon can be. From 1990 to 1998, when global oil and natural gas use grew at a rate of 2 percent annually, and coal consumption grew not at all, wind energy grew at an annual rate of 22 percent, and photovoltaics at

16 percent.[10] Denmark has banned coal and now gets 18 percent of its electricity from wind. Germany is the world's leader in wind energy generation, with wind supplying 3.5 percent of German electricity today and plans to go to 25 percent by 2025. Globally, wind energy is already generating a tenth of the electricity of all nuclear power plants. The growth of electricity from photovoltaic cells jumped to more than 30 percent a year globally between 1998 and 2001, and several European countries as well as Japan have subsidy programs to promote photovoltaic systems.[11] (Electricity prices from photovoltaic systems are still several times normal rates, but the gap is closing.) Because energy is at the root of so many of our environmental ills, transformation of the energy sector must rank as the highest priority.

In his book *Eco-Economy*, Lester Brown identifies eco-economy industries that he sees destined for large investments and rapid growth. Here are some on his list:

Industry	Description
Wind farm construction	Wind electric generation, including off-shore wind farms will grow rapidly over the next few decades, until wind is supplying most of the world's electricity.
Wind turbine manufacturing	Today the number of utility-scale wind turbines is measured in the thousands, but soon it will be measured in the millions, creating an enormous manufacturing opportunity.
Hydrogen generation	As the transition from a carbon-based to a hydrogen-based energy economy progresses, hydrogen generation will become a huge industry as hydrogen replaces coal and oil.
Fuel cell manufacturing	As fuel cells replace internal combustion engines in automobiles and begin generating power in buildings, a huge market will evolve.

Solar cell manufacturing	For many of the 2 billion people living in rural Third World communities who lack electricity, solar cells will be the best bet for electrification.
Light rail construction	As people tire of the traffic congestion and pollution associated with the automobile, cities in industrial and developing countries alike will be turning to light rail to provide mobility.[12]

In a similar exercise, the World Resources Institute has identified a cluster of environmentally critical technologies and called for their rapid development:

- energy capture, including photovoltaics and wind;
- energy storage and applications, including batteries, high-temperature superconductors, hydrogen storage, heat storage, and fuel cells;
- special energy end-uses, including new technologies for superefficient vehicles and buildings;
- improved agricultural techniques, including precision farming (which uses information technology to target inputs of fertilizers, pesticides, and water) and alternative agriculture (which takes advantage of natural cycles, crop rotations, and integrated pest management);
- "lean" and "intelligent" manufacturing systems, which rely heavily on information and control technologies to minimize waste;
- separations processes in manufacturing, including new membrane systems, supercritical fluid extraction, and affinity separation;
- precision fabrication, including thin films and nanolithography; and
- materials design and processing, including new metals, polymers, ceramics, and composites.[13]

There are numerous public policy options to speed the technology revolution: adoption of a national environmental technology policy, a sea change in the level and the pattern of R&D funding and cooperation with the private sector, use of government purchasing power to promote innovative technologies, new regulatory and tax incentives for investments in clean technologies and for retirement of outmoded ones, technology-forcing regulations and requirements, and new policies to transfer clean technology from country to country.[14] (What we do not need are efforts to shift old technology to the developing world, such as General Motors' current production of Buick Regals and Centurys in China.) The needed regulatory and economic incentives should include both a shift away from technology-based standards (such as the requirement for "best practicable control technology" in the Clean Water Act) toward standards that provide incentives for continuous technological improvements as well as a shift to full-cost pricing, where full environmental costs are incorporated in prices. These are major areas for policy improvement in the United States and elsewhere. Every new investment should embody the best environmental technology available.

The process by which cutting-edge, green technologies get introduced —green innovation—is now being studied by a group at the Massachusetts Institute of Technology. Early findings suggest the importance of what the researchers call "public entrepreneurship networks" —informal partnerships of public agencies, private companies, NGOs, and others that form around a particular objective. One key finding: the commitment of the top corporate management is indispensable when there are significant economic uncertainties, and there usually are.[15]

In their book *Cradle to Cradle*, William McDonough and Michael Braungart carry the idea of environmental design further, seeing human industry as a force to be encouraged, not restrained: "We see a world of abundance, not limits. In the midst of a great deal of talk about reducing the human ecological footprint, we offer a different vision. What if humans designed products and systems that celebrate an abundance of human creativity, culture, and productivity? That are so intelligent and safe, our species leaves an ecological footprint to delight in, not lament? . . .

"We would like to suggest a new design assignment. Instead of fine-tuning the existing destructive framework, why don't people and industries set out to create the following:

- Buildings that, like trees, produce more energy than they consume and purify their own waste water
- Factories that produce effluents that are drinking water
- Products that, when their useful life is over, do not become useless waste but can be tossed onto the ground to decompose and become food for plants and animals and nutrients for soil; or, alternately, that can return to industrial cycles to supply high-quality raw materials for new products
- Billions, even trillions, of dollars' worth of materials accrued for human and natural purposes each year
- Transportation that improves the quality of life while delivering goods and services
- A world of abundance, not one of limits, pollution, and waste."[16]

In effect, McDonough and Braungart are challenging us to transform economic investment from a negative environmental force into a positive one—an exciting, challenging assignment for the new generation.

Transition 4: Environmentally Honest Prices

The fourth transition is a transition in the public management of the economy and in the use of market forces. It can be described at the level of traditional "neoclassical economics" and at a more far-reaching nontraditional level of "ecological economics." In the neoclassical description, we seek a market transition to a world in which market forces are harnessed to environmental ends, particularly by making prices reflect the full environmental costs. My colleagues at Yale's environment school Marian Chertow and Daniel Esty have properly noted that "the triumph of market economics makes all the more clear the need for laws and rules to ensure that pollution harms do not go unaccounted for."[17] The revolution in technology just discussed will not happen unless there is a parallel revolution in pricing. As discussed in chapter 6, full-cost pricing is everywhere thwarted today by the failure of governments to eliminate environmentally perverse subsidies and to ensure that external environmental costs—including damages to public health, natural resources, and ecosystem services—are captured in market prices. The corrective most needed now is environmentally honest prices.

Environmental economists make a powerful case for full-cost pricing and have identified a variety of economic instruments that are available to move in this direction. They advocate securing property rights to overcome the "tragedy of the commons" problem, tradable emission permits, pollution taxes, user fees, shifting subsidies from environmentally damaging activities to beneficial ones, and making polluters and others financially liable for the damages they cause.[18] Traditional "command and control" regulation, as well as outright bans, will still be essential in various contexts, in part because many environmental assets, such as endangered species, cannot and should not be valued in dollars and cents. The World Trade Organization can play a constructive role in this area by promoting negotiations to reduce perverse subsidies. No shortage exists in techniques to "get the prices right," and doing so is fundamental to the transition to sustainability.

A great many other changes need to be made for our economic system to properly value the environment. One is reform of national income and product accounts. Governments live or die by their success with GDP, so it is very important to measure it properly. A National Academy of Sciences panel chaired by economist William Nordhaus offered an important corrective: "The intuitive idea behind the desire to broaden the U.S. national accounts is straightforward. Natural resources such as petroleum, minerals, clean water, and fertile soils are assets of the economy in much the same way as are computers, homes, and trucks. An important part of the economic picture is therefore missing if natural assets are omitted in creating the national balance sheet.

Likewise, consuming stocks of valuable subsoil assets such as fossil fuels or water or cutting first-growth forests is just as much a drawdown on the national wealth as is consuming aboveground stocks of wheat, cutting commercially managed forests, or driving a truck. . . .

"The panel concludes that developing a set of comprehensive nonmarket economic accounts is a high priority for the nation. Developing nonmarket accounts to address such concerns as environmental impacts [and] the value of nonmarket natural resources . . . would illuminate a wide variety of issues concerning the economic state of the nation."[19]

Are we making progress in adopting these prescriptions to correct the market? Here we encounter something of a paradox. On one hand we are in the midst of a sea change in the formulation of environmental policy: there is definitely a major shift toward use of economic instruments and away from the older command and control approach. The OECD has noted that "over the last decade, economic instruments have been playing a growing role in environmental policies of OECD countries. In this context, a distinctive feature is the increasing role of environmentally related taxes. All countries have introduced environmental taxes to a varying extent. . . . The revenue from environmentally related taxes averages roughly 2% of GDP in Member Countries."[20] One of the most hopeful developments is the tax shift idea adopted in Germany and other European nations. Moving in four stages starting in 1999, Germany is shifting the tax burden from something one wants to encourage—work and the wages that result—to something one wants to discourage—energy consumption and the pollution that results.[21]

The flowering of market-based approaches is an important and encouraging development. But, paradoxically, we do not yet seem to be in the midst of a shift to full-cost, environmentally honest prices. Economic instruments such as those mentioned previously are increasingly being used, but mostly to achieve greater efficiency in environmental protection and not rigorously to get the prices right. If environmentally honest prices were the goal, more emphasis would be given to subsidy elimination, strict regulation, and the accounting of environmental costs, such as the economic value of the loss of ecosystems services when wetlands are destroyed.

Earlier I indicated that there was a more far-reaching, less traditional path of economic reform. It has been developed in part by the new school of "ecological economics."[22] Sustainable development in their view requires that natural capital be maintained intact—that we live off nature's income and do not consume natural capital. Herman Daly has explained what this means for management of renewable natural resources: "First, that harvest rates should equal regeneration rates (sustained yield). Second, that waste emission rates should equal the natural assimilative capacities of the ecosystems into which the wastes are emitted. Regenerative and assimilative capacities must be treated as natural capital, and failure to maintain these capacities must be treated as capital consumption, and therefore not sustainable."[23]

And for sustainable use of nonrenewable resources, Daly explains that "use of nonrenewables requires that any investment in the exploitation of a nonrenewable resource must be paired with a compensating investment in a renewable substitute (e.g. oil extraction paired with tree planting for wood alcohol). The idea is to divide the net receipts from the nonrenewable into an income component that can be consumed currently each year, and a capital component that must be invested in the renewable substitute. The division is made in such a way that the renewable will be yielding, by the end of the life of the nonrenewable, an annual sustainable yield equal to the income component of the nonrenewable receipts."[24]

Ecological economists focus on the economy "throughput"—what we extract from the natural world to put through our economic system and what we return to the environment. They are therefore always concerned about the scale of the human enterprise in relation to its environmental setting, whether local or global. And they tend to believe that even full-cost, environmentally honest pricing will not get a society all the way to sustainable development. Other policy measures are still necessary to ensure that the rates of extraction of resources do not exceed regenerative capacities and to ensure that wastes do not exceed the environment's assimilative capacities.[25]

Paul Hawken and Amory and Hunter Lovins have argued that the fundamental economic shift we need requires a major reorientation of conventional thinking: "Following Einstein's dictum that problems can't be solved within the mind-set that created them, the first step toward any comprehensive economic and ecological change is to understand the mental model that forms the basis of present economic thinking. The mind-set of the present capitalist system might be summarized as follows:

- Economic progress can best occur in free-market systems of production and distribution where reinvested profits make labor and capital increasingly productive.
- Competitive advantage is gained when bigger, more efficient plants manufacture more products for sale to expanding markets.
- Growth in total output (GDP) maximizes human well-being.
- Any resource shortages that do occur will elicit the development of substitutes.
- Concerns for a healthy environment are important but must be balanced against the requirements of economic growth, if a high standard of living is to be maintained.
- Free enterprise and market forces will allocate people and resources to their highest and best uses."[26]

Natural capitalism and the possibility of a new industrial system, in their view, are based on "a very different mind-set and set of values than conventional capitalism. Its fundamental assumptions include the following:

- The environment is not a minor factor of production but rather is 'an envelope containing, provisioning, and sustaining the entire economy.'

- The limiting factor to future economic development is the availability and functionality of natural capital, in particular, life-supporting services that have no substitutes and currently have no market value.
- Misconceived or badly designed business systems, population growth, and wasteful patterns of consumption are the primary causes of the loss of natural capital, and all three must be addressed to achieve a sustainable economy.
- Future economic progress can best take place in democratic, market-based systems of production and distribution in which all forms of capital are fully valued, including human, manufactured, financial, and natural capital.
- One of the keys to the most beneficial employment of people, money, and the environment is radical increases in resource productivity.
- Human welfare is best served by improving the quality and flow of desired services delivered, rather than by merely increasing the total dollar flow.
- Economic and environmental sustainability depends on redressing global inequities of income and material well-being.
- The best long-term environment for commerce is provided by true democratic systems of governance that are based on the needs of people rather than business."[27]

Hawken and the Lovinses are proposing a fundamental transformation in the way Americans and many others commonly think about the economy and the environment. They are saying, in essence, that it is time for a Declaration of Dependence—the economy's dependence on the environment.

Transition 5: Sustainable Consumption

The fifth transition is a transition in consumption from unsustainable patterns to sustainable ones. Individual consumers and households can exercise enormous power in the marketplace, and they can shift their preferences with remarkable speed, as fashion fads and the unfortunate example of SUVs make plain. We must work for a new "sustainable living movement"—the rapid spread of consumers and households that are environmentally smart and socially aware. Such a sustainable living movement may offer the best chance we have of achieving rapid change in many of the areas where it is needed. A sustainable diet campaign could help transform agribusiness and the fishing industry. A consumer commitment to sustainable energy systems could force changes in energy production while helping protect climate, and a commitment to toxic-free home and workplace environments could drive the chemical industry to new, safer products.

Even at levels of consumption that are high and growing, consumers can insist on at least two green things. First, we can shift purchases to products and services where the making and the use of the product are carried out in an environmentally friendly way. And, second, we can insist that provisions be made for the recycle and reuse of consumer products. When the consumer is done with the television, fridge, range, or computer, the manufacturer should take it back and see that it is reused, recycled, or disposed of in an environmentally responsible way. At a more basic level, we need a change in values that sees overconsumption and waste as morally wrong—I will say more about this in chapter 10.

There are hopeful signs in these areas. Product certification, green labeling, and product biographies have made a start.[28] Notable developments include the Forest Stewardship Council's efforts promoting the certification and labeling of wood products as having been produced in sustainably managed forests and the Marine Stewardship Council's program certifying sustainable fishery practices. Increasingly, consumers are voting green in the marketplace, and that is driving change. A group of experts assembled by the Center for a New American Dream sees "the emergence of an alternative in farmers' markets, worker cooperatives, healthy communities, land-use planning, socially responsible businesses, organic cotton, hybrid electric vehicles, barter networks, micro-enterprise, flexible work arrangements, simple living, reduced television watching, environmentally certified wood and fish, and a cultural renaissance of poetry, storytelling, dance, and reconnection to wild places. The new system is being built from the local level up."[29]

Another hopeful sign is the new legislation in Europe and Japan requiring that consumer durables be recycled. Some of these laws require that the product be returned to the producer, "cradle to cradle," all of which has the effect of encouraging the producer to think about reusing components and materials from the outset. The European Parliament has adopted laws obliging manufacturers to pay for the recycling of electrical appliances such as shavers, refrigerators, and computers.[30] In 2002 Dell announced a voluntary program of computer recycling. The consumer is responsible only for shipping charges to the nearest recycling center. Dell plans to recycle and reuse 98 percent of the original materials.[31]

A report prepared in 2003 for a group of U.S. foundations, the Environmental Grantmakers Association, encouraged investment in five areas to promote sustainable consumption:

- *Increase consumer awareness and choice.* "Grantmakers need to underwrite communications campaigns, school curricula, and other investments in cultural currency to raise awareness and engage citizens and consumers for this cause. Consumers also need to understand how to buy environmentally friendly products, and how to signal to producers that a growing constituency of green consumers is on the move."
- *Promote innovative policies.* "This grantmaking approach involves increasing the political support for sustainability initiatives, possibly beginning with a focus on model policy initiatives at the local and state levels. There are many new, innovative policies that can provide incentives, assess more accurate prices (tax policy) and eliminate subsidies of wasteful or unsustainable practices."
- *Accelerate demand for green products.* "Businesses, governments, uni-

versities and other institutions are major consumers of goods and services. This purchasing power is a fundamental level for change because suppliers must listen to their customers. . . . When billions of dollars—from governments, universities, and companies—are redirected to sustainably harvested and produced products, the market responds and producers change their practices."

• *Demand corporate accountability.* "One key lever for change focuses on emerging corporate campaigns and initiatives that spur companies to be accountable to their socially responsible investors and customers. Consumer campaigns, boycotts and shareholder advocacy are effective ways to influence corporate behavior, because corporations want to protect their brand value and company reputation."

• *Encourage sustainable business practices.* "NGOs, governments and others can help companies 'green' their products and services—through such means as mapping their environmental footprints; rethinking resource extraction, use and recycling; sustainable re-design of products; and analysis of supply-chains and their environmental impacts."[32]

This is an excellent agenda. It deserves support by consumers, businesses, and governments, not only foundations. And, by the way, we should not think of the sustainable consumption agenda as something relevant only for the rich countries of the OECD. Asia now has more consumers with annual incomes exceeding seven thousand dollars than North America and Europe combined.

Transition 6: Knowledge and Learning

The sixth transition is a transition in knowledge and learning. Here the goals are to create the new knowledge that is needed for the transition to sustainability, ensure that every student who emerges from school is environmentally literate, close the widening gap between science and the public, and train a new generation of environmental professionals.

In their work with the National Academy of Sciences, William Clark and Roberts Kates have called for a dramatic strengthening of "sustainability science." They call for "a capacity for long-term, intelligent investment in the production of relevant knowledge, know-how, and the use of both must be a component of any strategy for the transition to sustainability. In short, this strategy must be one not just of thinking but also of doing. Our explorations suggest that this strategy should include a spectrum of initiatives, from curiosity-driven research addressing fundamental processes of environmental and social change, to focused policy experiments designed to promote specific sustainability goals."[33] These goals deserve strong support in federal science funding.

The science-based analytical work of the Intergovernmental Panel on Climate Change has proven indispensable to climate negotiators and citizens alike. A comparable large-scale effort—the Millennium Ecosystem Assessment—is now under way, seeking to provide a comprehensive evaluation of the natural capital of the earth, how it has changed, and at what cost.

Physicist Murray Gell-Mann has stressed the importance of general education. He urges not just a transition in knowledge and understanding but "in dissemination of that knowledge and understanding. . . . Only if there is a higher degree of comprehension, among ordinary people as well as elite groups, of the complex issues facing humanity is there any hope of achieving sustainable quality."[34] If we had invested generously in environmental education at all levels over the past three decades, we would not be in as dangerous a situation as we find ourselves in today. A simple understanding of the impacts on climate change of various daily activities can cause people to act to reduce those impacts—as well as bring the issue of climate change into the political system. The print media, television, and others who reach the general public have an obligation to make the global-scale threats come alive as they did with the domestic threats of the 1970s. Otherwise they are not reporting the news.

With so many public issues today driven by science and technology (or the rejection of them), a well-ordered democracy demands much larger investments in scientific and environmental literacy. The Roper opinion polling organization reported in 2002 that only a third of American adults passed a simple quiz on environmental topics, while only 12 percent passed a quiz on basic energy knowledge.[35]

A further dimension is professional training in environmental management. Managing human interactions with the natural world, from levels local to global, demands extraordinary sophistication and high levels of expertise. Many solutions to today's environmental challenges lie outside the established "environmental sector." Environmental objectives now need to be incorporated into corporate planning, energy strategy, technology policy, R&D funding, tax policy, international trade and finance, development assistance, and other matters that once seemed far removed. While environmental dimensions can and should be introduced into business and other professional schools, institutions as diverse as the Yale School of Forestry and Environmental Studies, the National University of Singapore, and the Tata Energy and Resources Institute in India have introduced special advanced degrees in professional environmental management to prepare young people for these challenges. A bedrock assignment is to empower a new generation of leaders with the best possible education and training for what they will face.

These six of the eight transitions are vital to the success of the effort to chart a new course in global environmental protection. But they will not get far without strong and effective government action motivated by an aroused and active citizenry. The needed transitions in governance and in public attitudes and motivation are taken up in the next two chapters.

9 Taking "Good Governance" Seriously

You know what good government is? It's the same old govern-
ment in a helluva fright. Heard in Canada

The seventh transition must take place in institutions and governance.
The World Business Council for Sustainable Development, a leading
international group of major corporations, has sketched several illus-
trative scenarios depicting different approaches to environmental governance. One they playfully call "FROG": First Raise Our Growth.
The FROG philosophy is to meet economic challenges first and worry
about the environment later. FROG is thus a business-as-usual scenario
leading to huge environmental costs. FROG leads not just to a wrecked
global ecosystem but to a wrecked global society as well. It is a path
to failure even in the eyes of the business-oriented WBCSD.[1]

In the WBCSD's other two scenarios, sustainability is successfully
pursued, but the approaches are very different. Under "GEOpolity,"
people turn to governments to focus the market on environmental and
social ends, and they rely heavily on intergovernmental institutions
and treaties. GEOpolity is the world of international environmental

law and global environmental agreements. Under "JAZZ," the third scenario, people and businesses create a world full of unscripted, voluntary initiatives that are decentralized and improvisational, like jazz. In the JAZZ world, information about business behavior is abundant, and good conduct is enforced by public opinion and consumer decisions. Governments facilitate more than regulate, environmental and consumer groups are very active, and businesses see strategic advantage in doing the right thing.

Employing this useful framework, we can say that the initial international response to global challenges has tried to move the world from FROG to GEOpolity. For reasons I reviewed in chapter 5, this move has not worked well. Nations have not yet genuinely embraced GEOpolity, and where GEOpolity approaches have been used, they have been too weak to be successful.

Getting serious about global environmental governance requires new action on two mutually supportive fronts: pursuing a very different approach to GEOpolity, and taking JAZZ to scale, enlarging it until it is a major part of the solution.

What does it mean to pursue GEOpolity differently? As we saw in chapter 5, the current world of GEOpolity is a world that is designed to fail. How can it be redesigned for success? Basically, two things must happen. First, we must alter the broad "external" context—the setting —from which we expect impressive legal regimes to emerge and in which we expect them to be effectively implemented. And second, "internal" to the GEOpolity process, we need very different international institutions, procedures, and core understandings. International environmental law is failing today on the big issues, but it need not.

Regarding the "external" context of GEOpolity, most basic is the transition in governance to capable, accountable, and democratic governments. The United Nations Development Programme estimates that today about 65 percent of the world's people live in countries with multiparty electoral systems and that 121 of 147 countries surveyed had some or all of the elements of formal democracy.[2] Progress on this front is sine qua non. It can be aided by development assistance focused on building capacities in government, on fighting corruption, on political and civil rights, and on elections and democratic reforms. When I was at UNDP, I saw over and over again the need for initiatives in these areas. By the time I left in 1999, we had over a third of our resources programmed to support "good governance" in developing countries, but we were able to meet only a small portion of the need.

Development progress in the poorer regions is essential for many reasons, but its relevance here is that GEOpolity will never succeed unless development is succeeding. The only world that works is one in which the aspirations of poor people and poor nations for fairness and opportunity are being realized. Developing country views in international negotiations on environment are powerfully influenced by their fear of the costs of environmental measures, their focus on their own compelling economic and social challenges, and their distrust of the intentions and policies of the industrial countries.[3] Sustained and sustainable human development, strongly supported by the international community, provides the only context in which the developing world has enough confidence, trust, and hope to ground the difficult measures needed to realize environmental objectives.

Beyond sharply improving overall development prospects, we need to bring both creativity and resources to the forging of "compacts" or "bargains" between the rich countries of the North and poorer countries of the South.[4] Under these arrangements, poorer countries would take impressive steps to halt deforestation and biodiversity loss, for example, while rich countries provide financial, political, and other support for these efforts (which will often be politically difficult and risky) as well as for the poorer countries' development priorities. With a portfolio of over sixteen billion dollars, the Global Environmental Facility assists developing countries in meeting international objectives, principally in climate and biodiversity protection, and can be thought of as a type of broad global compact. It should be supplemented by a flowering of country-specific compacts, incorporating and linking priority goals of industrial and developing countries. I discussed one type of such compacts, involving the protection of forests, in chapter 2. To succeed, these compacts must put providing sustainable livelihoods for the poor at the heart of conservation planning.

Regarding arrangements "internal" to GEOpolity, there must be new procedures, institutions, and understandings if GEOpolity is to do the job. Strengthening GEOpolity first requires international acceptance of certain fundamental, underlying principles. Professionals in international environmental law have called for a binding covenant incorporating basic international environmental law principles.[5] The following are among the most important:

Fundamental human right. All human beings have a right to an environment adequate for their health and well-being.

Common concern. The global environment is a common concern of humanity.

Common but differentiated responsibilities. In view of their different contributions to global environmental degradation and their different capacities to support solutions, states have common but differentiated responsibilities.

Duty not to cause environmental harm. States have the responsibility to ensure that activities within their jurisdiction or control do not damage the environment of other states or of areas beyond the limits of national jurisdiction.

Integration. In order to achieve sustainable development, environmental protection shall constitute an integral part of the development process and cannot be considered in isolation from it.

The polluter pays principle. National authorities should promote the internalization of environmental costs and the use of economic instruments, taking into account the approach that the polluter should, in principle, bear the cost of pollution.

The precautionary principle. Where there are threats of serious or irreversible damage, lack of full scientific certainty shall not be used as a reason for postponing cost-effective measures to prevent environmental degradation.

Public participation. Environmental issues are best handled with the participation of all concerned citizens, at the relevant level.

Right to development. The right to development must be fulfilled so as to equitably meet developmental and environmental needs of present and future generations.

It is worth noting that these are essentially the "Rio Principles" adopted informally at the Earth Summit more than a decade ago. That legal scholars and others see the need to elevate them to the level of a binding agreement is yet another reflection of how much of what was agreed at the Rio Earth Summit has never been implemented. Within this framework, the precautionary principle could not be more important, given how rapidly potentially hazardous chemicals and technologies can be introduced and spread.

Today's GEOpolity approach can also be redesigned for success by insisting on new procedures for setting international requirements and on new institutions, including a World Environment Organization.

There are many innovative ways the decision-making process in GEOpolity can be improved. As has happened with the Montreal Protocol and the Stockholm Convention on Persistent Organic Pollutants, the Conference of the Parties to a convention can be empowered to make certain types of regulatory decisions that would not need to be ratified as separate treaties, and decision-making procedures can be adopted whereby a two-thirds supermajority, a double majority (a majority of both industrial and developing countries), or even a mere majority of the COP members could make decisions binding for all. Conceivably a COP could even delegate certain rulemaking or standard-setting powers to an expert body, provided there were safeguards ensuring broad public participation. The COP would then limit itself to providing the general policy framework and providing a check against abuse of discretion, much as Congress and the federal courts supervise decision-making in U.S. regulatory agencies. Under all of these arrangements, enforcement procedures could be introduced whereby the COP, the treaty secretariat, or an aggrieved party (government or nongovernment) can take a government before a court or some adjudicatory body to compel action.

The European Community/European Union has seen a progression in which environmental policy has moved from being the separate province of each European country to being more common throughout Europe. The extent of the change is reflected in a *New York Times* article of 2001: "The European Commission plans to take eight countries to the European Court for not implementing water standards. Britain, Belgium, Spain and Luxembourg failed to meet the December 2000 deadline for drinking water; France, Greece, Germany and Ireland failed to meet standards for waste water or bathing water."[6]

There was a moment in 1989 when the world seemed ready to change. Motivated primarily by concern over global warming, twenty-four countries—among them France, Germany, Brazil, India, and Japan—signed the Hague Declaration, which called for an international body that could make non-unanimous decisions needed to protect the global environment.[7] Forty countries eventually signed the declaration, but conspicuous by their absence were most of the permanent members of the U.N. Security Council—the United States, China, Russia, and Britain. So the Hague Declaration died an early death. But this history does remind us that sometimes seemingly far-out ideas can quickly gather strength and prominence.

What may be the next steps forward for GEOpolity? Over the past decade, the leaders of France, Germany, and other countries have called for the creation of a World Environment Organization. UNEP, as we have seen, is very far from that today. It is strange to have a WHO, WTO, WIPO, ILO, and so on and not have a WEO. If one were writing on a clean slate—approaching afresh the question of what international regulatory organizations should be created—the case for a WEO would be among the very strongest. Many of the arguments brought forth in the 1970s for federalizing U.S. environmental law apply to the need for globalizing environmental protection in a world where pollution knows no boundaries and where trade, deployment of technology, and investment flows are increasingly international. Imagine: what if nations had put as much energy into a WEO as they have put into the WTO?

There are several models of a WEO, ranging from quite modest to quite powerful.[8] In one model, UNEP would become a larger and more independent entity by becoming a "specialized agency" of the United Nations. (WHO and FAO are prominent specialized agencies.) These steps would increase the stature of the agency, enlarging its financial resources and providing for a more efficient and effective structure for governance and leadership. The next ratchet up would bring the various environmental treaties together under a WEO, and the most ambitious idea would create a world environment agency entrusted with setting international standards and enforcing them against laggard countries.

If we are to ever see a WEO, it will probably be essential to start at the modest end of the spectrum and strengthen the new organization over time as the need arises and as trust and confidence build. I would favor beginning with a new U.N. specialized agency that would incorporate UNEP, reflect modern organizational concepts, and *initially* do the following:

- provide an international vehicle for national environmental ministers, much as WHO is the focal point for health ministries around the world;
- promote international environmental law, including new treaties, and provide a common secretariat and dispute resolution services for the various existing treaty regimes;
- serve as a global environmental watchdog, ombudsman, and catalyst;
- provide global monitoring of conditions and trends, as well as foresight and early warning;
- develop consensus around informal international goals and mobilize financing and launch campaigns related to them;

- assess and report on national and international performance and progress; and
- coordinate and sponsor relevant scientific research.

Further, WEO would provide an international center of expertise on what works and what does not in environmental law, policy, and management. Countries setting up environmental programs at national and regional levels could seek advice and assistance. Information and data banks could be accessed by all. Thanks to an outpouring of scholarship, we now know much better the criteria for success in international environmental regimes. Future efforts in global environmental governance will have to build on this knowledge, pursue science-based and data-driven approaches to "smart regulation," and use market-based mechanisms such as emissions trading, which has been successfully deployed against acid rain and is now being used to protect climate.[9] More focused agreements involving smaller numbers of parties should be one avenue of pursuit; another should be agreements that address explicitly the need for technology transformation.

Having a well-funded World Environment Organization such as this would make a major difference, and its mandate should be strengthened as experience is gained and responsible performance proven. Institutional development is also essential in another area. We urgently need to devise new, innovative arrangements associated with the United Nations where the environmental and social rules of the road for economic globalization can be debated and devised and where the often-conflicting objectives under the sustainable development umbrella can be brought together. Current arrangements for addressing these issues are woefully inadequate.

Created after the Earth Summit in Rio, the U.N.'s Commission on Sustainable Development was supposed to take up such issues, but I saw in the United Nations that it had become little more than a talk shop. Nor are the mega-meetings of the United Nations up to the task. The 2002 World Summit on Sustainable Development in Johannesburg was a true sustainable development summit in the sense that advocates of all three dimensions of sustainable development—the "triple bottom line" of economy, environment, and society—were there under one roof arguing their cases, raising real issues, and confronting those with different interests and perspectives.[10] It was not a social summit dealing only with poverty, social exclusion, and human rights. It was not an economic and globalization summit addressing only trade and investment, finance for development, and transfer of technology. And it was not an environmental summit focusing only on large-scale biotic impoverishment and pollution. Johannesburg was instead a summit about the intersections of these issues, and it was as sprawling and unwieldy as the sustainable development concept itself. But, because of this, it accurately reflected the dynamics of these issues as they are in reality today. Johannesburg revealed a world greatly divided on key issues: corporate accountability, globalization and the WTO, trade and subsidies, climate and energy, development priorities and aid, and many others. The summit debates raised the key issues in making economic globalization supportive of sustainable development, but in the end delegates could only agree on platitudes and on-one-hand-on-the-other-hand. What my students and I saw at Johannesburg was that the main interest of many governments there was damage limitation—avoiding anything that looks like a real commitment to which they would be held accountable, especially if it would cost money.

With more leadership, better preparation, and a more focused agenda, future efforts could resolve real-world issues of inevitable difficulty and complexity. But today the United Nations lacks a forum for these negotiations. It is certainly not the Commission on Sustainable Development or another mega-conference like Johannesburg. Using modern organizational design concepts, it should be possible to create new and innovative arrangements associated with the United Nations to address these issues. That is a good challenge for the new generation.

Most broadly, the international push for liberalized trade and investment flows should be complemented by equally concerted efforts on the environmental and social fronts. Norms and rules of the road are needed to guide globalization—to protect and benefit poor countries and poor people, the environment, workers, consumers, and investors. The WTO should be reformed to make it more open and broadly accountable, with different principles and procedures to guide its decisions. An international polity should evolve and become as robust as the international economy. While efforts to promote economic globalization proceed apace through the WTO and elsewhere, policy-makers should pursue, with equal determination, reforms and institutions needed in the social and environmental areas.

Building a new GEOpolity also involves giving the public access to the governance process, including information needed for responsible participation.[11] International environmental law is still far too dominated by the outmoded idea that only governments get to play. Principle 10 of the Rio Declaration began to break with this orthodoxy: "Environmental issues are best handled with the participation of all concerned citizens. . . . At the national level each individual shall have appropriate access to information concerning the environment . . . and the opportunity to participate in the decision making processes. . . . Effective access to judicial and administrative proceedings . . . shall be provided."[12]

Rio's Principle 10 focuses mostly on access at the national level, but access at the international level is just as important. Until citizens can have their say in international fora, get the information they need, submit petitions for action and complaints for noncompliance, participate in hearings and initiate judicial proceedings to enforce international law—all the things that are available in many countries at the national level—international environmental law and policy will never have the dynamism it so badly needs. Law professors David Hunter and Durwood Zaelke have called for an international administrative procedures treaty to set minimum norms on how intergovernmental organizations relate to citizens.[13]

Environmental organizations and other NGOs have been indispensable to the development of the major international environmental agreements. They have brought issues to the fore, built public support for action, suggested treaty provisions, and even offered draft language. I enjoyed an analysis of ozone protection by Reiner Grundmann. He argues that, if you want an agreement as tough as the Montreal Protocol you will need both NGOs and scientists on your side, you've got to fight doggedly for it, and you must outmaneuver the opposition.[14] Grundmann observes, I believe correctly, that the Montreal Protocol battle was won because the proponents of action:

- defined the problem on their terms as a very serious cancer and other public health threats;
- made the "precautionary principle" the decision rule, rather than the "wait-till-certainty" approach;
- were given a big boost by a major "focusing event"—the discovery of the ozone hole over Antarctica; and
- had a better network and more hustle than the opposition.

  Grundmann explains: "The U.S. position for the international negotiations . . . was confirmed in the spring of 1987. Shortly before that, the anti-regulation network, rallying within the Domestic Policy Council, had sparked off a new controversy within the federal government. The Secretary of the Interior, Hodel, apparently favored a 'personal protection plan' [that is, sun screen and broad-brimmed hats!] instead of international regulation. The NRDC exploited this rumor by making it public, which backfired on Hodel and his allies. In an article with the catchy headline 'Advice on Ozone May Be: Wear Hats and Stand in the Shade' *The Wall Street Journal* quoted Hodel as saying: 'People who don't stand out in the sun—it doesn't affect them.' The attempt to redefine the situation as one of personal risk ended in ridicule once it was made public. EPA administrator Lee Thomas confirmed the U.S. option of a 95 percent reduction in CFC production, which was supported by the Secretary of State, Shultz. Shultz appointed Richard Benedick as the State Department's Deputy Assistant Secretary for Environmental, Health, and Natural Resource Issues, and as chief negotiator for the international talks. As this episode shows, the U.S. adopted its leadership role willy-nilly. Beneath the governmental level, an active policy network influenced the course of action of the U.S., and also of other countries. Apart from visible scientists such as Molina and Rowland, the network consisted of quieter scientists acting as policy advisers (such as Bob Watson), people at NRDC (David Doniger), WRI (Alan Miller and Irving Mintzer), the EPA (Steven Anderson, James Hofmann, Steve Seidel), and of course, at UNEP. They also had contacts across the Atlantic to their European colleagues. This network spread vital pieces of information around the globe at a critical juncture of the international negotiation process."[15]

I was president of WRI at the time, and from my perspective Grundmann accurately describes how it happened. It is interesting to contrast these circumstances with those that have plagued agreement on climate change. Certainly, one notable contrast is the failure to get the precautionary principle as the decision rule for climate change.

MIT's environmental treaty authority, Lawrence Susskind, argues for formal recognition of the role of nongovernmental interests. He sees full-fledged advisory and monitoring roles as indispensable. "Although important questions remain about how specific organizations and their representatives should be selected (in response to questions about accountability), these should not be used as an excuse to keep unofficials on the sidelines any longer."[16]

Susskind also advocates an interesting and important institutional innovation: an Amnesty International for the global environment.[17] To be successful in preparing periodic reports on each nation's environmental performance, the effort would have to be well funded, independent of other organizations, and totally committed to fearless but objective reporting. Such an effort could prove enormously valuable in galvanizing national and world opinion, especially on large-scale projects of high environmental risk, and would be a strong complement to the Environmental Sustainability Index and other efforts to measure country-by-country progress toward sustainability.[18]

If these are the types of things that need to happen to take GEOpolity seriously, what about the other path, JAZZ, and taking JAZZ to scale?

For my money, green JAZZ is the most exciting arena of ongoing action today. Environmental groups, consumer groups, and other NGOs, private businesses, state and local governments, foundations, religious organizations, investors, and others are behind a remarkable outpouring of initiatives that are the most hopeful things happening today.

At the state and local levels, initiatives are flourishing: the smart growth movement, sustainable cities, state and local greenplans, state climate protection initiatives, innovative state regulatory approaches and green purchasing programs, and environmental standards in building codes, to mention some of the developments.[19] Through the International Council for Local Environmental Initiatives, about 140 local governments are now part of a Climate Protection Campaign to reduce greenhouse gas emissions.[20] The Pew Climate Center has identified twenty-six separate state initiatives that address the challenge of climate change.[21] Thirteen states now require electric power utilities to include renewable energy as a portion of their business.

Chicago under Mayor Richard Daley has declared that it wants to be America's greenest city—and this time not by dumping green dye in the Chicago River on Saint Patrick's Day.[22] In February 2003, seven states announced plans for a lawsuit to force the federal government to regulate carbon dioxide emissions from power plants, the latest in a series of state and city legal actions challenging the Bush administration's go-slow approach to global climate change.[23]

The product certification movement is an example of still another pathbreaking phenomenon: the rise of information-rich, nonregulatory governance, even nongovernmental governance. Forest certification is occurring with governments watching from the sidelines. Political scientist Benjamin Cashore has called attention to this "startling new phenomenon . . . the emergence of domestic and transnational private governance systems that derive their policymaking authority not from the state, but from the manipulation of global markets and attention to customer preferences. From forests to fisheries to coffee to food production and even tourism, nongovernmental organizations have developed governance structures and social and environmentally focused rules concerning the production and sale of products and services."[24] In late 2002, the Mitsubishi Corporation, one of the largest forestry companies in the world, announced its commitment to third-party certification of its forestry operations using strict Forest Stewardship Council standards.

A long list of techniques—the U.S. Toxics Release Inventory and other "right to know" disclosures, third-party auditing, market creation by government entities and consumers, product boycotts and bad publicity—coupled with the Internet and an increasingly sophisticated international NGO community, can form powerful combinations, as Mitsubishi learned when it tried to establish a salt-mining operation in whale-calving waters in Mexico. An unprecedented outpouring of opposition from Mexican civil society, the Natural Resources Defense Council, and other environmental and consumer groups forced the industrial giant to withdraw in 2000.[25]

Environmental groups, philanthropic foundations, and others—they are the real maestros of JAZZ, and their number, size, and reach have grown dramatically in the past two decades. The World Wildlife Fund, for example, now has a 3,800-person staff and annual expenditures exceeding $340 million. With other such international groups as the Nature Conservancy and Conservation International, they are seeking to protect ecoregions of unprecedented size.[26]

In April 2001, hundreds of thousands of letters generated by environmental organizations paid off when agreement was reached to halt clear-cut logging on 3.5 million forest acres in British Columbia until an ecologically sensitive management plan is developed. The plan includes setting aside a large swath of ancient rainforest as a sanctuary for the rare white spirit bear. Consumer pressure was important in this campaign. The environmental groups targeted U.S. companies that are the market for most British Columbia timber, and companies like Home Depot, Andersen, Lowe's, and others pledged to stop buying products from endangered forests.[27]

NGOs are growing stronger and more organized at the international level. About thirty thousand NGOs are operating internationally today. Timed to coincide with—and thus challenge—the elite annual meeting of the World Economics Forum in Davos, Switzerland, the 2003 World Social Forum held in Porto Alegre, Brazil, attracted 120,000 social activists from around the world when it met in January. Key themes emerging from the discussions in Porto Alegre included the effects of economic globalization on the poor and the environment, the human right to clean water for all, and corporate accountability.

What may be most surprising, and certainly heartening, is the amount of green JAZZ being played today by businesses and investors. There are now many examples:

- Seven large companies—DuPont, Shell, BP Amoco, and Alcan among them—have agreed to reduce their greenhouse gas emissions to 15 percent below their 1990 levels by 2010.[28] Indeed, Alcoa is reported to be on track to reduce its emissions 25 percent below 1990 levels by 2010, and DuPont is on schedule to reduce emissions by 65 percent by 2010. At least thirty-eight major corporations have adopted energy or emission reduction targets, and a baker's dozen of North American companies—including International Paper, MeadWestvaco, and Motorola—have joined the Chicago Climate Exchange with a commitment to reduce their greenhouse gas emissions by 4 percent by 2006.[29]
- Eleven major companies—DuPont, GM, and IBM among them—have formed the Green Power Market Development Group and have committed to develop markets for a thousand megawatts of renewable energy over the next decade.[30]
- Home Depot, Lowe's, Andersen, and others have agreed to sell wood (to the degree that it is available) only from sustainably managed

forests certified by an independent group against rigorous criteria. Unilever, the largest processor of fish in the world, has agreed to the same regarding fish products.[31]

- Today, more than $2 trillion reside in socially and environmentally screened funds. In October 2002, institutional investors managing over $4.5 trillion in assets wrote the five hundred largest global companies asking for full disclosure of their emissions of climate-changing gases and their policies on global climate change.[32] Shareholders, bond ranking agencies, insurance companies, and state pension-fund managers are now coming to see the risks of inaction on climate change; meanwhile a quiet campaign is building to get the Securities and Exchange Commission to require more disclosure of company exposure to potential environmental costs.[33]

- Major corporations are now routinely issuing "sustainability reports" to stakeholders, scores of them following the rigorous practices recommended by the Global Reporting Initiative for reporting their environmental and social impacts.[34]

We are thus far beyond the old days of environmentalism as pollution control compliance. The environment is becoming more central to business strategic planning. Companies are beginning to develop sustainable enterprise strategies that are leading to profitable new processes and products.[35] New partnerships between corporations and environmental NGOs are being forged. Civil society organizations have played important roles in many of the corporate initiatives just presented.[36]

How can we reinforce these positive developments and take JAZZ to scale? Many things can be done. JAZZ requires an information-rich, wired environment, so Internet access and connectivity should be increased internationally. Initiatives like the U.S. Toxics Release Inventory and other government-mandated disclosures can ensure that the public gets new and accurate information. Ecolabeling should be improved, and systems should be built to provide product biographies covering the full life cycle of consumer goods. Securing corporate reporting through the Securities and Exchange Commission and the voluntary Global Reporting Initiative will help to encourage compliance and responsibility.[37] NGOs can build on their growing expertise in environmental and consumer campaigns, achieving new levels of effectiveness.

Beyond information, governments can change their tax and other laws to encourage citizen group activity in JAZZ. Government and private foundation spending can promote public-private partnerships, and purchasing by governments and others can build markets for green products. The media can provide highly visible recognition for taking the right steps. Foundations can link otherwise isolated "sustainability actors" at the national and regional levels, as the AVINA foundation does in Latin America.

Last, each one of us can contribute to JAZZ every day. We can drive hybrid vehicles rather than SUVs (I love my Toyota Prius), know the seafood on the menu, become active in environmental causes and organizations, vote after checking with the League of Conservation Voters, and generally try to escape the enthrallment of utopian materialism. In business, customer-driven change occurs very rapidly. The more that we consumers demand products that have less environmental impact, the faster change will occur.

Is there a link between GEOpolity and JAZZ? One reason we are hearing so much JAZZ, especially from the business community, is because of all the classical music being played over in GEOpolity Hall. And what is it when jazz and classical music are brought together? It's called FUSION, of course, and we are beginning to see it as well. JAZZ and GEOpolity are not mutually exclusive; they can reinforce each other. GEOpolity actions, proposed or actual, can stimulate JAZZ, and successful JAZZ can pave the way for further GEOpolity initiatives that create a framework where individual initiatives can flourish.

Two useful FUSION ideas have come forward, and one has already achieved some success. The World Bank's vice president for Europe, J. F. Rischard, has proposed that the best way to address many global issues is through what he calls "global issue networks."[38] These would be ad hoc, self-starting groups with participants from civil society organizations, governments, and businesses that would together produce norms, standards, and policies needed to address particular issues. These norms would be enforced by public scrutiny and other pressures, and could lead to implementation through national legislation. Why not try out Rischard's proposal on the global nitrogen problem discussed in chapter 3? Another good project for a new generation.

The 2002 Johannesburg Summit pioneered a FUSION initiative—using a classic GEOpolity process, a U.N. mega-conference, to promote voluntary partnerships. The summit encouraged what were called "type 2 outcomes," public-private and other partnership initiatives for sustainable development. Hundreds of these individual initiatives were showcased at Johannesburg. The United States highlighted numerous U.S.-based partnership initiatives, said to be worth $2.4 billion over several years. (Because it offered so little else in the traditional "type 1" negotiations among governments, critics accused the United States of seeking to derail the main purpose of the meeting with "type 2" agreements.) UNEP presented awards for the ten best partnerships, including ones involving Alcan for school-based recycling in Asia and the Americas and Shell for a gas exploration project in the Philippines. The United States committed thirty-six million dollars over three years to help protect Congo Basin forests.[39]

I would like to close with an extraordinary example of JAZZ beginning to go to scale. In August 2000, a group of leading scientists convened by the NGO Conservation International in Pasadena, California, endorsed a multibillion dollar plan to focus conservation efforts on biodiversity hot spots.[40] The basic idea, pioneered by Norman Myers, is that twenty-five areas around the globe, representing only 1.4 percent of the earth's land, are home to 44 percent of all plants, 35 percent of nonfish vertebrates, and 60 percent of all terrestrial species.[41] Hot spot advocates claim that the best investment for saving species is to protect these areas, most of which are threatened by development and other pressures. About 40 percent of hot spot area is already in some protected status, though these are often little more than paper parks. Prominent among the hot spots are areas of Madagascar, the Philippines, Indonesia, Brazil's Atlantic forest, the Caribbean, India, and Southeast Asia.

This attractive concept has now developed legs beyond the imaginings of even optimistic observers. In August 2000 the World Bank and the Global Environment Facility joined with Conservation International to launch a $150 million fund to protect hot spots. And then the Moore Foundation in San Francisco announced that it was making the largest environmental grant in history—$261 million—to CI to help launch the hot spot strategy. All of which has led even cautious observers to conclude that it just might work.

We can draw at least two important lessons from the hot spots initiative. One is to think big, even if you are a small NGO. The other is that if you have a really good and promising idea, like saving half the world's species with investments that are relatively modest, the world might just respond. Apathy is a shield people use to protect themselves against despair and powerlessness. It is not so much the product of indifference as inability. When you empower people with the possibility of action on the scale of the problem, things can happen.

The hot spots will not be saved, however, unless in a larger sense we save the world, too. A world thrown into disarray ecologically and socially by global climate change will not favor hot spot conservation. The ecosystems services on which we depend will not be provided by 1.4 percent of the land. Every place, every locale, has its endemic populations of plants and animals, genetically suited to function in that place.[42] Their loss is unconscionable, too. So while we give the hot spot initiative our fullest support, we should not neglect the larger context.

IO The Most Fundamental Transition of All

We are Nature, long have we been absent, but now we return. Walt Whitman

Confirm thy soul in self-control. "America the Beautiful"

The most fundamental transition is the transition in culture and consciousness. The change that is needed can be best put as follows: in the twentieth century we were from Mars but in the twenty-first century we must be from Venus—caring, nurturing, and sustaining.

Paul Raskin and his colleagues in the Global Scenario Group have envisioned a future when these and other human values are realized. "Here is a civilization of unprecedented freedom, tolerance and decency. The pursuit of meaningful and fulfilling lives is a universal right, the bonds of human solidarity have never been stronger and ecological sensibility infuses human values. . . . Preferred lifestyles combine material sufficiency with qualitative fulfillment. Conspicuous consumption and glitter are viewed as vulgar throwbacks to an earlier era. The pursuit of the well-lived life turns to the quality of existence—creativity, ideas, culture, human relationships and a harmonious relationship with nature. . . . The economy is understood as the means to these ends, rather than an end in itself."[1] A new consciousness such as this breaks with the anthropocentrism and contempocentrism discussed in chapter 6 and embraces a perspective on life and the world that prizes the two central ideas of environmental ethics: the protection for their own sake of the living communities that evolved here with us and our trusteeship of the earth's natural wealth and beauty for generations to come.

To realize such a future, societies will have to free themselves from a variety of pernicious habits of thought, including the enchantment of limitless material expansion and what John Kenneth Galbraith has called the "highly contrived consumption of an infinite variety of goods and services."[2] On the subject of ruling ideas that contributed to our current predicament, none will be more difficult to erode than the undisputed primacy of economic growth, which historian J. R. McNeill has called "easily the most important idea of the twentieth century."[3]

Imagine a group of countries where citizens rank at the top among today's countries in terms of purchasing power, health, longevity, and educational attainment; where income inequality between the top and the bottom of society is low and poverty virtually eliminated; and where fertility rates are at replacement levels or below, and the challenge is not unemployment but deploying innovative technologies to remain competitive and increase the productivity of a shrinking labor force. Should these countries not declare victory on the economic growth front and concentrate instead on protecting current standards of living (that's very different from resting on one's laurels in today's fast-moving world) and on enjoying the nonmaterial things that peace, economic security, education, freedom, and environmental quality make possible? Can a country make a decision that enough is enough? Or is our current system so geared to high economic growth that it is either up, up, and away or down, down, and out? I suspect that questions like these will emerge increasingly as our century unfolds. It is important for this discussion to begin, soon.

The Global Scenario Group believes that many scenarios of world economic, social, and environmental conditions are possible, including scenarios where there are no fundamental changes in values. But they favor a "new sustainability" scenario where society turns "to nonmaterial dimensions of fulfillment . . . the quality of life, the quality of human solidarity and the quality of the earth. . . . Sustainability is the imperative that pushes the new agenda. Desire for a rich quality of life, strong human ties and a resonant connection to nature is the lure that pulls it toward the future."[4]

The revolution Raskin and his colleagues see coming a quarter-century away is primarily a revolution in attitudes and values. Charles Reich, far ahead of his time, wrote of such a new consciousness in 1970 in *The Greening of America*. "The new consciousness," Reich wrote, "seeks restoration of the non-material elements of man's existence, the elements like the natural environment and the spiritual that were passed by in the rush of material development."[5] Let us hope that Raskin and his colleagues, in seeing these changes finally occurring a half-century after Reich wrote about them, have given our species enough time to grow up. It is doubtful that the planet can take much more of our heedless childhood.

The most sophisticated and participatory effort to date to frame values and principles for a sustainable future has been the effort to draft the Earth Charter. Part of the unfinished business of the Rio Earth Summit, the now final Earth Charter is an eloquent statement of the ethical principles needed to "bring forth a sustainable global society founded on respect for nature, universal human rights, economic justice, and a culture of peace."[6] By 2003 the Earth Charter had been endorsed by 725 organizations representing forty million people.

Paul Ehrlich has observed that "our global civilization had better move rapidly to modify its cultural evolution and deal with its deteriorating environmental circumstances before it runs out of time."[7] He

The Earth Charter Preamble

We stand at a critical moment in Earth's history, a time when humanity must choose its future. As the world becomes increasingly interdependent and fragile, the future at once holds great peril and great promise. To move forward we must recognize that in the midst of a magnificent diversity of cultures and life forms we are one human family and one Earth community with a common destiny. We must join together to bring forth a sustainable global society founded on respect for nature, universal human rights, economic justice, and a culture of peace. Towards this end, it is imperative that we, the peoples of Earth, declare our responsibility to one another, to the greater community of life, and to future generations.

Earth, Our Home

Humanity is part of a vast evolving universe. Earth, our home, is alive with a unique community of life. The forces of nature make existence a demanding and uncertain adventure, but Earth has provided the conditions essential to life's evolution. The resilience of the community of life and the well-being of humanity depend upon preserving a healthy biosphere with all its ecological systems, a rich variety of plants and animals, fertile soils, pure waters, and clean air. The global environment with its finite resources is a common concern of all peoples. The protection of Earth's vitality, diversity, and beauty is a sacred trust.

The Global Situation

The dominant patterns of production and consumption are causing environmental devastation, the depletion of resources, and a massive extinction of species. Communities are being undermined.

The benefits of development are not shared equitably and the gap between rich and poor is widening. Injustice, poverty, ignorance, and violent conflict are widespread and the cause of great suffering. An unprecedented rise in human population has overburdened ecological and social systems. The foundations of global security are threatened. These trends are perilous—but not inevitable.

The Challenges Ahead

The choice is ours: form a global partnership to care for Earth and one another or risk the destruction of ourselves and the diversity of life. Fundamental changes are needed in our values, institutions, and ways of living. We must realize that when basic needs have been met, human development is primarily about being more, not having more. We have the knowledge and technology to provide for all and to reduce our impacts on the environment. The emergence of a global civil society is creating new opportunities to build a democratic and humane world. Our environmental, economic, political, social, and spiritual challenges are interconnected, and together we can forge inclusive solutions.

Universal Responsibility

To realize these aspirations, we must decide to live with a sense of universal responsibility, identifying ourselves with the whole Earth community as well as our local communities. We are at once citizens of different nations and of one world in which the local and global are linked. Everyone shares responsibility for the present and future well-being of the human family and the larger living world. The spirit of human solidarity and kinship with all life is strengthened when we live with reverence for the mystery of being, gratitude for the gift of life, and humility regarding the human place in nature.

notes that the potential for conscious evolution is evident in great social movements that societies have already experienced, such as the abolition of slavery, the civil rights movement, and the collapse of communism and the Soviet empire.

Is it possible that we are seeing the birth of something new—a change of consciousness—in the antiglobalization protests, in the far-reaching and unprecedented initiatives being taken by some private corporations, in the strength and vitality of civil society organizations in the growing advocacy for sustainable consumption patterns, in the social movements of the landless and others in the developing world, in scientists speaking up and speaking out, and in the outpouring of environmental initiatives by the religious community? We must hope that the answer is yes, for contrary to the conventional perspective, it is business as usual that is utopian, whereas creating a new consciousness is a pragmatic necessity.[8]

In the end, what can reliably be said about the prospect for humans and nature? A pessimist might conclude that the drivers of deterioration are too powerful to counter, that our economy is too dependent on unguided growth and laissez-faire, that our politics cannot accommodate long-term thinking, and that our society responds only to major crises and in this case the crises will come too late.

Weighed against this, there are hopeful signs and encouraging developments in each of the eight areas of transition. Scientific understanding is greatly improved. Population growth is slowing, and the proportion of the world's people in poverty is being reduced. Technologies that can bring a vast environmental improvement in manufacturing, energy, transportation, and agriculture are either available or close at hand. We are learning how to harness market forces for sustainability, and major schemes for capping and trading the right to emit climate-changing gases are emerging. International environmental law has expanded and is ready for a new phase. Environmental and other civil society organizations have developed remarkable new capacities for leadership and effectiveness. Private businesses, environmental organizations, and local governments the world over are taking impressive initiatives often far ahead of international agreements or other government requirements. Environment is emerging as a force in business strategic planning. The JAZZ world is full of life and energy. Europe, at least, is providing real leadership on the policy front. So, despite the gravity of our predicament, the situation is far from hopeless, and some areas such as a green consumer movement and emissions trading to control greenhouse gases may be poised for takeoff. Solutions—including the policy prescriptions and other actions needed to move forward—abound. We need but use them.

Helpful trends outside the environmental arena are becoming discernable. Globalization of many descriptions is eroding sovereignty. We are seeing the slow but steady emergence of a global civil society, as like-minded organizations in many countries come together. The nation-state, it has been said, is too little for the big things and too big for the little things. "Glocalization" is emerging, with action shifting to local and global levels. In many places, especially in Europe, one can see psychological disinvestment in the nation-state and the strengthening of local and global citizenship. These trends should enhance prospects for international cooperation, both official and unofficial.[9]

One thing is clear: the needed changes will not simply happen. No hidden hand is guiding technology or the economy toward sustainability. The issues on the global environmental agenda are precisely the type of issues—long-term, chronic, complex—where genuine, farsighted leadership from elected officials is at a premium. But we have not seen this leadership emerge, and we have waited long enough. What we need now is an international movement of citizens and scientists, one capable of dramatically advancing the political and personal actions needed for the transition to sustainability. We have had movements against slavery and many have participated in movements for civil rights and against apartheid and the Vietnam War.[10] Environmentalists are often said to be part of "the environmental movement." We need a real one.

It is time for we the people, as citizens and as consumers, to take charge.

Eventually, leaders in the political and business worlds will see that it is powerfully in their self-interest to promote the eight transitions. But the clear evidence to date is that, absent some new force in the picture, they will be much too late in coming to this realization. The best hope we have for this new force is a coalescing of a wide array of civic, scientific, environmental, religious, student, and other organizations with enlightened business leaders, concerned families, and engaged communities, networked together, protesting, demanding action and accountability from governments and corporations, and taking steps as consumers and communities to realize sustainability in everyday life.

A new movement of consumer and households committed to sustainable living could drive a world of change. Young people will almost certainly be centrally involved in any movement for real change. They always have been. New dreams are born most easily when the world is seen with fresh eyes and confronted with impertinent questions. The Internet is empowering young people in an unprecedented way—not just by access to information but by access to each other, and to a wider world.

One goal should be to find the spark that can set off a period of rapid change, like the flowering of the domestic environmental agenda in the early 1970s. Part of the challenge is changing the perception of global-scale concerns so that they come alive with the immediacy and reality of our domestic challenges of the 1970s. In the end, we need to trigger a response that in historical terms will come to be seen as revolutionary—the Environmental Revolution of the twenty-first century. Only such a response is likely to avert huge and even catastrophic environmental losses.

There is an important body of scholarly literature on political change in the United States. Political scientists Frank Baumgartner and Bryan Jones in their book *Agendas and Instability in American Politics* make the distinction between normal periods characterized by incremental change, when negative feedback stalls proposals for large changes, on one hand, and on the other those special periods when proposals for change generate positive feedback and major change sweeps through the system.[11] They write: "Much recent literature, both scholarly and popular, has offered discouraging assessments of the ability of democratic institutions to deal with change. This line of argument, summarized in the question 'Can the government govern?' contends that democratic government in the United States (and elsewhere) is so plagued with lackluster politicians beholden to powerful interest groups that heroic policy actions have become impossible, at least in domestic affairs. . . . Other arguments blame the inability of the government to govern on the increasing complexities of modern society. . . .

"We disagree profoundly with this straightjacket view of government. . . . Our primary thesis is that the American political system . . . [has been] continually swept by policy change. . . . During quiet periods of policymaking, negative feedback dominates; policy innovations seldom capture the imagination of many individuals, so change is slow or rare. During periods of rapid change, positive feedback dominates; each action generates disproportionately large responses, so change accelerates. . . . Punctuated equilibrium, rather than stability and immobility characterizes the American political system."[12]

Clearly, the global environment has been addressed incrementally in our politics whereas we want and need major change—a rapid shift to a new equilibrium. Baumgartner and Jones analyze periods of major shifts in American politics and conclude that sweeping policy change happens when a major wave of new and previously apathetic citizens are attracted to an issue. These newly activated participants almost all enter on one side of the issue. They are motivated to enter the fray because the issue has been redefined, with new dimensions added that the new participants find attractive and compelling. A major event or "crisis" can help redefine the issue and attract wide attention. (Forced to guess, I would say that if an environmental "crisis" of some type occurs, it is likely to have its origins in global climate change. We must hope that a serious threat or precrisis—such as the very real prospect of losing most of the coral reefs—will suffice in spurring action.)

When the perception of an issue is systematically altered to engage a new and broader audience, perhaps by a crisis or major event, far-reaching change becomes possible. A new vocabulary or way of discussing the issue can help this along. No group could be better suited to undertake such a redefinition and new articulation than the young people I see on campuses across the country. I hope that they can lead in making the grand challenges of today have the same immediacy as the local environmental threats of the 1970s.

One dimension of this redefinition with potentially broad appeal is environmental restoration—freeing rivers, restoring wetlands, replanting forests, recharging groundwaters, regenerating wastelands, reclaiming urban brownfields, reintroducing species, removing invasives. There is much to be done, and whatever the pace of the transition to sustainability, much more damage will need to be corrected. While efforts to prevent future damage continue, a new, broad and decidedly positive aspect of our planetary stewardship is environmental restoration.[13]

If we want to move forward, it is important to be clear about the barriers. Can we pinpoint what has stymied real progress on the global environmental front? Is the main barrier simply the United States, which has dragged its feet on issue after issue since initially giving leadership in protecting Earth's ozone shield? Or are we confronting a typical situation in politics where noneconomic goals need higher priority, more urgency, and some new policies and approaches? Or is the problem deeply structural, rooted fundamentally in our economic system and our international system of sovereign states? My conclusion, reflected in the preceding chapters, is that it is all three. This conclusion makes progress a serious challenge, but it also suggests a strategy forward.

An immediate priority should be to get the United States back into the game with Europe and Japan. In the long run the United States being an outlier is not helping U.S. industry or the U.S. economy. We are falling behind, for example, in environmental and energy technology —a big business—as well as new approaches to environmental protection—both areas where the United States once had the lead. More fundamentally, the world will not get far in this field without American leadership. Not only are we Americans a big source of problems (as with climate change), but we are also essential to cooperative solutions (as with reversing resource deterioration in the developing world). The world needs a United States that leads by example and diplomacy, with generosity and compassion.

We should vigorously pursue the agenda for action reflected in the eight transitions—the eightfold way. I believe it is a fair conclusion that we know what we have to do, at least to a rough approximation. The many initiatives discussed in chapters 8 and 9 should be pursued together. Positive developments in one area can reinforce those in another. There will be no single solution—no magic bullet. We cannot know now what will work best. A revitalized GEOpolity, for example, might succeed without JAZZ, or JAZZ might go to scale while GEOpolity sputters. More likely, they will reinforce each other.

The initiatives that are recommended to advance the eight transitions do not fundamentally threaten the prevailing economic and international systems. Mostly they seek to make those systems succeed at their long-term purposes of furthering human welfare. Deeper changes may be necessary one day, but I suspect they will accrue over time and will be the result of a change in public values and aspirations.

A phenomenal expansion of economic activity is projected for the decades immediately ahead. Down one path, this growth can protect, regenerate, and restore the environment. It can provide sustainable livelihoods for the world's poor and lead to large improvements in quality of life for all. There is still world enough and time to realize this future. But it will not be won without a profound commitment to urgent action. President John F. Kennedy often told the story of the aged Marshal Lyautey of France debating with his gardener the wisdom of planting a certain tree.

"It will not bloom," the gardener argued, "for decades."

"Then," said the marshal, "plant it this afternoon."

Resources for Citizens

With the assistance of Kelly Levin, 2003 graduate of the Yale School of Forestry and Environmental Studies, and Heather Creech, International Institute for Sustainable Development

The immensity of global-scale challenges, their seeming remoteness from everyday life, and the inaccessibility of the policy processes that address them make it hard for individuals to think that they can make a difference. The good news is that Web-based resources, outstanding organizations, and other levers make it possible today as never before for citizens to affect the outcome of global challenges.*

For example, globalization can in fact be played in reverse. *New York Times* columnist Thomas Friedman has noted that globalization is shrinking the world, linking events here with those far away. The great and legitimate fear of many is that the process is homogenizing and hollowing out local economies, communities, and cultures. Yet today's technology is also empowering individuals to combine their forces in

---

*Resources for Citizens is available on-line, with linkages to the Web-sites mentioned here, at www.redskyatmorning.com.

unprecedented ways and to link up with others seeking constructive change around the world. Positive local change can go global—spreading, seeking larger goals, and asserting itself until the world is changing.

The biggest threat to our environment is global climate disruption, and the greatest problem in that context is America's energy use and the policies that undergird it. So, in terms of bottom-up, citizen-driven action—the green JAZZ discussed in chapter 9—there is no riper target than the U.S. energy scene. And, indeed, the energy-climate problem provides the best example available of how citizen initiative and local action are beginning to address a global-scale problem. Most of the examples offered in chapters 3 and 9 of JAZZ in action have to do with energy and climate. We can imagine goals being set for renewable energy use and for reductions in greenhouse gas emissions by businesses and universities, by communities and states, then by groups of states and national associations and organizations of many types, all supported by worried insurers and institutional investors, to the point that local actions are indeed going to scale and changing the world. This is not a distant vision: it is a process that has already begun in the United States.

We are not powerless to affect even the most remote and global challenges. This guide presents, briefly and incompletely, some of the things that citizens can do to promote and further the eight transitions—the eightfold way—sketched in chapters 8, 9, and 10. Even this limited agenda will strain the time and stretch the energies of most of us. There is much to be done—and much that we can do.

Areas for Citizen Action

Before turning to the eight transitions, let's take up the various ways that individuals can make an impact on global environmental challenges:

As voters. The League of Conservation Voters (www.lcv.org) is devoted to evaluating the "greenness" of political candidates and to supporting those with strong environmental credentials. Their Environmental Scorecard evaluates the votes and positions of elected officials.

In addition to the national level, League of Conservation Voters are springing up at the state level around the country and are increasingly becoming involved in state and local level elections. Voting itself is but the finale. More important, individuals can become involved in the political process—up to and including becoming candidates for elected posts. There is good news here: it is easier to become involved politically at local and state levels, and, as discussed in previous chapters, it is at these levels of government where the action is the most impressive today.

As investors. This door is opening dramatically. Numerous groups now provide information to investors on finding green companies and environmentally screened mutual funds. Individuals can also get involved in the decisions of pension funds and other institutional investors. On the cutting edge is a burgeoning movement of investors who are taking shareholder petitions and resolutions to annual meetings. (Resources for green investing are presented under Transition 7, below.)

As consumers. The first stop here is the information published and available on-line regarding the greening of household consumer purchases. In addition, consumers can support eco-labeling and product certification. Eco-labels range from those denoting sustainable forest products to those identifying energy-saving technologies to those labeling sustainable food choices. Labeling schemes, such as fair trade labeling, have also been designed to promote sustainable development abroad. In addition to everyday household products, larger purchases present greater opportunities to affect global environmental challenges. Consumers can choose hybrids and other fuel-efficient vehicles, take green vacations and support ecotourism, build green homes and green yards, create green office environments, participate in consumer boycotts, and more. And, of course, we can opt for mass transit, bicycles, and other lifestyle changes. Many good books address lifestyle issues, among them, Union of Concerned Scientists, *The Consumer's Guide to Effective Environmental Choices* (New York: Three Rivers Press, 1999; www.ucsusa.org/publication.cfm?publicationID=130), Denis Hayes, *The Official*

Earth Day Guide to Planet Repair (Washington, D.C.: Island Press, 2000), The Ecologist, ed., *Go Mad! 365 Daily Ways to Save the Planet* (London: Think Publishing, 2001), and Julia Butterfly Hill, *One Makes the Difference* (San Francisco: Harper Collins, 2002). (Additional resources on sustainable consumption are presented under Transition 5, below.)

As family members. Let's face it: the polls show that women are more concerned about environmental issues than men and young people more than their parents. Many businessmen have reported that they got educated on the environment by their families.

As association members. Americans are a nation of joiners—we are members of a wide variety of voluntary associations. And these groups can take action in response to global environmental challenges. How green is your high school, college, or university? Your church, synagogue, or other place of worship? Your gym or golf course? Your lodge or club? Most of us don't want to be pests, but the groups to which we belong can and should have energy and climate goals, reduce their use of toxic chemicals, participate in building markets for climate-friendly products and cutting-edge green technologies, and encourage their regional and national counterparts to sponsor larger efforts.

As workers. According to the Center for Small Business and the Environment (www.geocities.com/aboutcsbe), small businesses can be an ideal source of environmental solutions because they are local, nonbureaucratic, creative, flexible, independent, and responsive to change. By contrast, large businesses wield tremendous power, and if employees of large companies can institute change, the ramifications will be large. In addition to business owners and managers, farmers and union workers can play a vital role in shaping global environmental change. Farmers can adopt sustainable farming techniques, shift to organic farming and shade-grown crops, and set aside land for wildlife and regeneration. The U.S. Farm Bill programs help guide farmers in green farming techniques. For information and inspiration on the greening of business, see www.GreenBiz.com or subscribe to *Tomorrow* (www.environmental

-center.com/magazine/tomorrow/index) and Green@work (www
.greenatworkmag.com). See also Resources for Promoting Global
Business Principles and Best Practices at www.csrwire.com/directory.
What can your office do to counter climate change? See Samantha Putt
del Pino and Pankaj Bhatia, "Working 9 to 5 on Climate Change: An
Office Guide," World Resources Institute, December 2002 (http://
pdf.wri.org/wri_co2guide.pdf), and SafeClimate for Business,
www.safeclimate.net. The Natural Step offers a framework for businesses to rethink their operations to become more sustainable, www
.naturalstep.org. The opportunities for an environmental career are
also expanding. The Environmental Careers Organization publishes
The Complete Guide to Environmental Careers in the Twenty-first Century
(Washington, D.C.: Island Press, 1999) and has a useful Web-site,
www.eco.org. See also the "Bytes of Note" columns by Thomas Parris
in the April 1999 and May 2003 issues of *Environment*. (Additional resources on the greening of business are presented under Transitions 3
and 7, below.)

As advocates of governmental policies and funding. Although one can
individually lobby elected officials on global environmental issues, the
next best thing is to join, support, and participate in the many outstanding nongovernmental organizations (NGOs) that "work" the global-
scale policy issues at local, state, national, and international levels.
There is no substitute for doing this. Although most of us could not
attend the meeting of the Conference of the Parties to the U.N. Framework Convention on Climate Change when it convened in New Delhi
in 2002, these meetings are attended by groups like the Natural Resources Defense Council (www.nrdc.org), Environmental Defense
(www.environmentaldefense.org/home.cfm), World Resources Institute (www.wri.org), World Wildlife Fund (www.worldwildlife.org),
Greenpeace (www.greenpeace.org), the World Conservation Union
(IUCN) (www.iucn.org), the Sierra Club (www.sierraclub.org), and
many other NGOs. Excellent directories of environmental organizations
are available (see, for example, *2003 Conservation Directory* [Washington,

D.C.: Island Press, 2003]; Jeff Standinger, *The Environmental Guidebook* [Menlo Park, Calif.: Environmental Frontiers, 2002]; and on-line directories listed below). Groups range from conservative to radical. An important action-oriented coalition of environmental organizations is SaveOurEnvironment.org (www.saveourenvironment.org). For a coalition active on energy and climate, see Climate Action Network (www.climatenetwork.org). Nontraditional environmental actors such as the National Religious Partnership for the Environment (www.nrpe.org), Physicians for Social Responsibility (www.psr.org), and the United Nations Association for the United States of America (www.unausa.org) should not be overlooked. (Additional resources on membership, advocacy, and other groups are presented under Transition 7, below.)

As conservationists and eco-developers. Individuals can also join, support, and engage in the activities of organizations that are working "on the ground" at sites around the world rather than pressuring legislators to draft policies that would achieve comparable goals. These "operational" organizations are diverse in nature—ranging from land trusts devoted to saving ecologically viable land from development and degradation (acting locally, such as the Trust for Public Land, www.tpl.org, and Land Trust Alliance, http://lta.org, and internationally, such as the Nature Conservancy, http://nature.org), to organizations working on international biodiversity issues (such as World Wildlife Fund, www.worldwildlife.org, and Conservation International, www.conservation.org/xp/CIWEB/home) to groups focusing on development projects that stress sustainable livelihoods and environmental regeneration (such as CARE, www.care.org, and Oxfam, www.oxfam.org.uk). Many other U.S. and international groups support sustainable development initiatives in developing countries, among them the National Wildlife Federation (www.nwf.org) and World Conservation Union (www.iucn.org). The Marine Conservation Biology Institute works to establish marine sanctuaries (www.mcbi.org).

As activists. You say you want a revolution? The eight transitions will not be made without activists. Two books may be of special interest on this subject: Todd Gitlin, *Letters to a Young Activist* (New York: Basic Books, 2003), and Randy Shaw, *The Activist's Handbook: A Primer* (Berkeley: University of California Press, 2001). See also the discussion of "global action networks" at www.gan-net.net. And see the resources under Transition 7, below.

As educators. We are all teachers—not only in our schools and other institutions of formal education but also in our families, among our friends and co-workers, and in our clubs and places of worship. We can spread the news—both good and bad—about the global environment and what can be done, and we can support educational programs in environmental studies and in science generally. It is unlikely that someone who rejects the science supporting evolution is going to place much stock in the science of global climate change. Excellent Web-based sources of general environmental news include Environmental News Network (www.enn.com), Environmental News Service (www.ens-news.com), Bonda Report (www.bondareport.com), and Planet Ark (www.planetark.org). U.N. Wire (www.unwire.org) also provides excellent coverage of U.N.-related news, including that pertaining to the environment. Excellent access to international environmental information is provided by IISD Linkages (www.iisd.ca.linkages) and Earth-Trends (http://earthtrends.wri.org). UNEP's Web-site (www.unep.org) is extremely valuable, as is its magazine *Our Planet* (www.ourplanet.com).

Eight Steps to Sustainability

Using the methods of citizen engagement just reviewed, individuals can do many things to promote each of the eight transitions to sustainability. The organizations and Web-based resources presented here provide an abundance of information along with ideas for membership, financial support, and personal initiative. (People's politics differ. The resources presented were not selected with the idea that they would appeal to everyone. Also, the focus here is primarily U.S. Web-based resources, and the numerous and often excellent resources maintained by federal and state governments in general are not presented simply for reasons of length.) The materials here supplement those cited in the Notes and recommended in For Further Reading: A Bookshelf.

Transition 1: A Stable or Smaller World Population

The Resource Clock of the International Development Research Centre has tracked the increase of human population and decrease of arable land since 1987, when the first clock was installed in the front lobby of IDRC's Ottawa headquarters. The clock also runs on-line on the front page of IDRC's Web-site at www.idrc.ca.

People and the Planet, at www.peopleandplanet.net, provides a global gateway to issues of family health as they relate to pressure on resources. The news service also covers feature articles and stories on population, environment, and development issues.

WEDO (Women's Environmental and Development Organization) is an international advocacy group that collaborates with policy-makers to empower women across the globe. Individuals can check out www.wedo.org to support their campaigns. Their Web-site is helpful in staying up-to-date with the challenges facing women's social and political empowerment today.

WomenWatch, a joint project between UNIFEM (www.unifem.org) and the Interagency Network on Women and Gender Equality (www.un.org/womenwatch/ianwge), provides a wealth of information regarding the empowerment of women. Individuals can educate themselves about women-related events around the world, read relevant publications and data, and discover upcoming meetings on women's issues on the WomenWatch Web-site, www.un.org/womenwatch. Information on the Beijing Platform for Action, the international agenda for women's empowerment, can be found at www.un.org/womenwatch/daw/beijing/platform/plat1.htm.

Founded in 1975, CEDPA (Center for Development and Population Activities) provides services to millions of women through partnerships with 138 organizations in forty countries. CEDPA focuses on access to reproductive health and voluntary family planning and strengthens community organizations to support, educate, and empower women. Visit www.cedpa.org for more information.

The Planned Parenthood Federation of America–International and Planned Parenthood Global Partners are the international arms of Planned Parenthood Federation of America, the largest voluntary reproductive health care organization in the world. Planned Parenthood provides access to family planning and safe abortion services and advocates for improvements in reproductive health care. In addition, Planned Parenthood has established contraceptive services and sex education programs throughout the world. Individuals can visit www.plannedparenthood.org/global/about, sign up for newsletters, and receive action alerts on pressing issues related to reproductive health.

The Population Council (www.popcouncil.org) is an international, not-for-profit institution that conducts research on three fronts: biomedical, social science, and public health. The council's research has been extremely successful in educating people about challenges related to reproductive health and population growth.

Population Action International (PAI) is a membership group that works to strengthen awareness and support for population and family planning programs. It also does pathbreaking work on environment-population linkages and interactions. Individuals can get involved by becoming a member of their Action Network and can keep track of news and relevant information, participate in lobbying campaigns, and more (www.populationaction.org).

The Population Reference Bureau is a membership organization that provides authoritative data and analyses on population trends and their implications, including publication of the annual *World Population*

Data Sheet (www.prb.org). For a directory of global population information, see www.popnet.org, and for population health and environment links, visit www.popplanet.org.

The Center for Environment and Population, a research center, addresses the relations among population, resource consumption, and environmental impacts. It played a major role in producing the *AAAS Atlas on Population and the Environment* (www.cepnet.org).

Two United Nations programs have proven themselves instrumental in tackling global population issues:

- UNFPA (United Nations Population Fund, see www.unfpa.org), the largest international fund for reproductive health and population programs, assists in family planning and in formulating reproductive health policies. It is the lead U.N. organization for the implementation of the Programme of Action of the Cairo International Conference on Population and Development (www.unfpa.org/icpd/summary.htm).
- UNIFEM (United Nations Development Fund for Women), the women's fund of the United Nations, works to strengthen women's organizations and networks, leverage political and financial support for women, and promote women's human rights, among other activities. Individuals can join national and local chapters of UNIFEM (www.unifem.org).

AWID (Association for Women's Rights in Development) is an international membership organization linking those working to promote women's empowerment, sustainable development, and women's human rights. Individuals can become members and participate in online discussions, receive newsletters, and create alliances with others working to further gender equality (www.awid.org/index.pl).

Other lobby groups include Pathfinder International (www.path find.org) (which also provides family planning and reproductive health services internationally) and Population Connection (www.population connection.org). Population Connection (formerly Zero Population Growth) provides education kits and citizen lobby programs.

Transition 2: Free of Mass Poverty

The annual *Human Development Report* includes a Human Development Index, a Gender-related Index, a Gender Empowerment-Measure, and a Human Poverty Index (http://hdr.undp.org). It also reports on progress toward meeting the poverty-oriented Millennium Development Goals approved by the U.N. General Assembly. On-line volunteers and contributions are possible through the United Nations Development Programme's (UNDP) NetAid. Individuals can sign up for online volunteering opportunities and receive a monthly newsletter (www.netaid.org). Poverty-oriented U.N. organizations like UNDP badly need stronger U.S. citizen support to secure their funding by Congress.

Regarding the Millennium Development Goals, www.development goals.org tracks MDG progress and initiatives. In addition, the World Bank's PovertyNet provides resources and support for people working to understand and alleviate poverty worldwide (www.worldbank .org/poverty).

An influential work on poverty and development, *Development as Freedom* (Oxford: Oxford University Press, 1999), by Nobel Prize–winning economist Amaryta Sen, has developed a functioning-capability-freedom framework, which addresses the challenges posed by poverty and inequality in a new light. To join the Sen-Capability listserv and follow its applications to international development, see www.iisd.org/economics/ pov_sd/senlistserv.asp.

The establishment of just and equitable trade regimes is an important component in the economic development of countries. To stay informed of the trade debates at the World Trade Organization, one can sign up for the weekly electronic newsletter *Bridges* (www.ictsd.org/weekly), published by the independent Geneva-based International Centre for Trade and Sustainable Development.

Many independent research organizations and think tanks focus on poverty alleviation, strengthening development assistance, the removal of perverse subsidies, the promotion of fair trade regimes, and the need for innovation in technology. Among these are the Center for Global Development (www.cgdev.org), World Resources Institute (www.wri.org), International Institute for Sustainable Development (www.iisd.org), International Institute for Environment and Development (www.iied.org), International Forum on Globalization (www.ifg.org), Institute for Agriculture and Trade Policy (www.iatp.org), and Worldwatch Institute (www.worldwatch.org).

A number of other groups work on the ground to develop appropriate technologies. For example, EnterpriseWorks (www.enterpriseworks.org) provides an informational database of best practices for those wanting to support sustainable development projects in Africa, Asia, and Latin America. The organization also provides tools for micro-entrepreneurs to make business plans, improve crop yields, and increase profits in a sustainable manner.

Contributions to support the excellent work of UNICEF can be made through the U.S. Fund for UNICEF (www.unicefusa.org). Save the Children US (www.savethechildren.org) specifically addresses poverty in the South but also covers wider child poverty issues in rural America. Individuals can join their action network, community sponsorship programs, and other activities.

HORIZON International maintains a useful Web-site that presents peer-reviewed examples of successful sustainable development projects (www.solutions-site.org).

Oxfam International (www.oxfam.org), another major international relief organization, provides not only grassroots support for poverty alleviation but also in-depth policy analyses and campaigns for fair trade, education for all, debt relief, and access to medicine. Individuals can join a campaign, contribute to emergency relief programs, and become a volunteer with their national Oxfam organization (located in the United States, Canada, United Kingdom, and several other countries).

Much of the grassroots fieldwork in developing countries is carried out by faith-based organizations, which have been successful in providing basic health, education, and support programs for entrepreneurship and community infrastructure. Individuals can inquire at local places of worship about how to best support their services by volunteering, contributing financially, or providing used equipment. Among many faith-based groups are Bread for the World (www.bread.org), Catholic Relief Services (www.catholicrelief.org), Christian Children's Fund (www.christianchildrensfund.org), American Jewish World Service (www.ajws.org), Church World Service (www.churchworldservice .org), and World Vision (www.worldvision.org).

InterAction is the largest alliance of U.S.-based NGOs working on poverty alleviation around the world. Its more than 160 member organizations have programs in all developing countries (www.interaction .org). One of the most effective tools for fighting poverty is the provision of small loans to the poor. An important U.S.-based effort to ensure that microcredit is available to one hundred million of the world's poorest families is the Microcredit Summit Campaign (www.micro creditsummit.org), a project of the poverty advocacy group Results (http://results.org).

One World is a global network of organizations advocating sustainable human development (www.oneworld.net).

Transition 3: Environmentally Benign Technologies

The Global Network of Environment and Technology (GNET), at www.gnet.org, contains information on government environmental technology assistance programs, innovative technologies, markets, and other information relevant to environmentally benign technologies. GNET's affiliates include Cool Companies (which focuses on energy-efficient technologies, www.cool-companies.org), TechKnow (which provides a database of environmental remediation technologies, www.techknow.org), and other companies working on the technology transition.

GreenBiz.com is another useful on-line resource providing information to the environmental technology community (www.greenbiz.com/index.cfm). Sustainable Alternatives Network (www.sustainable alternatives.net) is available to business experts working in emerging markets. The network is unique in its focus on exchange of know-how, helping to secure the financing of cleaner technologies.

Inventors at the Rocky Mountain Institute (www.rmi.org) are developing "new design assignments" every day. The institute has been recognized for its innovative green building design and energy-efficient and climate-friendly technologies for the twenty-first century and beyond. See also the Web-sites described by Amory Lovins in his letter to *Business Week*, quoted in chapter 3.

Key multilateral groups include the United Nations Environment Programme's Production and Consumption Branch, which maintains the Cleaner Production Web-site (www.unepie.org/pc/cp), with training packages on strategies, policies, and processes for greener production techniques. Also see UNEP's MAESTRO database at www.unep.or.jp/maestro2.

The Greening of Industry Network facilitates discussion among civil society, government, and the private sector to speed progress on adopting sustainable industries. Individuals can join the network and help GIN carry out its mission (www.greeningofindustry.org/join/membership.cfm).

Rather than focusing on end-of-pipe pollution abatement techniques, the National Pollution Prevention Roundtable (www.p2.org), a membership organization, is devoted to source reduction.

An energy and climate audit for homes and businesses is described on these sites: Safe Climate for Individuals (www.safeclimate.net/individual.php) and Safe Climate for Business (www.safeclimate.net/business/index.php).

At BuildingGreen.com, individuals can sign up for the "Environmental Building News," providing updates on green building developments. Visitors to this site can browse through information on more than 1,700 green building products (www.buildinggreen.com).

Opportunities for those seeking to adopt cutting-edge pest management approaches are presented on the USDA Regional Pest Management Centers Information System Web-site (www.ipmcenters.org).

An excellent source of information on leading-edge environmental technologies and their commercial potential is Clean Edge (www.clean edge.com), and the intriguing design ideas of Bill McDonough and Michael Braungart discussed in chapter 8 are presented at www.mbdc .com.

Transition 4: Environmentally Honest Prices

SubsidyWatch has a mailing list of news stories and journal articles monitoring perverse subsidies (www.iisd.org/subsidywatch).

Green Scissors is a campaign led by Friends of the Earth (www.foe .org), Taxpayers for Common Sense (www.taxpayer.net), and the U.S. Public Interest Research Group (www.uspirg.org) that works to put a stop to environmentally degrading and wasteful spending. Their Web-site (www.greenscissors.org) allows individuals to sign up for their e-bulletin and receive updates on how to take action on their campaigns.

Many of the independent research institutes mentioned previously also focus on eliminating perverse subsidies and internalizing external environmental costs. Among those developing policy options are the Rocky Mountain Institute (www.rmi.org), the World Resources Institute (www.wri.org), the International Institute for Sustainable Development (www.iisd.org), and the Wuppertal Institute (www.wupperinst.org). At the multilateral level, the OECD Environment Directorate (www .oecd.org) is another important player in this field.

The U.S. Society for Ecological Economics (www.ussee.org) addresses policy research, curriculum development, and citizen education. It is a member of the International Society for Ecological Economics (www.ecologicaleconomics.org) and is open not only to academics but also to grassroots organizations and concerned individuals.

Though it may be a personal challenge, it is possible, at least in some respects, to pay for the full cost of one's lifestyle. We can pay a part off the external environmental costs the next time we take a plane. A Climate Ticket will support "climate protection projects," which reduce greenhouse gas emissions elsewhere. Visit www.climateticket.com/en/Kauf_en.php for more information. One can also invest in green tags, which offset one's environmental damages, such as those sold by the Bonneville Environmental Foundation (see www.greentagsusa.org/GreenTags/index.cfm).

Transition 5: Sustainable Consumption

The Web-based resources to support this transition may be more plentiful than any other. To focus on greening consumer purchases, good places to begin include the Center for a New American Dream (www.newdream.org), a leading organization devoted to helping Americans consume responsibly. They provide extensive resources on lifestyle shifts including guides on how to buy green, parent in a consumer society, and more. The center also advocates for changes that support more sustainable consumption in government and business practices, and it has an Action Network. Co-op America's Responsible Shopper allows consumers to make the green choice for buying clothing, personal care products, housewares, and other items. Individuals can visit their Web-site (www.responsibleshopper.org), choose a product or company, and make a decision based on its environmental ratings. Co-op America also maintains Green Pages Online, www.greenpages.org. Another valuable point of departure is BuyGreen, a guide to green products and services, www.buygreen.com. The "Living Green" section of *E-The Environmental Magazine* is very useful (www.emagazine.com). On eco-labeling and product certification programs, see "The Consumers Union Guide to Environmental Labels," www.eco-labels.org, and the Environmental Law Institute 2003 report "Harnessing Consumer Power," available at www.elistore.org/reports_detail.asp?ID=10841. A growing number of useful sites address green certification and labeling. For example:

- fish: Marine Stewardship Council, www.msc.org, and Salmon Safe, www.salmonsafe.org;
- forest products: Forest Stewardship Council, www.fscoax.org;
- energy: Energy Star, www.energystar.gov; renewables, www.green-e .org;
- buildings: U.S. Green Building Council, www.usgbc.org;
- tropical fruit: Rain Forest Alliance Certified, www.rainforest-alliance .org/programs/cap/index.html; and
- fair trade: TransFair, www.transfairusa.org.

Consumers International (www.consumersinternational.org/home page.asp) runs campaigns and programs on world trade, environmental issues, consumer education, and corporate social responsibility. It works closely with the United Nations Environment Programme on consumption issues. The United Nations Environment Programme's Production and Consumption Branch manages an extensive sustainable consumption program (www.uneptie.org/pc/sustain).

On a sustainable food supply, see www.foodroutes.org to learn where food comes from. The Find Good Food map will locate local farmers and food markets near you. The United States Department of Agriculture's organic seal (www.ams.usda.gov/nop/Consumers/Seal.html) has now been introduced. The Natural Resources Defense Council's Web-site lists stores and mail-order suppliers that sell organic foods (www.nrdc.org/health/farming/gorgdir.asp). In addition, its Web-site lists overharvested fish that should be avoided when making seafood choices (www.nrdc.org/wildlife/fish/gwhichfi.asp). Information on shade-grown or certified coffee is available at the Environmental Defense site (www.environmentaldefense.org/more/10526).

Useful sites to consult on eco-tourism include the International Eco-tourism Society (TIES) (www.ecotourism.org) and Ecotravel.com Online Magazine (www.ecotravel.com).

On reducing energy consumption (and greenhouse gas emissions), the previously mentioned SafeClimate Web-sites provide useful guidance on emissions reductions. Travelers can check their car pollution at Environmental Defense's Tailpipe Tally, www.environmentaldefense.org/go/more, and the greenhouse gas cost of the next plane trip can be calculated at http://chooseclimate.org/flying. A database for state incentives for renewable energy installation is at www.dsireusa.org, and renewable energy dealers and home power ideas can be found at www.homepower.com. The American Council for an Energy-Efficient Economy (www.aceee.org) offers a "Consumer Guide to Home Energy Savings" as well as a Web-site that provides an environmental guide to cars and trucks, www.greenercars.com. Information on solar energy can be found in Solar Today (www.solartoday.org); the Web-site for the American Wind Energy Association is www.awea.org. See also www.eere.energy.gov.

There is much that can be done to conserve water at home. An interesting Web-site is www.h2ouse.org. On reducing packaging wastes and impacts, see Daniel Imhoff, "Thinking Outside of the Box," *Whole Earth* (Winter 2002), 9, and the Web-sites provided there.

Transition 6: Knowledge and Learning

The important work of environmental education in our schools and more broadly is supported by the National Environmental Education and Training Foundation, www.neetf.org. EE-Link (http://eelink.net) is a gateway to a full range of environmental education programs, products, and services. See also Thomas Parris' "Bytes of Note" on K–12 education in the November 2002 issue of *Environment*.

The extraordinary efforts of the National Academies (Science, Engineering, and Medicine) to bring credible science into the policy process and public arena are reflected at www.nas.edu (click on "Environmental Issues" or visit other areas of the site). At the international level, environmental science has always featured prominently in the work of the International Council for Science, www.icsu.org.

A group that has done innovative work on greening America's colleges and universities is Second Nature, www.secondnature.org. The National Council for Science and the Environment (http://NCSEonline.org) is the leading group seeking to support stronger federal funding for environmental research and better links among environmental science, policy decisions, and public understanding. An excellent source of information on the science of sustainability is maintained by the Initiative on Science and Technology for Sustainability, http://sustsci.harvard.edu.

Almost all U.S. universities carry out significant scientific and policy research related to the environment; it is impossible to list them. There are also many independent research centers whose work is highly relevant to policy concerns. Several prominent organizations in the northeast, for example, are the Woods Hole Marine Biological Laboratory (and its Ecosystems Center) (www.mbl.edu), Woods Hole Oceanographic Institution (www.whoi.edu), Woods Hole Research Center (www.whrc.org), Institute of Ecosystem Studies (www.ecostudies.org), Wildlife Conservation Society (http://wcs.org), and New York Botanical Garden (www.nybg.org), just to mention a few known to me.

Many of the leading organizations developing new knowledge and solutions for sustainability are members of one of the oldest and most respected environmental bodies, IUCN—The World Conservation Union (www.iucn.org). (IUCN maintains the "Red List," the global list of endangered species.)

Multilateral agencies and NGOs have recently come together and created partnerships with researchers around the world to undertake the Millennium Ecosystem Assessment (www.millenniumassessment.org/en/index.htm). This massive scientific endeavor is devoted to assessing the condition of the world's ecosystems comprehensively— including the pressures we are placing on them, our dependency on their services, and the gaps in our knowledge. The assessment draws on the knowledge of local experts, natural and social scientists, government officials, business leaders, and academics.

The Web-site www.actionbioscience.org contains science lessons designed for middle school, high school, and undergraduate students. Subjects range from biodiversity and biotechnology to evolution and the environment.

The World Resources Institute has, with some success, championed the greening of U.S. business schools (see http://bell.wri.org and www.beyondgreypinstripes.org).

For descriptions of what some American universities are doing in the area of professional training for environmental management and leadership, see www.yale.edu/environment, www.env.duke.edu, www .snre.umich.edu, www.esm.ucsb.edu, http://environmentalsciences .berkeley.edu, and www.ksg.harvard.edu.

Transition 7: Taking "Good Governance" Seriously

As developed in chapter 9, the governance transition has two main aspects: transforming the way we do environmental governance at the international level ("GEOpolity") and pushing bottom-up, voluntary initiatives to scale (green "JAZZ").

The best way by far for individuals to help promote the transformation of today's GEOpolity is to support and, wherever appropriate, join and contribute to those organizations that are working to make GEOpolity succeed. Although not always recognized, the United Nations is at the center of almost all of the main environmental treaties and intergovernmental environmental organizations. The success of global environmental governance is inseparably linked to the success of the United Nations. The principal private U.S. group supporting the United Nations overall is the United Nations Association of the United States of America (www.unausa.org). The Better World Campaign (www.betterworldfund.org) has also become increasingly important in building public support and recognition for the United Nations.

The U.N. landscape is complicated, to say the least, but three parts of the United Nations deserve special attention and support. The United Nations Environment Programme (www.unep.org) has been extraordinarily effective, given its size and niche in the United Nations structure. The principal environmental treaties have secretariats that are increasingly important, among them the U.N. Framework Convention on Climate Change (www.unfccc.int), U.N. Convention on Biological Diversity (www.biodiv.org), and U.N. Convention to Combat Desertification (www.unccd.int/main.php). The Commission on Sustainable Development, part of the U.N. Economic and Social Council (www.un.org/esa/sustdev/csd/csd12/csd12.htm; www.un.org/esa/coordination/ecosoc), generates much useful information, if little action. The United Nations University (www.ias.unu.edu) also deserves recognition for its thoughtful work in this field.

Environmental governance at the international level is managed through the myriad of conventions and protocols negotiated, signed, and ratified by countries. The best way to follow these international negotiations is to read the Earth Negotiations Bulletin (www.iisd.ca/linkages/vol22/enb2221e.html). Considered the "Hansard" of international development, the ENB publishes daily reports and analysis when the parties and technical bodies meet to review progress on implementation.

Prominent among the many environmental NGOs based in North America working with (or against) governments and the United Nations to make GEOpolity succeed are Environmental Defense (www.environmentaldefense.org), Natural Resources Defense Council (www.nrdc.org), World Resources Institute (www.wri.org), Environmental Law Institute (www.eli.org), IUCN—The World Conservation Union (www.iucn.org), Earth Action (www.earthaction.org), International Institute for Sustainable Development (www.iisd.org), Center for International Environmental Law (www.ciel.org), World Wildlife Fund (www.worldwildlife.org), Sierra Club (www.sierraclub.org), Friends of the Earth (www.foe.org), Greenpeace (www.greenpeace.org), and the National Wildlife Federation (www.nwf.org).

A good entry point for a wide range of environmental concerns is Earth Day Network (www.earthday.org). Led by Denis Hayes, the organizer of the first Earth Day in 1970, the network brings together five thousand groups around the world that address environmental and sustainability issues.

Some advocacy groups focus on particular issues, such as the Rainforest Alliance (www.rainforest-alliance.org), Oceana (www.oceana.org), and Institute for Agriculture and Trade Policy (www.iatp.org).

Think tanks and policy research centers are growing stronger in this field. Many are based at universities; among those that are not are such diverse organizations as the Worldwatch Institute (www.worldwatch.org), World Business Council for Sustainable Development (www.wbcsd.ch), International Forum on Globalization (www.ifg.org), American Enterprise Institute (www.aei.org), Resources for the Future (www.rff.org), Woods Hole Research Center (www.whrc.org), Heinz Center (www.heinzcenter.org), World Resources Institute (www.wri.org), Union of Concerned Scientists (www.ucsusa.org), Tellus Institute (www.tellus.org), the Center for International Sustainable Development Law (www.cisdl.org), International Institute for Environment and Development (www.iied.org), Carnegie Endowment for International Peace (www.ceip.org), and Earth Policy Institute (www.earth-policy.org). The World Wildlife Fund (www.worldwildlife.org) and World Conservation Union (www.iucn.org) also address a wide range of GEOpolity issues.

A number of useful reports are prepared every year or two that offer different measures of progress toward sustainability. They provide benchmarks against which government officials, private corporations, and even the public should be measured. They include:

- the Environmental Sustainability Index (includes twenty indicators on environmental sustainability, www.ciesin.columbia.edu/indicators/ESI);
- the Living Planet Index (includes indexes on animal species and ecosystem change, www.panda.org/news_facts/publications/general/livingplanet/lpr02.cfm);

- the Ecological Footprint (estimates consumption of natural resources, www.rprogress.org); see also www.ecofoot.net;
- the Compass of Sustainability (provides a Sustainable Development Index, www.iisd.org/cgsdi/compass.htm);
- the Dashboard of Sustainability (provides a Policy Performance Index, http://iisd.ca/cgsdi/dashboard.htm); and
- the Wellbeing Assessment/Barometer of Sustainability (measures human and ecosystem wellbeing together, www.iucn.org/info_and _news/press/wonback.doc); see also Robert Prescott-Allen, *The Wellbeing of Nations* (Washington, D.C.: Island Press, 2001).

The JAZZ future is one in which individuals, NGOs, corporations, cities, states, and associations of all varieties are initiating voluntary actions around the world to "just do it," not waiting on Washington and the international agreement process. Many of the ideas and initiatives presented previously when discussing the sustainable technology and the sustainable consumption transitions are part of the growing JAZZ world.

As mentioned in chapter 9, NGOs are the real maestros of green JAZZ. The Natural Resources Defense Council (www.nrdc.org) is working at the state level to get action on climate disruption; the International Center for Local Environmental Initiatives (www.iclei.org) is doing the same at the city level; and groups like Clean Air–Cool Planet (www.cleanair-coolplanet.org) are working for action at both state and local levels from a regional perspective. Environmental Defense (www.environmentaldefense.org), the Pew Climate Center (www .pewclimate.org), and World Resources Institute (www.wri.org) are effective in partnerships with the private sector. Conservation International (www.conservation.org/xp/CIWEB/home), the Nature Conservancy (http://nature.org), and the World Wildlife Fund (www .worldwildlife.org) are cooperating with international agencies, developing country governments, and NGOs in protecting threatened natural areas. America's private foundation community has been active in supporting these NGO initiatives. See the Environmental Grant-making Foundations directory at www.environmentalgrants.com.

JAZZ depends very much on citizen access to information and to the Internet. WRI's Access Initiative (www.accessinitiative.org) and its Digital Dividend project (www.digitaldividend.org) address these two issues.

Voluntary climate initiatives by individuals, organizations, and businesses are encouraged and supported by several initiatives: SafeClimate for Business (www.safeclimate.net), Climate Neutral Network (www.climateneutral.com), the Pew Climate Center (www.pewclimate.org), and the Chicago Climate Exchange (www.chicagoclimatex.com).

Other initiatives and groups advocating, encouraging, or supporting the greening of business include Environmental Defense (www.environmentaldefense.org), the Rainforest Action Network (www.ran.org), Biogems Initiative (www.savebiogems.org), the Natural Religious Partnership for the Environment (www.nrpe.org), the Global Reporting Initiative (www.globalreporting.org), the Coalition for Environmentally Responsible Economies (www.ceres.org), INFORM (www.informinc.org), the Greening of Industry Network (www.greeningofindustry.org), and Sustainable Business.com (http://sustainable business.com), Greenpeace (www.greenpeace.com), and Corporate Watch (www.corpwatch.org).

Many of the groups mentioned here support initiatives by local communities. Others working in this area include the Sustainable Communities Network (www.sustainable.org), Institute for Local Self-Reliance (www.ilsr.org), Local Government Commission (www.lgc.org), and E. F. Schumacher Society (www.smallisbeautiful.org).

Investors are now an important part of the world of green JAZZ. Useful resources on environmentally responsible investing are available from the Investor Responsibility Research Center (www.irrc.org), Carbon Disclosure Project (www.cdproject.net), Clean Yield Group (www.cleanyield.com), Socially Responsible Investing (www.enn.com/sri), Dow Jones Sustainability Indexes (www.sustainability-indexes

.com), Social Investment Forum (www.socialinvest.org), and the Social Venture Network (www.svn.org).

Republicans interested in promoting good environmental governance can explore REP America (www.repamerica.org). Those more Democratically inclined at present can look into MoveOn.org (www.moveon.org) and the Campaign for America's Future (www.ourfuture.org). For social and political criticism that includes environmental issues, see *The Ecologist* (www.theecologist.org), the Turning Point Project (www.turnpoint.org), *Earth Island Journal* (www.earthisland.org), *Mother Jones* (www.motherjones.com), *The American Prospect* (www.prospect.org), TomPaine.com (www.tompaine.com), and *Grist* (www.gristmagazine.com).

Transition 8: Transition in Culture and Consciousness

Among the good places to turn to think about new values and revitalizing old ones are the National Religious Partnership for the Environment (www.nrpe.org) and Earth Charter Commission (www.earthcharter.org). The Tellus Institute (www.tellus.org) has also been thinking deeply about the values we need for the twenty-first century, and the Harvard Divinity School has sponsored a ten-volume set of books on "religions of the world and ecology," published by Harvard University Press. Each volume addresses a different world religion. Apart from nature itself, inspiration for this transition is best found in novels, song, and poetry and in books like Thomas Berry's *Great Work: Our Way into the Future* (New York: Random House, 1999), which has a wonderful annotated bibliography.

But nature itself is best. My wife and I were fishing last summer behind the barrier islands northeast of Charleston, South Carolina. It was hot and humid as always in the summertime there, and the calm water was perfectly flat and glassy. Several porpoises surfaced around our boat, breaking the stillness. Nearby, two black skimmers began weaving back and forth, cutting the water's surface with their beaks. A hundred yards away, a brown pelican watched from atop a post that marked a channel. Oystercatchers gathered on the oyster banks exposed by the tide. A great blue heron stood motionless peering into the shallow waters near the marsh grass. Mullet were jumping not far from the great blue. It was hard to leave, but the tide was going out, and soon there would be mudflats where we were. We didn't catch any fish that day, but it didn't matter, not much anyhow.

Abbreviations

AEC	Atomic Energy Commission
AIDS	acquired immunodeficiency syndrome
C	Celsius
CEQ	Council on Environmental Quality
CFCs	chlorofluorocarbons
CI	Conservation International
CO_2	carbon dioxide
COP	conference of the parties (to various treaties)
DDT	dichlorodiphenyltrichloroethane (a persistent organo-chlorine pesticide)
DOE	U.S. Department of Energy
ECOSOC	United Nations Economic and Social Council
EDSs	endocrine disrupting substances
EPA	U.S. Environmental Protection Agency
F	Fahrenheit
FAO	Food and Agriculture Organization
FROG	"First Raise Our Growth," a business-as-usual scenario

G-7	Group of Seven: Canada, France, Germany, Italy, Japan, the United Kingdom, and the United States
GDP	gross domestic product
GEF	Global Environment Facility
GEOpolity	a scenario stressing intergovernmental environmental agreements
Global 2000	*Global 2000 Report to the President*
HIV	human immunodeficiency virus
ILO	International Labour Organization
IPAT	Impact $=$ Population $\times$ Affluence $\times$ Technology
IUCN	International Union for the Conservation of Nature and Natural Resources, the World Conservation Union
JAZZ	a scenario stressing voluntary environmental protection actions by businesses, NGOs, and others
LDCs	less developed countries
MIC	methyl isocyanate
MIT	Massachusetts Institute of Technology
mpg	miles per gallon
N_2	biologically inactive nitrogen
NAACP	National Association for the Advancement of Colored People
NAS	National Academy of Sciences
NASA	National Aeronautics and Space Administration
NEPA	National Environmental Policy Act of 1969
NGO	nongovernmental organization, usually a not-for-profit one
NRDC	Natural Resources Defense Council
O_3	ozone
ODA	official development assistance
OECD	Organisation for Economic Co-operation and Development
OPEC	Organization of Petroleum Exporting Countries
PBDE	polybrominated diphenylether

PCBs	polychlorinated biphenyls
POPs	persistent organic pollutants
ppm	parts per million
PV	photovoltaic
R&D	research and development
SEC	Securities and Exchange Commission
SIPI	Scientists' Institute for Public Information
SST	supersonic transport
SUVs	sport utility vehicles
UN	United Nations
UNDP	United Nations Development Programme
UNEP	United Nations Environment Programme
UV-B	ultraviolet-B radiation
WAIS	West Antarctic Ice Sheet
WBCSD	World Business Council for Sustainable Development
WEO	World Environment Organization
WHO	World Health Organization
WIPO	World Intellectual Property Organization
WRI	World Resources Institute
WSSD	2002 United Nations World Summit on Sustainable Development
WTO	World Trade Organization
WWF	World Wide Fund for Nature/World Wildlife Fund

Notes

Prologue

1. U.S. Council on Environmental Quality and U.S. Department of State, *The Global 2000 Report to the President—Entering the Twenty-First Century*, 2 vols. (Washington, D.C.: Government Printing Office, 1980), 1:iii. *Global 2000* was originally suggested by CEQ scientist Lee Talbott. Gerald O. Barney was the report's study director.

2. George M. Woodwell et al., "The Carbon Dioxide Problem: Implications for Policy in the Management of Energy and Other Resources," July 1979, 1.

3. National Research Council, *Carbon Dioxide and Climate: Report of an Ad Hoc Study Group on Carbon Dioxide and Climate* (Washington, D.C.: National Academy of Sciences, 1979), viii.

4. U.S. Council on Environmental Quality, *Global Energy Futures and the Carbon Dioxide Problem* (Washington, D.C.: Government Printing Office, 1981), iii–viii.

5. *Global 2000*, 1:1–3, 37. See also *Global 2000*, 2:328–331, for *Global 2000*'s analysis of species loss, prepared by Thomas E. Lovejoy. Tropical deforestation rates are reported at Food and Agriculture Organization, *State of the World's Forests, 2001* (Rome: FAO, 2001), 44. Loss of forests and biodiversity are discussed in chapter 2, as are uncertainties in the data.

6. Stuart L. Pimm and Peter H. Raven, "Extinction by Numbers," *Nature* 403 (2000): 843.

7. U.S. Council on Environmental Quality and U.S. Department of State, *Global*

2000, 2–3. On desertification, see Gretchen C. Daily, "Restoring Value to the World's Degraded Lands," *Science* 269 (1995): 351. See also U.N. Environment Programme, *Status of Desertification and Implementation of the United Nations Plan of Action to Combat Desertification* (Nairobi: UNEP, 1991), and Harold Dregne et al., "A New Assessment of the World Status of Desertification," *Desertification Control Bulletin* 20, no. 6 (1992). On soil degradation, see World Resources Institute et al., *World Resources, 1998–99* (Oxford: Oxford University Press, 1998), 157; World Resources Institute et al., *World Resources, 2000–2001* (Washington, D.C.: WRI, 2000), 62; and David Pimentel et al., "Environmental and Economic Costs of Soil Erosion and Conservation Benefits," *Science* 267 (1995): 1117.

8. *Global 2000*, 1:37.
9. Projections of global warming are discussed in chapter 3.
10. See the discussion of this period in chapter 4.
11. *Global 2000*, 1:4.
12. Willy Brandt et al., *North-South: A Program for Survival* (Cambridge, Mass.: MIT Press, 1980), 13.
13. These events are recounted, along with President Carter's remarks, in James Gustave Speth, "A New Institute for World Resources," *American Oxonian* 70, no. 1 (1983): 2.
14. U.S. Council on Environmental Quality and U.S. Department of State, *Global Future: Time to Act* (Washington, D.C.: Government Printing Office, 1981).

Chapter 1: A World of Wounds

1. Worldwatch Institute, *Vital Signs, 2002* (New York: W. W. Norton, 2002), 88.
2. Worldwatch Institute, *Vital Signs, 2002* (New York: W. W. Norton, 2002), 59.
3. J. R. McNeill, *Something New Under the Sun: An Environmental History of the Twentieth-Century World* (New York: W. W. Norton, 2000), 15, 360.
4. James Gustave Speth, "Environmental Pollution," in *Earth '88: Changing Geographic Perspectives* (Washington, D.C.: National Geographic Society, 1988), 266–267, and the sources cited therein.
5. John Wargo, *Our Children's Toxic Legacy: How Science and Law Fail to Protect Us from Pesticides* (New Haven and London: Yale University Press, 1998), 3.
6. Precise estimates of the loss of the earth's original forest cover are not possible, and estimates vary somewhat. See Emily Matthews et al., *Pilot Analysis of Global Ecosystems: Forest Ecosystems* (Washington, D.C.: WRI, 2000), 15–16; Kees Klein Goldewijk, "Estimating Global Land Use Change over the Past Two Hundred Years: The HYDE Database," *Global Biogeochemical Cycles* 15, no. 2

(2001): 417–433; World Commission on Forests and Sustainable Development, *Our Forests, Our Future* (Cambridge: Cambridge University Press, 1999), 3; and George M. Woodwell, "The Functional Integrity of Normally Forested Landscapes," *Proceedings of the National Academy of Sciences* 99, no. 21 (2002): 13600. See also David G. Victor and Jesse H. Ausubel, "Restoring the Forests," *Foreign Affairs* 79, no. 6 (2000): 127–129.

For wetland and mangrove losses globally, only estimates are possible. See Carmen Revenga et al., *Pilot Analysis of Global Ecosystems: Freshwater Systems* (Washington, D.C.: WRI, 2000), 3, 21–22; World Resources Institute et al., *World Resources, 2000–2001* (Washington, D.C.: WRI, 2000), 72, 107; Lauretta Burke et al., *Pilot Analysis of Global Ecosystems: Coastal Ecosystems* (Washington, D.C.: WRI, 2001), 19.

7. U.N. Environment Programme, *Global Environmental Outlook 3* (London: Earthscan, 2002), 64–65. See also sources cited in the prologue, n. 7, above.

8. Jane Lubchenco, "Waves of the Future: Sea Changes for a Sustainable World," in *Worlds Apart: Globalization and the Environment* (Washington, D.C.: Island Press, 2003), 25. See also Ransom A. Myers and Boris Worm, "Rapid World-wide Depletion of Predatory Fish Communities," *Nature* 423 (2003): 280, and Fred Pearce, "Oceans Raped of Their Former Riches," *New Scientist*, 2 August 2003, 4.

9. International Union for Conservation of Nature and Natural Resources, *The 2000 IUCN Red List of Threatened Species*, accessible at www.redlist.org.

10. Stuart L. Pimm et al., "The Future of Biodiversity," *Science* 269 (1995): 347; J. H. Lawton and R. M. May, *Extinction Rates* (Oxford: Oxford University Press, 1995). See also F. Stuart Chapin III et al., "Consequences of Changing Biodiversity," *Nature* 405, no. 11 (2000): 234; Walter V. Reid, "Biodiversity, Ecosystem Change, and International Development," *Environment* 43, no. 3 (2001): 22–23; and the discussion in E. O. Wilson, *The Future of Life* (New York: Alfred A. Knopf, 2002), 96–102.

11. Aldo Leopold, *Round River* (New York: Oxford University Press, 1953), 165.

12. William McKibben, *The End of Nature* (New York: Doubleday, 1999).

13. On climate change, see generally John Firor and Judith E. Jacobsen, *The Crowded Greenhouse* (New Haven and London: Yale University Press, 2002); Eileen Claussen, ed., *Climate Change: Science, Strategies and Solutions* (Boston: Brill, 2001); F. Sherwood Rowland, "Climate Change and Its Consequences," and John P. Holdren, "The Energy-Climate Challenge," both in Donald Kennedy and John A. Riggs, eds., *U.S. Policy and the Global Environment* (Washington, D.C.: Aspen Institute, 2000). And see also Al Gore, *Earth in the Balance* (New York: Penguin Books, 1993).

14. On the biological effects of global climate change, see Camille Parmesan and Gary Yohe, "A Globally Coherent Fingerprint of Climate Change Impacts Across Natural Systems," *Nature* 421 (2003): 37; Terry L. Root et al., "Fingerprints of Global Warming on Wild Animals and Plants," *Nature* 421, no. 2 (2003): 57; and Gian-Reto Walther et al., "Ecological Responses to Recent Climate Change," *Nature* 416 (2002): 389.

15. Peter M. Vitousek et al., "Human Alteration of the Global Nitrogen Cycle: Sources and Consequences," *Ecological Applications* 7, no. 3 (1997): 737–750.

16. Lubchenco, "Waves of the Future," 24; C. Yoon, "A 'Dead Zone' Grows in the Gulf of Mexico," *New York Times*, 20 January 1998, F1.

17. Peter M. Vitousek et al., "Human Appropriation of the Products of Photosynthesis," *Bioscience* 36, no. 6 (1986): 368; S. Rojstaczer et al., "Human Appropriation of Photosynthesis Products," *Science* 294 (2001): 2549.

18. Sandra L. Postel et al., "Human Appropriation of Renewable Fresh Water," *Science* 271 (1996): 785; Nels Johnson et al., "Managing Water for People and Nature," *Science* 292 (2001): 1071.

19. Matthews et al., *Pilot Analysis of Global Ecosystems*, 4.

20. U.N. Environmental Programme, *Global Environmental Outlook 3*, 150.

21. J. R. Malcolm and L. F. Pitelka, *Ecosystems and Global Climate Change: A Review of Potential Impacts of U.S. Terrestrial Ecosystems and Biodiversity* (Washington, D.C.: Pew Center on Global Climate Change, 2000), 11.

22. U.S. National Assessment Synthesis Team, *Climate Change Impacts on the United States: The Potential Consequences of Climate Variability and Change* (Cambridge: Cambridge University Press, 2000), 116–117. See also L. R. Iverson and A. M. Prasad, "Potential Changes in Tree Species Richness and Forest Community Types Following Climate Change," *Ecosystems* 4 (2001): 193.

23. U.S. National Assessment Synthesis Team, *Climate Change Impacts*, 28–29. See also D. Bachelet et al., "Climate Change Effects on Vegetation Distribution and Carbon Budget in the United States," *Ecosystems* 4 (2001): 169.

24. Jane Lubchenco, "Entering the Century of the Environment," *Science* 279 (1998): 492.

25. The statement is reprinted in *Renewable Resource Journal*, Summer 2001, 16.

26. U.S. Energy Information Administration, U.S. Department of Energy, Report No. DOE/EIA-0484 (2003), *International Energy Outlook, 2003*, 4–5.

27. Organisation for Economic Co-operation and Development, *OECD Environmental Outlook*, 159 (1995 is the base year). The Pew Center on Global Climate Change estimates that without mandatory controls, U.S. emissions will rise between 15 and 50 percent over the period 2000–2035. "U.S. CO$_2$ Emissions Will Rise Absent Strong Policy," *Environment News Service*, July 11, 2003.

28. Organisation for Economic Co-operation and Development, *OECD Environmental Outlook,* 171 (1998 is the base year).

29. Organisation for Economic Co-operation and Development, *OECD Environmental Outlook,* 126.

30. UNESCO et al., *Water for People — Water for Life: World Water Development Report* (Paris: UNESCO, 2003).

31. Peter Aldhous, "The World's Forgotten Crisis," *Nature* 422 (2003): 251.

32. UNESCO et al., *Water for People — Water for Life,* "Executive Summary," 33.

33. The view that economic growth is a panacea for improving environmental quality got a boost from studies showing that, as incomes rise, local air pollution first worsens and then improves—the so-called environmental Kuznets curve. There are many problems of making too much of these data. We know, for example, that it is usually much cheaper to prevent environmental decline than to cure it. And some environmental and human losses can never be repaired, even with money. The Kuznets pattern may hold true at certain times and places, but it is not the inevitable outcome. And many negative environmental trends remain positively correlated with increasing incomes even at high levels. See D. I. Stern et al., "Economic Growth and Environmental Degradation: The Environmental Kuznets Curve and Sustainable Development," *World Development* 24, no. 7 (1996): 1151, and Kenneth Arrow et al., "Economic Growth, Carrying Capacity and the Environment," *Science* 268 (1995): 520.

34. Peter M. Vitousek et al., "Human Domination of Earth's Ecosystems," *Science* 277 (1997): 494.

35. See Paul Harrison and Fred Pearce, *AAAS Atlas of Population and Environment* (Berkeley: University of California Press, 2000), 7–9; Robert W. Kates, "Population and Consumption: What We Know, What We Need to Know," *Environment* 42, no. 3 (2000): 10; and Marian Chertow, "The IPAT Equation and Its Variants: Changing Views of Technology and Environmental Impacts," *Journal of Industrial Ecology* 4, no. 4 (2000): 13.

36. Data from Worldwatch Institute's *Vital Signs* series, *Vital Signs: The Trends That Are Shaping Our Future* (New York: W. W. Norton, 1992–2002), and from the World Resources Institute Database.

37. Stuart Pimm and Peter Raven, "Extinction by Numbers," *Nature* 403 (2000): 843.

Chapter 2: Lost in Eden

1. Quoted in Norman Myers, ed., *Gaia: An Atlas of Planetary Management* (New York: Anchor/Doubleday, 1984), 159. See also Peter H. Raven, "Science, Sustainability, and the Human Prospect," *Science* 297 (2002): 954.

2. Roderick Frazier Nash, *The Rights of Nature* (Madison: University of Wisconsin Press, 1989), 63–77, provides a useful analysis of the evolution of Leopold's ethics.

3. Aldo Leopold, *A Sand County Almanac* (London: Oxford University Press, 1949), 204.

4. Leopold, *Sand County Almanac*, 211.

5. International Union for the Conservation of Nature and Natural Resources et al., *World Conservation Strategy* (Gland, Switzerland: IUCN, 1980); International Union for the Conservation of Nature and Natural Resources et al., *Caring for the Earth: A Strategy for Sustainable Living* (Gland, Switzerland: IUCN, 1991).

6. World Resources Institute et al., *Global Biodiversity Strategy* (Washington, D.C.: WRI, 1992).

7. Walter V. Reid, "Biodiversity, Ecosystem Change, and International Development," *Environment* 43, no. 3 (2001): 22.

8. World Resources Institute et al., *World Resources, 2000–2001* (Washington, D.C.: WRI, 2000), 3–4.

9. World Resources Institute et al., *World Resources, 2000–2001*, viii.

10. Gretchen Daily, ed., *Nature's Services: Societal Dependence on Natural Ecosystems* (Washington, D.C.: Island Press, 1997), 373.

11. Harold A. Mooney and Paul R. Ehrlich, "Ecosystem Services: A Fragmentary History," in Daily, ed., *Nature's Services*, 17.

12. Robert Costanza et al., "The Value of the World's Ecosystem Services and Natural Capital," *Nature* 387 (1997): 253.

13. Stephen R. Kellert, *The Value of Life: Biological Diversity and Human Society* (Washington, D.C.: Island Press, 1996), 12.

14. Stephen R. Kellert, *Kinship to Mastery: Biophilia in Human Evolution and Development* (Washington, D.C.: Island Press, 1997), 1–2.

15. Carl Safina, *Song for the Blue Ocean* (New York: Henry Holt, 1997), xiii.

16. See generally the material and sources in E. O. Wilson's books, *Biophilia* (Cambridge, Mass.: Harvard University Press, 1984); *The Diversity of Life* (Cambridge, Mass.: Harvard University Press, 1992); and *The Future of Life* (New York: Alfred A. Knopf, 2002). See also John Tuxill, *Nature's Cornucopia: Our Stake in Plant Diversity* (Washington, D.C.: Worldwatch Institute, 1999), and Mark J. Plotkin, *Medicine Quest: In Search of Nature's Healing Secrets* (New York: Viking, 2000). And see "Tree Bark Yields Two Possible AIDS Treatments," *Times of India*, 21 February 2000, 15; "Wormwood Is the Basis for Cancer Fighting Pill," *Environmental News Network*, 28 November 2001.

17. Michael Byrnes, "Bio-Prospectors Seek Treasure in Australian Forests," *Reuters*,

8 November 2002; Rob Turner, "Salient Facts: Biomimicry," *New York Times Magazine*, 13 January 2002, 16; Kenneth Chang, "In Experiment, Mammal Cells Produce Silk Like a Spider's," *New York Times*, 18 January 2002, A15.

18. Valuable reviews of the best available information on forest and other land-use changes and wetland alterations can be found in U.N. Environment Programme, *Global Environmental Outlook 3* (London: Earthscan, 2002) (land, 62–69; forests, 90–97; wetlands, 155–157), and World Resources Institute et al., *World Resources, 2000–2001* (Washington, D.C.: WRI, 2000) (land, 56, 122, 141–142; forests, 87–92; wetlands, 72–74, 106–107).

19. U.N. Environment Programme, *Global Environmental Outlook 3*, 64–65.

20. U.N. Environment Programme, *Global Environmental Outlook 3*, 150–152; *World Resources, 2000–2001*, 103–112. For additional detail, see Carmen Revenga et al., *Pilot Analysis of Global Ecosystems: Freshwater Systems* (Washington, D.C.: World Resources Institute, 2000).

21. U.S. Geological Survey, *The Status and Trends of the Nation's Biological Resources* (Washington, D.C.: U.S. Government Printing Office, 1998), 593–644.

22. World Resources Institute et al., *World Resources, 2000–2001*, 106. And see Fred Pearce, "Replumbing the Planet," *New Scientist*, 7 June 2003, 30.

23. U.S. Geological Survey, *Status and Trends of the Nation's Biological Resources*, 117–129; Alfonso Alonso et al., *Biodiversity: Connecting with the Tapestry of Life* (Washington, D.C.: Smithsonian Institution, 2001), 17.

24. *Biodiversity: Connecting with the Tapestry of Life*, 17. On reasons behind over-fishing, see Oran R. Young, "Taking Stock: Management Pitfalls in Fisheries Science," *Environment* 45, no. 3 (2003): 24.

25. Osvaldo E. Sala et al., "Global Biodiversity Scenarios for the Year 2100," *Science* 287 (2000): 1770.

26. Gian-Reto Walther et al., "Ecological Responses to Recent Climate Change," *Nature* 416 (2002): 394. See also Camille Parmesan and Gary Yohe, "A Globally Coherent Fingerprint of Climate Change Impacts Across Natural Systems," *Nature* 421 (2003): 37, and Terry L. Root et al., "Fingerprints of Global Warming on Wild Animals and Plants," *Nature* 421 (2003): 57. And see J. Alan Pounds, "Climate and Amphibian Declines," *Nature* 410 (2001): 639; Valerie A. Barber et al., "Reduced Growth of Alaska White Spruce in the Twentieth Century from Temperature Induced Drought Stress," *Nature* 405 (2000): 668; "Pacific Too Hot for Corals of World's Largest Reef," *Environmental News Service*, 23 May 2001; and "Warmer Water in Narragansett Bay Killing Winter Flounder," *Environmental News Network*, 17 September 2001.

27. Kendall Powell, "Warming Planet Shifts Life North and Early," *Nature News Service*, 6 January 2003. See also Oswald J. Schmitz, "Top Predator Control

of Plant Biodiversity and Productivity in an Old-Field Ecosystem," *Ecology Letters* 6 (2003): 156.

28. Reg Watson and Daniel Pauly, "Systematic Distortions in World Fisheries Catch Trends," *Nature* 414 (2001): 534. See also "Fishy Figures," *The Economist*, 1 December 2001, 75. See generally Daniel Pauly and Reg Watson, "Counting the Last Fish," *Scientific American*, July 2003, 42, and the references cited therein.

29. Catherine Lazaroff, "America's Vanishing Biodiversity," *Environmental News Service*, 21 September 1999 (reporting data from the U.S. Geological Survey, *Status and Trends of the Nation's Biological Resources*). See also Bruce A. Stein, "A Fragile Cornucopia: Assessing the Status of U.S. Biodiversity" *Environment* 43, no. 7 (2001): 13. For a global analysis, see Carmen Revenga and Greg Mock, "Freshwater Biodiversity in Crisis," *Earth Trends*, World Resources Institute, October 2000.

30. Food and Agriculture Organization, *State of the World's Forests, 2001* (Rome: FAO, 2001), 44.

31. See Frederic Achard et al., "Determination of Deforestation Rates of the World's Humid Tropical Forests," *Science* 297 (2002): 999; and Philip M. Fearnside and William F. Laurance, "Comment," and Frederic Achard et al., "Response to Comment," *Science* 299 (2003): 1015.

32. Janet N. Abramovitz, "Trends in Forest Area and Quality," in Worldwatch Institute, *State of the World, 1998* (New York: W. W. Norton, 1998), 22–24.

33. Bernice Wuethrich, "Combined Insults Spell Trouble for Rainforests," *Science* 289 (2000): 35; Daniel C. Nepstad et al., "Large-Scale Impoverishment of Amazonian Forests by Logging and Fire," *Nature* 398 (1999): 505; Lisa M. Curran et al., "Impact of El Niño and Logging on Canopy Tree Recruitment in Borneo," *Science* 286 (1999): 2184.

34. "Survey Confirms Coral Reefs Are in Peril," *Science* 297 (2002): 1622; Dirk Bryant et al., *Reefs at Risk* (Washington, D.C.: World Resources Institute, 1998), 20.

35. Tim Radford, "Scientist Warns of Sixth Great Extinction of Wildlife," *Guardian* (U.K.), 29 November 2001. See also Nigel C. A. Pitman and Peter M. Jorgensen, "Estimating the Size of the World's Threatened Flora," *Science* 298 (2002): 989, and F. Stuart Chapin III et al., "Consequences of Changing Biodiversity," *Nature* 405 (2000): 234. See generally Stuart L. Pimm, *The World According to Pimm* (New York: McGraw-Hill, 2001); Beverly Peterson Stearns and Stephen C. Stearns, *Watching, from the Edge of Extinction* (New Haven and London: Yale University Press, 1999); and the writings of E. O. Wilson cited in n. 16, above.

36. George M. Woodwell, "On Purpose in Science, Conservation and Government," *Ambio* 31, no. 5 (2002): 432.

37. Wilson, *Biodiversity*, 20–21.

38. World Resources Institute et al., *World Resources, 2000–2001*, 51.

39. Rosa M. Lemos de Sá, "Amazon Protected Areas Program," *Arborvitae* 15, International Union for the Conservation of Nature and Natural Resources, September 2000, 5.

40. Nepstad et al., "Large-Scale Impoverishment of Amazonian Forests," 505.

41. See Weuthrich, "Combined Insults Spell Trouble for Rainforests," 35; William F. Laurance et al., "The Future of the Brazilian Amazon," *Science* 291 (2001): 438; Georgia O. Cavalho et al., "Frontier Expansion in the Amazon: Balancing Development and Sustainability," *Environment* 44, no. 3 (2002): 34; "Managing the Rainforests," *The Economist*, 12 May 2001, 83; "Brazil: Still Chopping," *The Economist*, 12 April 2000, 36.

42. Nepstad et al., "Large-Scale Impoverishment of Amazonian Forests," 505.

43. Raymond Bonner, "Indonesia's Forests Going Under the Ax for Flooring," *New York Times*, 13 September 2002, A3. See also Paul Jepson et al., "The End for Indonesia's Lowland Forests?" *Science* 292 (2001): 859.

44. For general discussions of the forces driving deforestation in the tropics, see Helmut Geist and Eric Lambin, "Proximate Causes and Underlying Driving Forces of Tropical Deforestation," *Bioscience* 52, no. 2 (2002): 143–150; Robert Repetto and Malcolm Gillis, *Public Policies and the Misuse of Forest Resources* (New York: Cambridge University Press, 1988); Roger D. Stone and Claudia D'Andrea, *Tropical Forests and the Human Spirit: Journeys to the Brink of Hope* (Berkeley: University of California Press, 2001); Michael R. Dove, "A Revisionist View of Tropical Deforestation and Development," *Environmental Conservation* 20, no. 1 (1993): 17; and World Commission on Forests and Sustainable Development, *Our Forests, Our Future* (Cambridge: Cambridge University Press, 1999).

Also see James C. Scott, *Seeing Like a State: How Certain Schemes to Improve the Human Condition Have Failed* (New Haven and London: Yale University Press, 1998), and William Ascher, *Why Governments Waste Natural Resources: Policy Failures in Developing Countries* (Baltimore: Johns Hopkins University Press, 1999).

45. *Tropical Forests and the Human Spirit*, 5. For a quite different approach, see Peichang Zhang et al., "China's Forest Policy in the Twenty-First Century," *Science* 288 (2000): 2135.

46. Andy White and Alejandra Martin, *Who Owns the World's Forests?* (Washington, D.C.: Forest Trends, 2002), 7. And see Jesse C. Ribot, *Democratic Decentralization of Natural Resources* (Washington, D.C.: World Resources Institute, 2002).

47. World Wildlife Fund, *The Forest Industry in the Twenty-First Century* (Washington, D.C.: World Wildlife Fund, 2001).

48. U.N. Environment Programme et al., *An Assessment of the Status of the World's Remaining Closed Forests* (Nairobi: UNEP, 2001). See also Dirk Bryant et al., *The Last Frontier Forests* (Washington, D.C.: World Resources Institute, 1997).

49. Sara J. Scherr et al., *Making Markets Work for Forest Communities* (Washington, D.C.: Forest Trends, 2002).

50. Jared Harder and Richard Rice, "Rethinking Green Consumerism," *Scientific American* 286, no. 5 (2002): 88.

51. Paul J. Ferraro and Agnes Kiss, "Direct Payments to Conserve Biodiversity," *Science* 298 (2002): 1718.

52. Andrew Balmford et al., "Economic Reasons for Conserving Wild Nature," *Science* 297 (2002): 950.

Chapter 3: Pollution and Climate Change in a Full World

1. Arnulf Grübler, "Trends in Global Emissions: Carbon, Sulfur and Nitrogen," *Encyclopedia of Global Environmental Change*, vol. 3 (West Sussex, U.K.: John Wiley and Sons, 2001), 42–47.

  The early portions of this chapter update materials originally in James Gustave Speth, "Environmental Pollution," in *Earth '88: Changing Geographic Perspectives* (Washington, D.C.: National Geographic Society, 1988), 262.

2. Grübler, "Trends in Global Emissions," 40.

3. David P. Hackett, "An Assessment of the Basel Convention on the Control of Transboundary Movements of Hazardous Wastes and Their Disposal," *American University Journal of International Law and Policy* 5 (1990): 294.

4. U.S. Census Bureau, *Statistical Abstract of the United States: 2001* (Washington, D.C.: U.S. Government Printing Office, 2001), 218.

5. U.S. Census Bureau, *Statistical Abstract: 2001*, 219.

6. For one overview of U.S. domestic accomplishments in environmental cleanup, see Steven Hayward, *2003 Index of Leading Environmental Indicators* (San Francisco: Pacific Research Institute, 2003). The data on sulfur emissions are from U.N. Environment Programme, *Global Environmental Outlook, 2000* (London: Earthscan Publications, 1999), 46.

7. U.S. Census Bureau, *Statistical Abstract: 2001*, 216.

8. John Heilprin, "EPA Says One-Third of Rivers in Survey Too Polluted for Swimming, Fishing," Associated Press, 1 October 2001. On remaining challenges, see Devra Davis, *When Smoke Ran Like Water* (New York: Basic Books, 2002). The answer to persistent pollution in the United States does not lie with merely ratcheting up existing approaches. Environmental law reform is overdue. See

James Gustave Speth, Russell E. Train, and Douglas M. Costle, "Pollution v. Payrolls: Going for the Gold," *Washington Post*, 4 October 1992.

9. Speth, "Environmental Pollution," 266.

10. Lynn R. Goldman, "Preventing Pollution? U.S. Toxic Chemicals and Pesticides Policies and Sustainable Development," in John C. Dernbach, ed., *Stumbling Toward Sustainability* (Washington, D.C.: Environmental Law Institute, 2002), 414.

11. Speth, "Environmental Pollution," 266.

12. U.S. Environmental Protection Agency, Office of Pollution Prevention and Toxics, *Chemical Hazards Data Availability Study: What Do We Really Know About the Safety of High Production Volume Chemicals?* April 1998. See also Noelle Eckley, "Traveling Toxics," *Environment* 43, no. 7 (2001): 35.

13. Samuel Loewenberg, "E.U. Starts a Chemical Reaction," *Science* 300 (2003): 405.

14. John Wargo, *Our Children's Toxic Legacy: How Science and Law Fail to Protect Us from Pesticides* (New Haven and London: Yale University Press, 1998), 3.

15. Paul Ehrlich and Anne Ehrlich, *Betrayal of Science and Reason* (Washington, D.C.: Island Press, 1996), 163–165.

16. See I. Denholm et al., "Insecticide Resistance on the Move," *Science* 297 (2002): 2222.

17. Eckley, "Traveling Toxics," 24; Jocelyn Kaiser and Martin Enserink, "Treaty Takes a POP at the Dirty Dozen," *Science* 290 (200): 2053.

18. Fred Pearce, "Northern Exposure," *New Scientist*, 31 May 1997, 25; Martin Enserink, "For Precarious Populations, Pollutants Present New Perils," *Science* 299 (2003): 1642. See also the data reported in Joe Thornton, *Pandora's Poison* (Cambridge, Mass.: MIT Press, 2000), 1–55.

19. Center for Children's Health and the Environment, Mount Sinai School of Medicine, "Multiple Low-Level Chemical Exposures," at www.childenvironment.org/position.htm.

20. "Global Environment Ministers Take Action on Mercury Pollution," *Capitol Reports/Environmental News Link*, at www.caprep.com/0203039.htm.

21. "State Department Supports United Nations' Action on Mercury Pollution," *Capitol Reports/Environmental News Link*, at www.caprep.com/0203049.htm; Randall Lutter and Elisabeth Irwin, "Mercury in the Environment: A Volatile Problem," *Environment* 44, no. 9 (2002): 24.

22. "California Authorities Sue Restaurant Chains over Mercury in Fish," *Planet Ark: World Environment News*, at www.planetark.org/avantgo/dailynewsstory.cfm?newsid=20463.

23. Center for Children's Health and the Environment, Mount Sinai School of

Medicine, "Endocrine-Disrupting Chemicals Act Like Drugs, but Are Not Regulated as Drugs," at www.childenvironment.org/position.htm. The question of EDSs was first brought to wide public attention by Theo Colborn et al., *Our Stolen Future* (New York: Dutton, 1996). The issue is discussed in Sheldon Krimsky, "Hormone Disruptors: A Clue to Understanding the Environmental Causes of Disease," *Environment* 43, no. 5 (2001): 22.

24. Natasha Loder, "Royal Society Warns on Hormone Disrupters," *Nature* 406 (2000): 4.

25. "EPA Adopts Aggressive Measures on Herbicide Atrazine," *Capitol Reports/ Environment News Link,* at www.caprep.com/0203016.htm. See also Tyrone Hayes et al., "Feminization of Male Frogs in the Wild," *Nature* 419 (2002): 895, and Rebecca Renner, "Conflict Brewing Over Herbicide's Link to Frog Deformities," *Science* 298 (2002): 938.

26. Center for Children's Health and the Environment, Mount Sinai School of Medicine, "Kids Are Especially Susceptible: Toxic Environmental Threats to Child Development," at www.childenvironment.org/position.htm. See also John Wargo and Linda Evenson Wargo, *The State of Children's Health and Environment, 2002* (Princeton, N.J.: Children's Health Environmental Coalition, 2002), 30.

27. Enserink, "For Precarious Populations, Pollutants Present New Perils," 1642.

28. Rachel Carson, *Silent Spring* (Boston: Houghton, Mifflin, 1962).

29. World Resources Institute et al., *World Resources, 1998–99* (New York: Oxford University Press, 1998), 63–65; Devra Davis et al., "Urban Air Pollution Risks to Children: A Global Environmental Health Indicator," World Resources Institute, September 1999. See also Eric Chivian et al., eds., *Critical Condition: Human Health and the Environment* (Cambridge, Mass.: MIT Press, 1993).

30. Speth, "Environmental Pollution," 267–268.

31. World Resources Institute et al., *World Resources, 1998–99*, 42.

32. Speth, "Environmental Pollution," 268–269.

33. See generally Gordon J. MacDonald, *Climate Change and Acid Rain* (McLean, Va.: Mitre, 1985), and John Firor, *The Changing Atmosphere: A Global Challenge* (New Haven and London: Yale University Press, 1990).

34. Charles T. Driscoll et al., "Acid Deposition in the Northeastern United States," *Bioscience* 51, no. 3 (2001): 180; Kevin Krajick, "Longterm Data Show Lingering Effects from Acid Rain," *Science* 292 (2001): 195; Charles T. Driscoll et al., *Acid Rain Revisited,* Hubbard Brook Research Foundation, Science Links Publications, 2001. See also John McCormick, "Acid Pollution: The International Community's Continuing Struggle," *Environment* 40, no. 3 (1998): 17.

35. World Bank, *Clear Water, Blue Skies: China's Environment in the New Century*

(Washington, D.C.: World Bank, 1997). On the effects of pollutants on forests and crops, see James J. MacKenzie and Mohamed T. El-Ashry, eds., *Air Pollution's Toll on Forests and Crops* (New Haven and London: Yale University Press, 1989).

36. World Resources Institute et al., *World Resources, 1998–99*, 182–183; Pottel, "Rampant Urban Pollution Blights Asia's Crops," *New Scientist*, 14 June 1997.

37. J. Lelieveld et al., "The Indian Ocean Experiment: Widespread Air Pollution from South and Southeast Asia," *Science* 291 (2001): 1035. See also Charles W. Petit, "A Darkening Sky," *U.S. News and World Report*, 17 March 2003, 46, and Keith Bradsher, "A Rosy Pink Cloud, Packed with Pollution," *New York Times*, 10 September 2002, A10.

38. Mark Schrope, "Successes in Fight to Save Ozone Layer Could Close Holes by 2050," *Nature* 408 (2000): 627.

39. National Research Council, *Climate Change Science: An Analysis of Some Key Questions* (Washington, D.C.: National Academy Press, 2001). Much of this report was a review of the work of the Intergovernmental Panel on Climate Change in its Third Assessment Report. For an overview of the IPCC report, see Kevin E. Trenberth, "Stronger Evidence of Human Influences on Climate: The 2001 IPCC Assessment," *Environment* 43, no. 4 (2001): 8.

On anthropogenic climate change, see also Thomas J. Crowley, "Causes of Climate Change over the Past Thousand Years," *Science* 289 (2000): 270; P. Falkowski et al., "The Global Carbon Cycle: A Test of Our Knowledge of Earth as a System," *Science* 290 (2000): 291; and Francis W. Zwiers and Andrew J. Weaver, "The Causes of Twentieth Century Warming," *Science* 290 (2000): 2081.

40. National Assessment Synthesis Team, *Climate Change Impacts on the United States: Overview* (Cambridge: Cambridge University Press, 2000), 51.

41. Victor Kennedy et al., *Coastal and Marine Ecosystems and Global Climate Change* (Washington, D.C.: Pew Center on Global Climate Change, 2002), iv.

42. Dennis Normile, "Warmer Waters More Deadly to Coral Reefs than Pollution," *Science* 290 (2000): 682.

43. Brian C. O'Neill and Michael Oppenheimer, "Dangerous Climate Impacts and the Kyoto Protocol," *Science* 296 (2002): 1971.

44. "Pacific Too Hot for Corals of World's Largest Reef," *Environment News Service*, 23 May 2002.

45. National Assessment Synthesis Team, *Climate Change Impacts on the United States*, 45; Report of the New England Regional Assessment Group, *Preparing for Climate Change: New England Regional Overview*, U.S. Global Change Research Program, August 2001, 39–42.

46. Jay Parini and Richard Brown, *A Vermont Christmas* (Boston: Little, Brown, 1988).

47. Report of the New England Regional Assessment Group, *Preparing for Climate Change: New England Regional Overview,* 58–61.

48. See the articles presented in "Trouble in Polar Paradise," *Science* 297 (2002): 1489, and James J. McCarthy and Malcolm C. McKenna, "How the Earth's Ice Is Changing," *Environment* 41, no. 10 (2000): 8. See also Konstantin Y. Vinnikov et al., "Global Warming and Northern Hemisphere Sea Ice Extent," *Science* 286 (1999): 1934; Dorthe Dahl-Jensen, "The Greenland Ice Sheet Reacts," *Science* 289 (2000): 404; and, for a popular account, Eugene Linden, *The Future in Plain Sight* (New York: Simon and Schuster, 1998).

49. "New Kind of Dam Rises in Switzerland: To Hold Back the Land," *New York Times,* 13 December 2002, A20.

50. Frederick E. Nelson et al., "Subsidence Risk from Thawing Permafrost," *Nature* 410 (2001): 889; Timothy Egan, "Warmth Transforms Alaska, and Even Permafrost Isn't," *New York Times,* 6 June 2002, A1; Erica Goldman, "Even in the High Arctic, Nothing Is Permanent," *Science* 297 (2002): 1493.

51. "Kilimanjaro: Researchers Predict Mountain Glaciers Will Be Gone by 2020," *U.N. Wire,* 18 October 2002.

52. Natasha McDowell, "Melting Ice Triggers Himalayan Flood Warning," *Nature* 416 (2002): 776.

53. Gilbert Chin, ed., "Climate Science: Deicing the Arctic," *Science* 298 (2002): 1301 (citing *Geophysical Research Letters* 19 [2002]: 1956).

54. Richard Kerr, "A Warmer Arctic Means Change for All," *Science* 297 (2002): 1490.

55. Kevin Krajick, "Arctic Life, on Thin Ice," *Science* 291 (2001): 424.

56. David G. Vanghan and John R. Spouge, "Risk Estimation of Collapse of the West Antarctic Ice Sheet," *Climate Change* 52 (2002): 65.

57. National Research Council, *Abrupt Climate Change: Inevitable Surprises* (Washington, D.C.: National Academy Press, 2002), 1.

58. Keith Alverson et al., *Environmental Variability and Climate Change,* International Geosphere-Biosphere Program Science Series No. 3, 2001.

59. Robert B. Gagosian, "Abrupt Climate Change: Should We Be Worried?" Woods Hole Oceanographic Institution, 27 January 2003, 8 (emphasis in original). See Wallace B. Broecker, "Thermohaline Circulation, the Achilles Heel of Our Climate System: Will Man-Made CO_2 Upset the Current Balance?" *Science* 278 (1997): 1582. And see Paul R. Epstein and James J. McCarthy, "Why the Global Deep Freeze," *Boston Globe,* 28 January 2003, op-ed page. Another area for nasty surprises stems from the possibility that terrestrial ecosystems may produce "positive feedbacks" on global warming, making the problem worse. Jonathan A. Foley et al., "Green Surprise? How Terrestrial Ecosystems

Could Affect Earth's Climate," *Frontiers in Ecology and the Environment* 1, no. 1 (2003): 38.

60. Gagosian, "Abrupt Climate Change," 8.

61. Bruce J. Peterson et al., "Increasing River Discharge to the Arctic Ocean," *Science* 298 (2002): 2171.

62. The climate impacts reported in National Assessment Synthesis Team, *Climate Change Impacts on the United States,* assume a carbon dioxide buildup in this century to about 700 ppm.

63. O'Neill and Oppenheimer, "Dangerous Climate Impacts and the Kyoto Protocol," 1971. At this point we can perceive only dimly all the possible consequences of global warming and climate change. Extreme weather events and abrupt climate change, for example, could have far-reaching effects on the stability of ecosystems. See, e.g., Marten Scheffer et al., "Catastrophic Shifts in Ecosystems," *Nature* 413 (2001): 591.

64. This analysis is based on Stephen Bernow et al., *America's Global Warming Solutions* (Washington, D.C.: World Wildlife Fund, 1999), 8–10.

Portions of the developing world are beginning to participate meaningfully in the effort to slow global warming—principally by increasing energy efficiency and decreasing carbon intensity. See, e.g., David G. Streets et al., "Recent Reductions in China's Greenhouse Gas Emissions," *Science* 294 (2001): 1835; Walter V. Reid and José Goldemberg, "Developing Countries Are Combating Climate Change," *Energy Policy* 26, no. 3 (1998): 233. Still, emissions from the developing world could begin to exceed those from the developed within the next two decades.

65. Robert U. Ayres, "The Energy We Overlook," *World-Watch,* November–December 2001, 30.

66. The environmental and security issues that face any revival of the nuclear option remain formidable. See Frank N. von Hippel, "Plutonium and Reprocessing of Spent Nuclear Fuel," *Science* 293 (2001): 2397; Luther J. Carter and Thomas H. Pigford, "The World's Growing Inventory of Civil Spent Fuel," *Arms Control Today,* January–February 1999, 8, and "Confronting the Paradoxes in Plutonium Policies," *Issues in Science and Technology,* Winter 1999–2000, 29; and Peter Bradford, "Too Close for Comfort," *On Earth,* Winter 2002, 29.

67. See, e.g., Andrew C. Revkin, "U.S. Seeking Cleaner Model of Coal Plant: Goal Is No Emissions of Greenhouse Gases," *New York Times,* 28 February 2003, A22.

68. Antonia Herzog et al., "Renewable Energy: A Viable Choice," *Environment* 43, no. 10 (2001): 15.

69. Herzog et al., "Renewable Energy," 11.

70. Mark Jacobson and Gilbert M. Masters, "Exploiting Wind Versus Coal," *Science* 293 (2001): 1438.

71. Marlise Simons, "Wind Turbines Are Sprouting Off Europe's Shores," *New York Times*, 8 December 2002, 3; "Germany Approves Second Offshore Wind Project," *Planet Ark News Service*, 27 March 2003.

72. "Buffett Firm Plans Largest Land Wind Farm, in Iowa," *Planet Ark News Service*, 27 March 2003.

73. John A. Turner, "A Realizable Renewable Energy Future," *Science* 285 (1999): 687. See also Stewart Boyle, "Daze in the Sun," *Tomorrow*, June 2001, 64.

74. Danny Hakin, "Fuel Economy Hit Twenty-Two-Year Low in 2002," *New York Times*, 3 May 2003, C1. For an overview of principles to guide future motor vehicle and fuel development, see *Bellagio Memorandum on Motor Vehicle Policy* (San Francisco: Energy Foundation, 2002).

75. On fuel cells and getting to the hydrogen economy, see Marc W. Jensen and Marc Ross, "The Ultimate Challenge: Developing an Infrastructure for Fuel Cell Vehicles," *Environment* 43, no. 3 (2001): 43; Mark Schrope, "Which Way to Energy Utopia?" *Nature* 414 (2001): 682; Peter Schwartz and Doug Randall, "How Hydrogen Can Save America," *Wired*, April 2003, 136; Malcolm A. Weiss et al., "Comparative Assessment of Fuel Cell Cars," Massachusetts Institute of Technology, Laboratory for Energy and the Environment, February 2003; and David W. Keith and Alexandra E. Farrell, "Rethinking Hydrogen Cars," *Science* 301 (2003): 315.

Hydrogen can be produced from fossil fuels or biomass (plants) or other renewable energy sources. The relative costs of these options at today's prices are presented in "Hydrogen Power: These Fuelish Things," *The Economist*, 15 February 2003, 73. New ways of producing hydrogen renewably are on the horizon. Shahed U. M. Khan et al., "Efficient Photochemical Water Splitting by a Chemically Modified n-TiO_2," *Science* 297 (2002): 2243; R. D. Cortright et al., "Hydrogen from Catalytic Reforming of Biomass-Derived Hydrocarbons in Liquid Water," *Nature* 418 (2002): 964.

A hydrogen future would likely not be free of all problems. See Tracey K. Tromp et al., "Potential Environmental Impact of a Hydrogen Economy on the Stratosphere," *Science* 300 (2003): 1740.

76. Pew Center on Global Climate Change, "Climate Change Activities in the United States," June 2002.

77. Jeff Gerth, "Growing U.S. Need for Oil from the Middle East Is Forecast," *New York Times*, 26 December 2002, A16. See also Charles C. Mann, "Getting Over Oil," *Technology Review*, January–February 2002, 33.

78. Quoted in John Carey, "Taming the Oil Beast," *Business Week*, 24 February 2003, 98.

79. Carey, "Taming the Oil Beast," 102–106.

80. Amory B. Lovins, "Energy Strategy: The Road Not Taken?" *Foreign Affairs* 55, no. 1 (1976): 65.

81. Amory B. Lovins, "Readers Report," *Business Week*, 17 March 2003, 20. Several excellent reports on sustainable energy strategies for the United States have appeared recently. See Timothy E. Wirth et al., "The Future of Energy Policy," *Foreign Affairs*, July–August 2003, 132; Natural Resources Defense Council and Union of Concerned Scientists, *Dangerous Addiction: Ending America's Oil Dependence* (New York: NRDC, 2002); and Howard Geller, *Energy Revolution: Policies for a Sustainable Future* (Washington, D.C.: Island Press, 2003). For a global perspective, see José Goldemberg, ed., *World Energy Assessment: Energy and the Challenge of Sustainability* (New York: United Nations Development Programme, 2001).

82. Peter M. Vitousek et al., "Human Alteration of the Global Nitrogen Cycle: Sources and Consequences," *Ecological Applications* 7, no. 3 (1997): 737.

83. Organisation for Economic Co-operation and Development, *OECD Environmental Outlook* (Paris: OECD, 2001), 90.

84. Ellis Cowling et al., "Optimizing Nitrogen Management in Food and Energy Production and Environmental Protection," Summary Statement from the Second International Nitrogen Conference, December 2001.

85. Robert H. Socolow, "Nitrogen Management and the Future of Food: Lessons from the Management of Energy and Carbon," *Proceedings of the National Academy of Sciences* 96 (1999): 6001.

86. Jocelyn Kaiser, "The Other Global Pollutant: Nitrogen Proves Tough to Curb," *Science* 294 (2001): 1268.

Chapter 4: First Attempt at Global Environmental Governance

1. U.S. Council on Environmental Quality, *Environmental Quality: Tenth Annual Report* (Washington, D.C.: U.S. Government Printing Office, 1979), 4.
This chapter draws upon my introductory chapter in James Gustave Speth, ed., *Worlds Apart: Globalization and the Environment* (Washington, D.C.: Island Press, 2003), 1.

2. Rachel Carson, *Silent Spring* (Boston: Houghton, Mifflin, 1962).

3. Ralph Nader, *Unsafe at Any Speed* (New York: Pocket Books, 1965).

4. Charles Reich, *The Greening of America* (New York: Random House, 1970), 18.

5. Philip Shabecoff, *A Fierce Green Fire: The American Environmental Movement* (New York: Hill and Wang, 1993), 118.

6. Study of Critical Environmental Problem, *Man's Impact on the Global Environment: Assessment and Recommendations for Action* (Cambridge, Mass.: MIT Press, 1970).

7. Richard Falk, *This Endangered Planet* (New York: Random House, 1971).

8. Garrett Hardin, *Exploring New Ethics for Survival: The Voyage of the Spaceship Beagle* (New York: Viking Press, 1972).

9. Donella H. Meadows et al., *The Limits to Growth* (New York: Universe Books, 1974).

10. Barbara Ward and Rene Dubos, *Only One Earth: The Care and Maintenance of a Small Planet* (New York: W. W. Norton, 1972).

11. Harrison Brown, *The Human Future Revisited* (New York: W. W. Norton, 1978).

12. Lester Brown, *The Twenty-Ninth Day: Accommodating Human Needs and Numbers to the Earth's Resources* (New York: W. W. Norton, 1978).

13. Sherwood Rowland and Mario Molina, "Stratospheric Sink for Chlorofluoromethanes: Chlorine Catalysed Destruction of Ozone," *Nature* 249 (1974): 810. Paul Crutzen joined in this Nobel Prize.

14. National Research Council, *Carbon Dioxide and Climate: Report of an Ad Hoc Study Group on Carbon Dioxide and Climate* (Washington, D.C.: National Academy of Sciences, 1979).

15. International Union for the Conservation of Nature and Natural Resources and U.N. Environment Programme, *World Conservation Strategy: Living Resource Conservation for Sustainable Development* (Gland, Switzerland: IUCN, 1980).

16. R. D. Munro, "Environmental Research and Management Priorities for the 1980s," *Ambio* 12, no. 2 (1983): 60.

17. Martin Holdgate et al., *The World Environment: 1972–82* (Nairobi: UNEP, 1982).

18. U.S. Council on Environmental Quality and U.S. Department of State, *The Global 2000 Report to the President—Entering the Twenty-First Century* (Washington, D.C.: Government Printing Office, 1980); U.S. Council on Environmental Quality and U.S. Department of State, *Global Future: Time to Act* (Washington, D.C.: U.S. Government Printing Office, 1981).

19. James Gustave Speth, "Environment, Economy, Security: The Emerging Agenda," in *Protecting Our Environment: Toward a New Agenda* (Washington, D.C.: Center for National Policy, 1985). A variety of useful perspectives on the global agenda and responses to it can be found in Nazli Choucri, ed., *Global Accord: Environmental Challenges and International Responses* (Cambridge, Mass.:

MIT Press, 1993); Paul Harrison, *The Third Revolution: Population, Environment and a Sustainable World* (London: Penguin Books, 1993); Jessica Tuchman Mathews, ed., *Preserving the Global Environment* (New York: W. W. Norton, 1991); and Robert Repetto, ed., *The Global Possible: Resources, Development, and the New Century* (New Haven and London: Yale University Press, 1985).

20. Lynton K. Caldwell, *International Environmental Policy: From the Twentieth to the Twenty-First Century* (Durham, N.C.: Duke University Press, 1996), 63–78. For accounts of the emergence of international environmental affairs, see Maurice Strong, "Stockholm Plus Thirty, Rio Plus Ten: Creating a New Paradigm of Global Governance," in Speth, ed., *Worlds Apart*, 33, and Philip Shabecoff, *A New Name for Peace: International Environmentalism, Sustainable Development, and Democracy* (Hanover, N.H.: University Press of New England, 1996).

21. World Commission on Environment and Development, *Our Common Future* (Oxford: Oxford University Press, 1987). (Jim MacNeill was secretary general of the commission.)

The World Charter for Nature was also adopted by the U.N. General Assembly in this period. A pioneering effort to frame a new global ethic, the charter was approved in 1980 by a vote of 111 to 1; the United States cast the only negative vote.

22. See generally David Hunter et al., *International Environmental Law and Policy* (New York: Foundation Press, 2002), for a discussion of major environmental treaties and other agreements.

23. See Richard Elliot Benedick, *Ozone Diplomacy* (Cambridge, Mass.: Harvard University Press, 1998). And see also Stephen O. Anderson and K. Madhava Sarma, *Protecting the Ozone Layer: The United Nations History* (London: Earthscan, 2002), and Hunter et al., *International Environmental Law and Policy*, 293–308.

For useful broader discussions of the international environmental agreement process, the actors in it, their motivations, and the conditions for success and failure, see Scott Barrett, *Environment and Statecraft: The Strategy of Environmental Treaty-Making* (Oxford: Oxford University Press, 2003); Marvin S. Soroos, "Global Institutions and the Environment: An Evolutionary Perspective," in Norman J. Vig and Regina S. Axelrod, *The Global Environment: Institutions, Law and Policy* (Washington, D.C.: Congressional Quarterly Press, 1999); Peter M. Haas et al., eds., *Institutions for the Earth: Sources of Effective International Environmental Protection* (Cambridge, Mass.: MIT Press, 1993); Peter M. Haas, "Environment: Pollution," in P. J. Simmons and Chantal de-Jonge Oudraat, eds., *Managing Global Issues: Lessons Learned* (Washington, D.C.: Carnegie Endowment for International Peace, 2001); Edith Weiss and

Harold K. Jacobson, *Engaging Countries: Strengthening Compliance with International Environmental Accords* (Cambridge, Mass.: MIT Press, 1988) (especially chap. 15); Miranda A. Schreurs and Elizabeth Economy, *The Internationalization of Environmental Protection* (Cambridge: Cambridge University Press, 1997); and Oran Young, ed., *The Effectiveness of International Environmental Regimes* (Cambridge, Mass.: MIT Press, 1999).

24. On the interplay between domestic considerations and international action, see Elizabeth R. DeSombre, *Domestic Sources of International Environmental Policy* (Cambridge, Mass.: MIT Press, 2000). On the work of Mostafa Tolba, see Mostafa K. Tolba, *Global Environmental Diplomacy: Negotiating Environmental Agreements for the World, 1973–1992* (Cambridge, Mass.: MIT Press, 1998).

25. Gareth Porter et al., *Global Environmental Politics* (Boulder, Colo.: Westview Press, 2000), 93.

26. I wish to thank Julia Peck, one of my students, for this point.

27. The complexities in assessing the effectiveness of international environmental law and arriving at balanced conclusions are discussed in Oran R. Young, ed., *The Effectiveness of International Environmental Regimes* (Cambridge, Mass.: MIT Press, 1999).

28. See *Global Environmental Politics*, 212–218. For another critique and proposals for change, see Lawrence E. Susskind, *Environmental Diplomacy: Negotiating More Effective Global Agreements* (Oxford: Oxford University Press, 1994). See also International Network for Environmental Compliance and Enforcement, www.inece.org.

Chapter 5. Anatomy of Failure

1. Simon A. Levin, *Fragile Dominion: Complexity and the Commons* (Reading, Mass.: Perseus Books, 1999), 2.

2. Environmental and other treaties awaiting ratification by the United States are discussed later in this chapter.

3. David Levy and Peter Newell, "Oceans Apart? Business Responses to Global Environmental Issues in Europe and the United States," *Environment* 42, no. 9 (2000): 9.

4. David Hunter et al., *International Environmental Law and Policy* (New York: Foundation Press, 2002), 677.

5. See Eric Pianin, "White House Move on Toxic Chemicals Pact Assailed," *Washington Post*, 12 April 2002, A13.

6. Anil Agarwal et al., *Green Politics: Global Environmental Negotiations* (New Delhi: Centre for Science and Environment, 1999), 2–4. See also Marian A. L.

Miller, *The Third World in Global Environmental Politics* (Boulder, Colo.: Lynne Rienner, 1995). For an overview of the requirements of a successful global environmental politics, see Maurice Strong, "Stockholm Plus 30, Rio Plus 10," in James Gustave Speth, ed., *Worlds Apart: Globalization and the Environment* (Washington, D.C.: Island Press, 2003).

7. Center for Global Development/*Foreign Policy*, "Ranking the Rich: Who Really Helps the Poor," *Foreign Policy*, May–June 2003, 56.

8. David Hunter, "Global Environmental Protection in the Twenty-first Century," in Martha Honey and Tom Barry, *Global Focus: U.S. Foreign Policy at the Turn of the Millennium* (New York: St. Martin's Press, 2000), 120.

9. "Stop the World, I Want to Get Off," *The Economist*, 28 July 2001, 35.

10. Benjamin R. Barber, "A Failure of Democracy, Not Capitalism," *New York Times*, 29 July 2002, A23.

11. J. William Futrell, "Now on the Endangered List: Environmental Law Itself," *Environmental Forum*, 19, no. 1 (2002): 64.

12. Fred L. Smith, Jr., et al., Letter to the Honorable George W. Bush, 2 August 2002.

13. James Gustave Speth, "Perspectives on the Johannesburg Summit," *Environment* 45, no. 1 (2003): 24.

14. Bjorn Lomborg, *The Skeptical Environmentalist* (Cambridge: Cambridge University Press, 2001), 4.

15. Douglas A. Kyser, "Some Realism About Environmental Skepticism," *Ecology Law Quarterly* 30 (2003): 227. See also John C. Dernbach, "Sustainable Versus Unsustainable Propositions," *Case Western Reserve Law Review* 53, no. 2 (2002): 449.

16. Peter H. Gleick, "Is the Skeptic All Wet?" *Environment* 44, no. 6 (2002): 36.

17. Gleick, "Is the Skeptic All Wet?" 36–38.

18. Kyser, "Some Realism About Environmental Skepticism," 233.

Chapter 6. Ten Drivers of Environmental Deterioration

1. The usefulness of the IPAT equation is reflected in Marian R. Chertow, "The IPAT Equation and Its Variants," *Journal of Industrial Ecology* 4, no. 4 (2000): 13; P. E. Waggoner and J. H. Ausubel, "A Framework for Sustainability Science: A Renovated IPAT Identity," *Proceedings of the National Academy of Sciences* 99, no. 12 (2002): 7860; and James Gustave Speth, "EPA Must Help Lead an Environmental Revolution in Technology," *Environmental Law* 21 (1991): 1449–1451.

2. Population-environment linkages are discussed in U.N. Fund for Population

Activities, *Footprints and Milestones: Population and Environmental Change* (New York: UNFPA, 2001); Richard E. Benedick, "Human Population and Environmental Stresses in the Twenty-First Century," *Environmental Change and Security Project Report* 6 (2000): 5; Robert Engelman et al., *People in the Balance* (Washington, D.C.: Population Action International, 2000); and Anne H. Ehrlich and James Salzman, "The Importance of Population Growth to Sustainability," *Environmental Law Reporter News and Analysis* 32 (2002): 10559.

3. Partha S. Dasgupta, "Population, Poverty and the Local Environment," *Scientific American* 272, no. 2 (1995): 27–28.

4. James K. Gasana, "Natural Resource Scarcity and Violence in Rwanda," Swiss Organization for Development and Cooperation, Bern, Switzerland (undated), 1.

5. See Richard P. Cincotta and Barbara B. Crane, "The Mexico City Policy and U.S. Family Planning Assistance," *Science* 294 (2001): 525.

6. John Kenneth Galbraith, "On the Continuing Influence of Affluence," in U.N. Development Programme, *Human Development Report, 1998* (New York: Oxford University Press, 1998), 42.

For overviews of consumption and environment linkages, see Robert W. Kates, "Population and Consumption: What We Know and What We Need to Know," *Environment* 42, no. 3 (2000): 10, and Alan Durning, *How Much Is Enough? The Consumer Society and the Future of the Earth* (New York: W. W. Norton, 1992). And see the exchange between Norman Myers and Jeffrey R. Vincent, "Consumption: Challenge to Sustainable Development . . . or Distraction?" *Science* 276 (1997): 53.

7. Norman Myers and Jennifer Kent, *Perverse Subsidies* (Washington, D.C.: Island Press, 2001), 187–193.

8. Paul R. Ehrlich, *Human Natures: Genes, Cultures and the Human Prospect* (Washington, D.C.: Island Press, 2000), 288.

9. Terry Burnham and Jay Phelan, *Mean Genes* (New York: Penguin Books, 2001), 246–247.

10. Paul Ekins, "The Sustainable Consumer Society: A Contradiction in Terms?" *International Environmental Affairs* 3, no. 4 (1991): 242. For an analysis of the widely shared objective "to put mass consumption at the center of . . . a prosperous postwar America," see Lizabeth Cohen, *A Consumers' Republic* (New York: Alfred A. Knopf, 2003), 11.

11. This discussion draws on J. G. Speth, "The Federal Role in Technology Assessment and Control," in Erica L. Dolgin and Thomas G. P. Gilbert, eds., *Federal Environmental Law* (St. Paul, Minn.: West Publishing, 1974), 420.

12. Speth, "Federal Role in Technology Assessment and Control," 421–422.

13. J. B. Bury, *The Idea of Progress* (New York: Dover Publishers, 1955), 324.

14. John Kenneth Galbraith, *The New Industrial State* (Boston: Houghton Mifflin, 1967), 343.

15. George Heaton et al., *Transforming Technology: An Agenda for Environmentally Sustainable Growth in the Twenty-First Century* (Washington, D.C.: World Resources Institute, 1991), vii.

16. Heaton et al., *Transforming Technology*, vii.

17. International Union for the Conservation of Nature and Natural Resources et al., *World Conservation Strategy: Living Resource Conservation for Sustainable Development* (Gland, Switzerland: IUCN, 1980), 1.

18. For useful reviews of environment-poverty linkages, see World Commission on Environment and Development, *Our Common Future* (Oxford: Oxford University Press, 1987); U.K. Department for International Development et al., *Linking Poverty Reduction and Environmental Management* (Washington, D.C.: World Bank, 2002); Akin L. Mabogunje, "Poverty and Environmental Degradation: Challenges Within the Global Economy," *Environment* 44, no. 1 (2002): 8; U.N. Environment Programme et al., *Protecting Our Planet, Securing Our Future* (Washington, D.C.: World Bank, 1998); and Thomas B. Johansson and José Goldemberg, *Energy for Sustainable Development: A Policy Agenda* (New York: U.N. Development Programme, 2002).

Some of the best analyses of environment and development linkages come from developing country NGOs. For example, in India, see Ashok Khosla, "Technological Leapfrogging," *Development Alternatives Newsletter*, March 2003, 1; R. K. Pachauri, "A Step to Eliminate Poverty by Integrating New and Sustainable Technologies," *TERI Globe, Newsletter of the Tata Energy and Resources Institute*, March 2001, 1; and Anil Agarwal et al., *Poles Apart: Global Environmental Negotiations 2* (New Delhi: Center for Science and Environment, 2001).

19. World Bank, *World Development Report, 2003* (Washington, D.C.: World Bank, 2003), 59.

20. Wallace E. Oates, "An Economic Perspective on Environmental and Resource Management," in Wallace E. Oates, ed., *The RFF Reader in Environmental and Resource Management* (Washington, D.C.: Resources for the Future, 1999), xiv.

21. Theodore Panayotou, *Instruments of Change: Motivating and Financing Sustainable Development* (London: Earthscan, 1998), 6. There are, of course, many dimensions of governmental failure beyond the failure to correct the market. Tad Homer-Dixon argues that "the complexity, unpredictability, and pace of events in our world" are outstripping capacity and ingenuity to deal with them. See Thomas Homer-Dixon, *The Ingenuity Gap* (New York: Alfred A. Knopf, 2000), 1.

22. See Herman E. Daly, "From Empty-World Economics to Full-World Economics," in Kilaparti Ramakrishna and George M. Woodwell, eds., *World Forests for the Future: Their Use and Conservation* (New Haven and London: Yale University Press, 1993), 79.

23. David W. Rejeski, "S&T Challenges in the Twenty-First Century: Strategy and Tempo," Remarks at the Twenty-Seventh Annual AAAS Colloquium on Science and Technology Policy, Washington, D.C., 11–12 April 2002.

24. J. R. McNeill, *Something New Under the Sun: An Environmental History of the Twentieth-Century World* (New York: W. W. Norton, 2000), 336 (emphasis added). And see Edith Tilton Penrose, *The Theory of the Growth of the Firm* (New York: John Wiley and Sons, 1959).

25. Jan Aart Scholte, "Beyond the Buzzword: Towards a Critical Theory of Globalization," in Eleonore Kofman and Gillian Youngs, eds., *Globalization: Theory and Practice* (London: Pinter, 1996), 55.

26. Lamont C. Hempel, *Environmental Governance: The Global Challenge* (Washington, D.C.: Island Press, 1996), 66.

27. On intergenerational obligations, see Edith Brown Weiss, *In Fairness to Future Generations* (Tokyo: United Nations University, 1989).

28. See David M. Potter, *People of Plenty: Economic Abundance and the American Character* (Chicago: University of Chicago Press, 1954).

Chapter 7. Globalization and the Environment

1. Thomas Friedman, "States of Discord: Techno Logic," *Foreign Policy*, March–April 2002, 64. See generally Thomas Friedman, *The Lexus and the Olive Tree: Understanding Globalization* (New York: Farrar, Straus and Giroux, 1999).

   Differing perspectives on globalization and the environment are reflected in the essays in James Gustave Speth, ed., *Worlds Apart: Globalization and the Environment* (Washington, D.C.: Island Press, 2003). This chapter draws on my introductory chapter in *Worlds Apart*, 1.

2. For useful overviews of globalization issues, see U.N. Development Programme, *Human Development Report, 1999* (New York: Oxford University Press, 1999), and John Byrne and Leigh Glober, "A Common Future or Towards a Future Commons: Globalization and Sustainable Development Since UNCED," *International Review for Environmental Strategies* 3, no. 1 (2002): 5. On environmental issues, see Hilary French, *Vanishing Borders: Protecting the Planet in the Age of Globalization* (New York: W. W. Norton, 2000).

3. John Gray, *False Dawn: The Delusions of Global Capitalism* (New York: New Press, 1998); William Greider, *One World, Ready or Not: The Manic Logic of*

Global Capitalism (New York: Simon and Schuster, 1996). See also International Forum on Globalization, *Alternatives to Economic Globalization: A Better World Is Possible* (San Francisco: Berrett-Koehler, 2002).

4. William Clinton, Speech at University of California–Berkeley, 30 January 2002.

5. World Commission on Environment and Development, *Our Common Future* (Oxford: Oxford University Press, 1987), 40.

6. Arthur P. J. Mol, *Globalization and Environmental Reform* (Cambridge, Mass.: MIT Press, 2001), 2.

7. Mol, *Globalization and Environmental Reform*, 199–200.

8. Martin Khor, "Globalization and Sustainable Development: The Choices Before Rio + 10," *International Review for Environmental Strategies* 2, no. 2 (2001): 210.

9. Khor, "Globalization and Sustainable Development," 210–212.

10. Jeffrey Sachs, "Global Capitalism: Making It Work," *The Economist*, 12 September 1998, 23.

11. John Micklethwait and Adrian Wooldridge, "Think Again: The Globalization Backlash," *Foreign Policy*, September–October 2001, 16.

12. Maurice Strong, *Where on Earth Are We Going* (New York: Texere, 2001), 26.

13. Joseph E. Stiglitz, *Globalization and Its Discontents* (New York: W. W. Norton, 2002), 214. See also Robert W. Kates, "The Nexus and the Neem Tree: Globalization and a Transition Toward Sustainability," in Speth, ed., *Worlds Apart*, 85.

14. Benjamin Cashore and Steven Bernstein, "Globalization, Four Paths of Internationalization and Domestic Policy Change: The Case of Eco-Forestry Policy Change in British Columbia, Canada," *Canadian Journal of Political Science* 33, no. 1 (2000): 67.

15. The New World Dialogue on Environment and Development in the Western Hemisphere, *Compact for a New World* (Washington, D.C.: World Resources Institute, 1991), 1.

Chapter 8. Attacking the Root Causes

1. See James Gustave Speth, "Environmental Security in Six Not-So-Easy Steps," *Issues and Ideas*, World Resources Institute, January 1990, and "The Transition to a Sustainable Society," *Issues and Ideas*, World Resources Institute, June 1991; See also William C. Clark, "America's National Interest in Promoting a Transition to Sustainability," *Environment* 43, no. 1 (2001): 18, and Paul Raskin et al., *Great Transition: The Promise and Lure of the Times Ahead* (Boston: Stockholm Environment Institute/Tellus Institute, 2002).

2. Martin Wolf, "People, Plagues and Prosperity," *Financial Times*, 27 February

2003, 11. See also the United Nations Population Website, www.un.org/esa/population/unpop. Unfortunately, a portion of this decline is due to the impact of HIV/AIDS.

3. John Bongaarts, "Population Policy Options in the Developing World," *Science* 263 (1994): 771–776; W. Lutz, ed., *The Future Population of the World: What Can We Assume Today?* (London: Earthscan, 1996), table 6. See also Joel E. Cohen's detailed treatment, *How Many People Can the Earth Support?* (New York: W. W. Norton, 1995), 66–74, 372–379. Cohen points out the strong correlation between availability of contraceptives and declining fertility rates.

4. See Bongaarts, "Population Policy and Options in the Developing World"; U.N. Fund for Population Activities, *Footprints and Milestones* (New York: UNFPA, 2001), 37–58; Partha S. Dasgupta, "Population, Poverty and the Local Environment," *Scientific American* 272, no. 2 (1995): 26; Robert Repetto, "Population, Resource Pressures, and Poverty," in Robert Repetto, ed., *The Global Possible: Resources, Development, and the New Century* (New Haven and London: Yale University Press, 1985), 131; and Lily Han and Linda Shi, "The Politics of Reproduction: Grappling with Global Population Control," *Yale Globalist*, April 2002, 16.

5. Barbara Crossette, "Population Estimates Fall as Poor Women Assert Control," *New York Times*, 10 March 2002, 3.

6. Data are from the U.N. Development Programme's *Human Development Report* series, e.g., *Human Development Report, 2002* (New York: Oxford University Press, 2002). And see James Gustave Speth, "Poverty: A Denial of Human Rights," *Journal of International Affairs* 52, no. 1 (1998): 277, and "The Plight of the Poor," *Foreign Affairs* 78, no. 3 (1999): 13.

7. Progress toward achievement of the Millennium Development Goals is tracked in UNDP's *Human Development Report* series. See *Human Development Report, 2002*, 13–49. See also Nancy Birdsall and Michael Clemens, "From Promise to Performance: How Rich Countries Can Help Poor Countries Help Themselves," Center for Global Development, Washington, D.C., April 2003; and United Nations et al., *A Better World for All: Progress Towards the International Development Goals* (New York: U.N. Development Group, 2000).

8. U.N. Development Programme, *Human Development Report, 1997* (New York: Oxford University Press, 1997), focuses on poverty eradication. For poverty and environmental strategies in development, see U.K. Department for International Development, *Eliminating World Poverty: White Paper on International Development* (London: DFID, 1997); Vinod Thomas et al., *The Quality of Growth* (Washington, D.C.: World Bank, 2000); United Nations University, *Making Integrated Solutions Work for Sustainable Development* (Tokyo: United

Nations University, 2002); U.K. Department for International Development et al., *Linking Poverty Reduction and Environmental Management* (London: Department for International Development, 2002); U.N. Development Programme, *Reconceptualising Governance* (New York: UNDP, 1997); UNDP, *Corruption and Integrity Improvement Initiatives in Developing Countries* (New York: UNDP, 1998); UNDP, *Integrating Human Rights with Sustainable Human Development* (New York: UNDP, 1998); and Kristin Helmore and Naresh Singh, *Sustainable Livelihoods* (Bloomfield, Conn.: Kumarian Press, 2001). See also James Gustave Speth, "Development Assistance and Poverty," in John Dernbach, ed., *Stumbling Towards Sustainability* (Washington, D.C.: Environmental Law Institute, 2002), 163.

9. James Gustave Speth, "The Greening of Technology," *The Bridge* (National Academy of Engineering, Summer 1989), and "EPA Must Help Lead an Environmental Revolution in Technology," *Environmental Law* 21 (1991): 1424; George Heaton et al., *Transforming Technology: An Agenda for Environmentally Sustainable Growth in the Twenty-First Century* (Washington, D.C.: World Resources Institute, 1991). On industrial ecology, see Thomas E. Graedel, "The Evolution of Industrial Ecology," *Environmental Science and Technology*, 1 January 2000, 28; and Reid J. Lifset, "Full Accounting," *Sciences* 40, no. 3 (2000): 32. See also Emily Matthews et al., *The Weight of Nations: Material Outflows from Industrial Economics* (Washington, D.C.: World Resources Institute, 2000). On dematerialization, see Jesse H. Ausubel, "Can Technology Spare the Earth?" *American Scientist* 84, no. 2 (1996): 166. On the limits of modest technological change, see Faye Duchin and Glenn-Marie Lange, *The Future of the Environment: Ecological Economics and Technological Change* (Oxford: Oxford University Press, 1994).

10. Worldwatch Institute, *Vital Signs, 2000* (New York: W. W. Norton, 2000), 53, 57, 59.

11. Worldwatch Institute, *Vital Signs, 2002* (New York: W. W. Norton, 2002), 42–45.

12. Lester R. Brown, *Eco-Economy* (New York: W. W. Norton, 2001), 87.

13. George R. Heaton, Jr., et al., *Backs to the Future: U.S. Government Policy Toward Environmentally Critical Technology* (Washington, D.C.: World Resources Institute, 1992), 9–16. A variety of recent reports carry these analyses forward. See, e.g., Joel Makower and Ron Pernick, *Clean Tech: Profits and Potential*, Clean Edge, Inc., April 2001 (www.cleanedge.com), and Joel Makower, *The Clean Revolution: Technologies from the Leading Edge*, presentation at a Global Business Network Worldview Meeting, 14–16 May 2001. Makower is editor of the *Green Business Letter*.

14. Of particular importance is what has been called "technological leapfrogging." Named after the children's game, leapfrogging proposes that developing countries leap over the tried and true, but dirty, technologies deployed yesterday and today in the industrial countries and move instead directly to environmentally advanced technology. A good example would be the spread of cellular telephones rather than land lines in developing countries. See José Goldemberg, "Energy and Sustainable Development," in James Gustave Speth, ed., *Worlds Apart: Environment and Globalization* (Washington, D.C.: Island Press, 2003), 59–60, and George R. Heaton, Jr., et al., *Missing Links: Technology and Environmental Improvement in the Industrializing World* (Washington, D.C.: World Resources Institute, 1994).

15. David Laws et al., *Public Entrepreneurship Networks*, Environmental Technology and Public Policy Program, Massachusetts Institute of Technology, April 2001.

16. William McDonough and Michael Braungart, *Cradle to Cradle: Remaking the Way We Make Things* (New York: Farrar, Straus and Giroux, 2002), 15–16, 90–91.

17. Marian R. Chertow and Daniel C. Esty, eds., *Thinking Ecologically: The Next Generation of Environmental Policy* (New Haven and London: Yale University Press, 1997), 7.

18. See Robert Stavins and Bradley Whitehead, "Market-Based Environmental Policies," in Chertow and Esty, eds., *Thinking Ecologically*, 105; Theodore Panayotou, *Instruments of Change: Motivating and Financing Sustainable Development* (London: Earthscan, 1998), 15; Allen V. Kneese and Charles L. Schultze, *Pollution, Prices, and Public Policy* (Washington, D.C.: Brookings Institute, 1975); and Frederick R. Anderson et al., *Environmental Improvements Through Economic Incentives* (Baltimore: Johns Hopkins University Press, 1977). See also Vijay Vaitheewaran, "The Great Race," *The Economist*, 6 July 2002, 3, and Hartmut Grassl et al., "Charging the Use of Global Commons," German Advisory Council on Global Change, Berlin, 2002.

19. National Research Council, *Nature's Numbers: Expanding the National Income Accounts to Include the Environment* (Washington, D.C.: National Academy of Sciences, 1999), 3, 19–20.

   Other tools of the modern economic trade also need to be refined. See, e.g., H. Spencer Banzhaf, "Green Price Indices," Resources for the Future, Washington, D.C., March 2002; Lawrence H. Goulder and Robert N. Stavins, "An Eye on the Future," *Nature* 419 (2002): 673.

20. Organisation for Economic Co-operation and Development, *Environmentally Related Taxes in OECD Countries: Issues and Strategies* (Paris: OECD, 2001), 9.

21. Lester R. Brown, *The Earth Policy Reader* (New York: W. W. Norton, 2002), 241. For the background to this innovation, see Ernst U. von Weizsäcker and Jochen Jesinghaus, *Ecological Tax Reform* (London: Zed Books, 1992), and Robert Repetto, *Green Fees: How a Tax Shift Can Work for the Environment and the Economy* (Washington, D.C.: World Resource Institute, 1992).

22. See Robert Costanza, ed., *Ecological Economics* (New York: Columbia University Press, 1991); AnnMari Jansson et al., eds., *Investing in Natural Capital* (Washington, D.C.: Island Press, 1994). See also Douglas A. Kysar, "Law, Environment, and Vision," *Northwestern University Law Review* 97, no. 2 (2003): 675, and Eric A. Davidson, *You Can't Eat GNP: Economics as if Ecology Mattered* (Cambridge, Mass.: Perseus Publishing, 2000).

For an interesting statement straddling the two worlds of neoclassical and ecological economics, see Kenneth Arrow et al., "Economic Growth, Carrying Capacity and the Environment," *Science* 268 (1995): 520. See also Partha Dasgupta et al., "Economic Pathways to Ecological Sustainability," *Bioscience* 50, no. 4 (2000): 339.

23. Herman E. Daly, "Toward Some Operational Principle of Sustainable Development," *Ecological Economics* 2 (1990): 2.

24. Daly, "Toward Some Operational Principle," 4.

25. See, e.g., Philip A. Lawn, "Ecological Tax Reform," *Environment, Development and Sustainability* 2 (2000): 143.

26. Paul Hawken and Amory and Hunter Lovins, *Natural Capitalism: Creating the Next Industrial Revolution* (Boston: Little, Brown, 1999), 6.

27. Hawken, Lovins, and Lovins, *Natural Capitalism*, 9–10.

28. Ecolabeling programs are reviewed in Dave Wortman, "Shop and Save," *Sierra*, November–December 2002, 58; Environmental Law Institute, *Harnessing Consumer Power* (Washington, D.C.: ELI, 2003). See also Lester R. Brown, *Eco-Economy* (New York: W. W. Norton, 2001), 244. And see "The Consumers Union Guide to Environmental Labels" at www.eco-labels.org.

29. Juliet B. Schor and Betsy Taylor, *Sustainable Planet: Solutions for the Twenty-First Century* (Boston: Beacon Press, 2002), xi. And see Donella Meadows, *The Global Citizen* (Washington, D.C.: Island Press, 1991). Not everyone agrees that green consumerism is on the rise. See the discussion in Edwin R. Stafford, "Energy Efficiency and the New Green Marketing," *Environment* 45, no. 3 (2003): 8.

30. Paul Ames, "E.U. Parliament Approves Law Making Companies Pay for Recycling Electronic Waste," Associated Press, 19 December 2002. See also Brown, *Eco-Economy*, 138–143.

31. Anon., "Dell Offers Recycling Option," *GreenBiz.com*, 31 October 2002.

32. Joel Makower and Deborah Fleischer, *Sustainable Consumption and Production: Strategies for Accelerating Positive Change* (New York: Environmental Grant-makers Association, 2003), 2–3.

33. National Research Council, *Our Common Journey: A Transition Toward Sustainability* (Washington, D.C.: National Academy Press, 1999), 10. See also Robert W. Kates et al., "Sustainability Science," *Science* 292 (2001): 641, and Deborah Schoen, "Assessing the Grand Environmental Challenges," *Environmental Science and Technology* 35, no. 3 (2001): 75A.

34. Murray Gell-Mann, *The Quark and the Jaguar* (New York: W. H. Freeman, 1994), 362.

35. National Environmental Education and Training Foundation and Roper ASW, "The Ninth Annual National Report Card on Environmental Attitudes, Knowledge and Behaviors," and "Americans' Low 'Energy IQ': A Risk to Our Energy Future" at www.neetf.org/roper/roper.shtm and www.neetf.org/roper/Roper2002.pdf.

Chapter 9. Taking "Good Governance" Seriously

1. World Business Council for Sustainable Development, *Exploring Sustainable Development: Global Scenarios, 2000–2050: Summary* (1997), 18.

2. U.N. Development Programme, *Human Development Report, 2002* (New York: Oxford University Press, 2002), 15.

3. Gareth Porter et al., *Global Environmental Politics* (Boulder, Colo.: Westview Press, 2000), 178.

4. See James Gustave Speth, "A Post-Rio Compact," *Foreign Policy* 88 (1992): 145, and "Coming to Terms: Toward a North-South Bargain for the Environment," *Environment*, June 1990, 16–20, 40–43.

5. See, e.g., David Hunter, "Global Environmental Protection in the Twenty-First Century," in Martha Honey and Tom Barry, *Global Focus: U.S. Foreign Policy at the Turn of the Millennium* (New York: St. Martin's Press, 2000), 123. The principles cited in the text are adapted from Hunter, 124–125.

6. "Water Standards Not Met," *New York Times*, 23 February 2002, A7.

7. See Lawrence E. Susskind, *Environmental Diplomacy* (New York: Oxford University Press, 1994), 107–109.

8. See Frank Biermann, "The Case for a World Environment Organization," *Environment* 42, no. 9 (2000): 22; Daniel C. Esty and Maria H. Ivanova, "Revitalizing Global Environmental Governance: A Function-Driven Approach," in Esty and Ivanova, eds., *Global Environmental Governance: Options and Op-*

portunities (New Haven: Yale School of Forestry and Environmental Studies, 2002), 181; Steve Charnovitz, "A World Environment Organization," *Columbia Journal of Environmental Law* 27, no. 2 (2002): 324. The concept of a WEO has not met with universal praise even among environmental leaders. See, e.g., Calestous Juma, "The Perils of Centralizing Global Environmental Governance," *Environment Matters: Annual Review,* July 1999–June 2000, 13.

9. See Daniel C. Esty, "Toward Data-Driven Environmentalism: The Environmental Sustainability Index," *Environmental Law Reporter: News and Analysis* 31, no. 5 (2001): 10603, and "Environmental Protection in the Information Age," *New York University Law Review* 79 (2004).

10. The Johannesburg Summit is discussed in James Gustave Speth, "Environment and Globalization After Johannesburg," in Speth, ed., *Worlds Apart: Globalization and the Environment* (Washington, D.C.: Island Press, 2003), 155.

11. See Elena Petkova et al., *Closing the Gap: Information, Participation and Justice in Decision-Making for the Environment* (Washington, D.C.: World Resources Institute, 2002); Carl E. Brunch and Roman Czebiniak, "Globalizing Environmental Governance," *Environmental Law Reporter News and Analysis* 32 (2002): 10428. On the general issue of public access to information, see Thomas Blanton, "The World's Right to Know," *Foreign Policy,* July–August 2002, 50. On the status of governmental environmental reports, see Konrad von Moltke, "Taking Stock in Europe," *Environment* 43, no. 1 (2001): 36.

12. David Hunter et al., *International Environmental Law and Policy* (New York: Foundation Press, 2002), 436; and testimony of Durwood Zaelke before the House Banking Subcommittee on International Labor, Development, Finance, Trade and Monetary Policy hearings on International Labor and Environmental Standards, March 23, 1994.

13. Hunter, "Global Environmental Protection," 136–137.

14. Reiner Grundmann, "The Strange Success of the Montreal Protocol," *International Environmental Affairs* 10, no. 3 (1998): 197.

15. Grundmann, "Strange Success of the Montreal Protocol," 211.

16. Susskind, *Environmental Diplomacy,* 131.

17. Susskind, *Environmental Diplomacy,* 114–116.

18. World Economic Forum, Yale Center for Environmental Law and Policy, and Center for Earth Science Information Network, "Environmental Sustainability Index, 2002" (Geneva: World Economic Forum) (annual releases in 2000–2002; available at www.yale.edu/envirocenter/esi); David Hales and Robert Prescott-Allen, "Flying Blind: Assessing Progress Toward Sustainability," in Esty and Ivanova, eds., *Global Environmental Governance,* 31.

19. See Robert W. Kates and Thomas J. Wilbanks, "Making the Global Local,"

Environment 45, no. 3 (2003): 12; and David Bollier, *How Smart Growth Can Stop Sprawl* (Washington, D.C.: Essential Books, 1998). And see the catalog of city and state green initiatives at the Center for a New American Dream, www.newdream.org/procure/activities.html.

20. See International Council for Local Environmental Initiatives, www.iclei.org and www.iclei.org/co2. See also Clean Air/Cool Planet, "Cool Solutions to Global Warming: Twenty-Four Success Stories from the Northeast" (Portsmouth, N.H.: Clear Air/Cool Planet, 2001).

21. Pew Center on Global Climate Change, "Climate Change Activities in the United States," Arlington, Va., June 2002.

22. "Chicago: Green Machine," *The Economist,* 17 August 2002, 25.

23. John Heilprin, "States to Sue EPA over Power Plant Emissions," Associated Press, 21 February 2003.

24. Benjamin Cashore, "Legitimacy and the Privatization of Environmental Governance: How Non State Market-Driven (NSMD) Governance Systems Gain Rule Making Authority," *Governance* 15, no. 4 (2002): 503–504.

25. Natural Resources Defense Council, BioGems: Laguna San Ignacio, www .savebiogems.org/baja.

On the federal Toxics Release Inventory program, see Mary Graham and Catherine Miller, Disclosure of Toxic Releases in the United States," *Environment* 43 (2001): 8, and David Roe, "Toxic Chemical Control Policy: Three Unabsorbed Facts," *Environmental Law Reporter News and Analysis* 32 (2002): 10232.

26. The biodiversity "hot spot" initiative is discussed later in this chapter, and the international initiative to protect the Amazon is presented in chapter 2. See also World Wildlife Fund, *The Living Planet Campaign: A Call to Action* (Washington, D.C.: WWF, 1999). On the growing role of NGOs in global environmental governance, see Paul Wapner, *Environmental Activism and World Civic Politics* (Albany: State University of New York Press, 1996).

27. Natural Resources Defense Council, BioGems: Great Bear Rainforest, www .savebiogems.org/greatbear.

28. Andrew C. Revkin, "Getting Gases Down," *New York Times,* 22 October 2000, 2WK.

29. Jeremy Grant, "Boardrooms Make Pact on Reduction of Emissions," *Financial Times,* 17 January 2003; Chicago Climate Exchange, "Members Make Unprecedented Voluntary Binding Commitment to Reduce and Trade Greenhouse Gas Emissions by 4 Percent by 2006," 16 January 2003, www.chicagoclimatex.com.

For companies making greenhouse-gas reduction commitments, see Pew Center on Climate Change, "Climate Change Activities in the United States," June 2002, and see www.pewclimate.org.

30. "Eleven Companies Cultivate a Greener Power Market," *Environment News Service,* 8 August 2000.

31. Home Depot has also adopted policies against buying wood from the ten most endangered forest ecoregions as identified by the World Wildlife Fund. See www.homedepot.com. See also Unilever, *Global Challenges, Local Actions* (London: Unilever, 2003), 2.

32. "First Global Survey of Business Leaders on Greenhouse Gas Emissions Released," *Capitol Reports/Environmental News Link,* 19 February 2003; Tony Tassell, "Investors Set Emission Goals," *Financial Times,* 19 August 2002, 2. See Carbon Disclosure Project, www.cdproject.net.

33. See Robert Repetto and Duncan Austin, *Coming Clean: Corporate Disclosure of Significant Environmental Risks* (Washington, D.C.: World Resources Institute, 2000); David Lazarus, "Insurers Getting Wise to Global Warming," *San Francisco Chronicle,* 9 June 2002, G1; Tim Gardner, "Investors Want U.S. Utilities to Disclose Emissions," *Planet Ark: World Environment News,* 20 January 2003; and Bernd Kasemir et al., "The Need Unseen Revolution: Pension Fund Investment and Sustainability," *Environment* 43, no. 9 (2001): 9.

34. See Global Reporting Initiatives, www.globalreporting.org. The GRI is an offshoot of the Coalition for Environmentally Responsible Economies, a coalition of seventy advocacy and investor groups. More than fifty major companies have endorsed the CERES Principles, a ten-point code of environmental conduct. See www.ceres.org.

35. The World Business Council for Sustainable Development is leading the way in many of these areas. See, e.g., Chad Holliday and John Pepper, *Sustainability Through the Market: Seven Keys to Success* (Geneva: WBCSD, 2001); World Resources Institute, U.N. Environment Programme, and WBCSD, *Tomorrow's Markets: Global Trends and Their Implications for Business* (Washington, D.C.: World Resources Institute, 2002); and International Institute for Environment and Development and WBCSD, *Breaking New Ground: Mining, Minerals and Sustainable Development* (Geneva: WBCSD, 2002). Two magazines on sustainability in business, *Tomorrow* and *Green@Work,* now reach large audiences in the business community.

36. Jim Carlton, "Business Interests, Green Groups Seek More Ways to Work Together," *Wall Street Journal,* 23 April 2003, B6B.

37. See the discussion of education, information, and voluntary measures in National Research Council, *New Tools for Environmental Protection* (Washington, D.C.: National Academy Press, 2002).

38. J. F. Rischard, *High Noon: Twenty Global Problems, Twenty Years to Solve Them* (New York: Basic Books, 2002).

39. "Environment and Globalization After Johannesburg," 159.
40. Rex Dalton, "Ecologist Back Blueprint to Save Biodiversity Hotspots," *Nature* 406 (2000): 926.
41. Norman Myers et al., "Biodiversity Hotspots for Conservation Priorities," *Nature* 403 (2000): 853.
42. I am indebted to George M. Woodwell on this point.

Chapter 10. The Most Fundamental Transition of All

1. Paul Raskin et al., *Great Transition: The Promise and Lure of the Times Ahead* (Boston: Stockholm Environment Institute/Tellus Institute, 2002), 44–45. See also Allen Hammond, *Which World? Scenarios for the Twenty-First Century* (Washington, D.C.: Island Press, 1998).
2. John Kenneth Galbraith, "On the Continuing Influence of Affluence," in U.N. Development Programme, *Human Development Report, 1998* (New York: Oxford University Press, 1998), 42.
3. See J. R. McNeill, *Something New Under the Sun: An Environmental History of the Twentieth-Century World* (New York: W. W. Norton, 2000), 33. See also J. Ronald Engel, "Liberal Democracy and the Fate of the Earth," in Steven C. Rockefeller and John C. Elder, *Spirit and Nature* (Boston: Beacon Press, 1992), 59.
4. Raskin et al., *Great Transition*, 43.
5. Charles Reich, *The Greening of America* (New York: Random House, 1970), 352.
6. Earth Charter Initiative, *The Earth Charter: Values and Principles for a Sustainable Future*, www.earthcharter.org.
7. Paul R. Ehrlich, *Human Natures: Genes, Cultures, and the Human Prospect* (Washington, D.C.: Island Press, 2000), 330. Peter Raven has also noted that "the basic conditions of change must clearly come from within us." Peter H. Raven, "Sustainability: Prospects for a New Millennium," *Science and the Future of Mankind* (Vatican City: Pontifical Academy of Science, 2001), 132.
8. Adapted from Raskin et al., *Great Transition*, 29.
9. See Ann Florini, *The Coming Democracy: New Rules for Running a New World* (Washington, D.C.: Island Press, 2003), and Ronnie D. Lipschutz, *Global Civil Society and Global Environmental Governance* (Albany: State University of New York Press, 1996). See also Oran R. Young, *Global Governance* (Cambridge, Mass.: MIT Press, 1997).
10. See Bill Moyer, *Doing Democracy* (Gabriola Island, B.C.: New Society, 2001); David S. Meyers and Sidney Tarrow, eds., *The Social Movement Society: Contentious Politics for a New Century* (New York: Rowman and Littlefield, 1998).

11. Frank R. Baumgartner and Bryan D. Jones, *Agendas and Instability in American Politics* (Chicago: University of Chicago Press, 1993), 9–21.
12. Baumgartner and Jones, *Agendas and Instability in American Politics*, 235–236.
13. See Andy P. Dobson et al., "Hopes for the Future: Restoration Ecology and Conservation Biology," *Science* 277 (1997): 515, and Jesse H. Ausubel, "The Great Reversal: Nature's Chance to Restore Land and Sea," *Technology in Society* 22 (2000): 289.

For Further Reading: A Bookshelf

*The sources listed here are primarily recent efforts aimed at a broad audience—
the general reader with interest in the subjects covered in this book. Many more
could have been included. Materials cited in the Notes overlap slightly with this
list, but the Notes also provide more technical references. In addition, much material
in* Environment, Science, New Scientist, *and other periodicals is accessible to
the nonspecialist. Web-sites of interest are described in "Resources for Citizens,"
following chapter 10.*

State of the Planet Reports: Conditions and Trends

Harrison, P., and F. Pearce. 2000. *AAAS Atlas of Population and Environment*. Berkeley: University of California Press.

Organization for Economic Co-Operation and Development. 2001.
OECD Environmental Outlook. Paris: OECD.

United Nations Environment Programme. 2002. *Global Environmental Outlook 3*. London: Earthscan.

World Resources Institute, et al. *World Resources*. Washington, D.C.:
World Resources Institute. Biennial series.

Worldwatch Institute. *Vital Signs: The Trends That Are Shaping Our Future.* New York: W. W. Norton. Annual series.

Background: Some Twentieth-Century History

McNeill, J. R. 2000. *Something New Under the Sun: An Environmental History of the Twentieth-Century World.* New York: W. W. Norton.

Shabecoff, P. 1993. *A Fierce Green Fire: The American Environmental Movement.* New York: Hill and Wang.

————. 1996. *A New Name for Peace: International Environmentalism, Sustainable Development, and Democracy.* Hanover, N.H.: University Press of New England.

Planetary Perspectives: Politics and Prospects

Gore, A. 1993. *Earth in the Balance.* New York: Penguin Books.

Hammond, A. 1998. *Which World? Scenarios for the Twenty-First Century.* Washington, D.C.: Island Press.

Hertsgaard, M. 1999. *Earth Odyssey.* New York: Broadway Books.

Kennedy, D., and J. A. Riggs, eds. 2000. *U.S. Policy and the Global Environment.* Washington, D.C.: Aspen Institute.

Linden, E. 1998. *The Future in Plain Sight.* New York: Simon and Schuster.

McKibben, W. 1999. *The End of Nature.* New York: Doubleday.

Pew Oceans Commission. 2003. *America's Living Oceans: Charting a Course for a Sea Change.* Arlington, Va.: Pew Oceans Commission.

Raskin, P., et al. 2002. *Great Transition: The Promise and Lure of the Times Ahead.* Boston: Stockholm Environment Institute / Tellus Institute.

Schor, J. B., and B. Taylor. 2002. *Sustainable Planet: Solutions for the Twenty-First Century.* Boston: Beacon Press.

Daily, G., and K. Ellison. 2002. *The New Economy of Nature.* Washington, D.C.: Island Press.

Davidson, E. 2000. *You Can't Eat GNP: Economics as If Ecology Mattered.* Cambridge, Mass.: Perseus.

Ehrlich, P. R. 2000. *Human Natures: Genes, Cultures and the Human Prospect.* Washington, D.C.: Island Press.

Elgin, D. 1993. *Voluntary Simplicity.* New York: William Morrow.

Florini, A. 2003. *The Coming Democracy: New Rules for Running a New World.* Washington, D.C.: Island Press.

French, H. 2000. *Vanishing Borders: Protecting the Planet in the Age of Globalization.* New York: W. W. Norton.

Hawken, P., A. Lovins, and H. Lovins. 1999. *Natural Capitalism: Creating the Next Industrial Revolution.* Boston: Little, Brown.

Homer-Dixon, T. 2000. *The Ingenuity Gap.* New York: Alfred A. Knopf.

Kellert, S. R., and T. Farnham, eds. 2002. *The Good in Nature and Humanity.* Washington, D.C.: Island Press.

McDonough, W., and M. Braungart. 2002. *Cradle to Cradle: Remaking the Way We Make Things.* New York: Farrar, Straus and Giroux.

Myers, N., and J. Kent. 2001. *Perverse Subsidies.* Washington, D.C.: Island Press.

National Research Council. 1999. *Our Common Journey: A Transition Toward Sustainability.* Washington, D.C.: National Academy Press.

Panayotou, T. 1998. *Instruments of Change: Motivating and Financing Sustainable Development.* London: Earthscan.

Rischard, J. F. 2002. *High Noon: Twenty Global Problems, Twenty Years to Solve Them.* New York: Basic Books.

Rockefeller, S. C., and J. C. Elder. 1992. *Spirit and Nature.* Boston: Beacon Press.

Speth, J. G., ed. 2003. *Worlds Apart: Globalization and the Environment.* Washington, D.C.: Island Press.

United Nations Development Programme. *Human Development Report.* New York: Oxford University Press. Annual series.

United Nations Environment Programme. 1998. *Protecting Our Planet, Securing Our Future*. Washington, D.C.: World Bank.

Conflicting Perspectives

On Growth

Daly, H. E. 1996. *Beyond Growth*. Boston: Beacon Press.

Hollander, J. M. 2003. *The Real Environmental Crisis*. Berkeley: University of California Press.

On Transnational Corporations

International Forum on Globalization. 2002. *Alternatives to Economic Globalization: A Better World Is Possible*. San Francisco: Berrett-Koehler.

Schmidheiny, S. 1992. *Changing Course: A Global Business Perspective on Development and the Environment*. Cambridge, Mass.: MIT Press.

Global Environmental Governance

Chertow, M. R., and D. C. Esty, eds. 1997. *Thinking Ecologically: The Next Generation of Environmental Policy*. New Haven and London: Yale University Press.

Choucri, N., ed. *Global Environmental Accord: Strategies for Sustainability and Institutional Innovation*. Cambridge, Mass.: MIT Press. This multivolume series, though aimed at specialists in the field, contains the leading collection of analyses of environmental treaties and international environmental institutions.

Esty, D. C., and M. Ivanova, eds. 2002. *Global Environmental Governance: Options and Opportunities*. New Haven: Yale School of Forestry and Environmental Studies.

Hempel, L. C. 1996. *Environmental Governance: The Global Challenge*. Washington, D.C.: Island Press.

Porter, G., et al. 2000. *Global Environmental Politics*. Boulder, Colo.: Westview Press.

Susskind, L. E. 1994. *Environmental Diplomacy: Negotiating More Effective Global Agreements*. Oxford: Oxford University Press.

Vig, N. J., and R. S. Axelrod. 1999. *The Global Environment: Institutions, Law and Policy*. Washington, D.C.: Congressional Quarterly Press.

Wapner, P. 1996. *Environmental Activism and World Civic Politics*. Albany: State University of New York Press.

Useful Textbooks

Botkin, D. B., and E. A. Keller. 2000. *Environmental Science: Earth as a Living Planet*. New York: John Wiley and Sons.

Hunter, D., J. E. Salzman, and D. Zaelke. 2002. *International Environmental Law and Policy*. New York: Foundation Press.

Miller, G. T., Jr. 2002. *Living in the Environment*. Belmont, Calif.: Wadsworth.

Raven, P. H., and L. R. Berg. 2004. *Environment*. Fort Worth, Tex.: Harcourt College.

Index

AAAS Atlas on Population and the Environment, 212
acid rain, 45, 52–54, 86, 90–91, 95
actionbioscience.org, 221–222
The Activist's Handbook: A Primer (Shaw), 209
affluence, 20, 120, 124. *See also* consumption
The Affluent Society (Galbraith), 125
Agenda 21. *See* Earth Summit
Agendas and Instability in American Politics (Baumgartner and Jones), 198–199
agriculture, 18, 29
  enacting environmental solutions, 159, 206–207
  and environmental deterioration, 14, 15, 30–31, 37, 39, 48, 85 (*see also* deforestation and forest destruction; pesticides)
  and poverty reduction, 155–156
  resources, 216, 218–219

Agriculture, U.S. Department of, 217, 219
air pollution, 44–46, 51–54, 72, 80(table), 86, 90–91. *See also* climate change; fossil fuels; greenhouse gases; pollution; *and specific emissions and pollutants*
Alaska, 59, 67
Alcan, 186, 189
Alcoa, 186
Aldhous, Peter, 18
Amazon, 36–38. *See also* Brazil; deforestation and forest destruction; forests
American Council for an Energy-Efficient Economy, 220
American Enterprise Institute, 224
American Jewish World Service, 215
The American Prospect, 227
American Wind Energy Association, 220
Andersen corporation, 186

Anderson, Steven, 183
Antarctica
    ice sheet, 59–60
    ozone hole, 55, 81(table), 94 (see
        also ozone: ozone depletion)
anthropocentrism, 138
Arctic, 59. See also Inuit people
Argarwal, Anil, 108
Asia, 72, 169. See also specific countries
Association for Women's Rights in
    Development, 212
Atomic Energy Commission, 127–129
automobiles
    fuel-cell vehicles, 67–68, 71, 159,
        248 n75
    fuel efficiency, 67, 70–71
    global production, 20, 160
AVINA foundation, 187
Ayres, Robert, 64

Barber, Benjamin, 111, 113
Basel Convention on the Control
    of Transboundary Movement
    of Hazardous Wastes, 81(table),
    90–91
Baumgartner, Frank, 198–199
Benedick, Richard, 182
Bernstein, Steven, 145–146
Berry, Thomas, 227
Better World Campaign, 222
biodiversity
    in the Amazon, 36
    catastrophic nature of biodiversity
        loss, 24, 190
    as concept, 25–26
    extinction rates, 6–7, 15 (see
        also species extinction/
        endangerment)
    failure of international convention,
        96

hot spots, 189–190
international agreements, 81(table),
    90, 110, 222–223
rationales for sustaining, 24–30
threats to, 30–36, 57 (see also
    specific ecosystems, species,
    and threats)
Biogems Initiative, 226
biomass burning, 53
biophilia, 28–29
biotechnology, 30
birds, 15, 50, 82
Bonneville Environmental Founda-
    tion, 218
Borneo, 34
Brandt Commission on International
    Development Issues, 8
Braungart, Michael, 160–161, 217
Brazil, 34, 36–38, 104, 153, 177
Bread for the World, 215
Bridges (electronic newsletter), 213
bridging institutions, 116
Brown, Harrison, 84
Brown, Lester, 84, 85, 158–159
Brown, Richard, 58
building design/technology, 159, 161,
    216, 219
BuildingGreen.com, 216
Burnham, Terry, 127
Bury, J. B., 129–130
Bush, George W., 62, 112
Bush administration (George W.)
    energy policies, 68–69, 111
    environmental policies, 6, 184
    and the Johannesburg Summit,
        112
    Kyoto Protocol rejected, 55–56,
        62, 110
    Mexico City Policy reinstated, 123
    unilateral approach, 110

business
corporations viewed as villains,
82–83
environmentally responsible practices, 185, 186–187, 196–197
multinationals' response to environmental concerns, 78–79, 107,
185, 186
opposition to global agenda, 88, 93,
107
production and environmental
deterioration, 125–126, 133–135,
160, 162, 175
resources for greening of, 206–
207, 215–216, 225–226
and sustainable consumption,
168–169, 185, 186–187, 196–
197 (*see also* consumption,
sustainable)
and technology, 131 (*see also*
technology)
See also economic growth; globalization; sustainability and sustainable development; *and*
specific corporations
Business Week, 70–71
BuyGreen, 218

Cairo conference. *See* Conference on
Population and Development
Caldwell, Keith, 86
California, 32, 34, 49, 68–69,
80(table), 83
Campaign for America's Future, 227
Canada, 54, 62, 91, 92. *See also* Inuit
people
carbon dioxide (CO_2) and CO_2
emissions
atmospheric levels, 7, 16, 62,
81(table), 247 n62

in developing vs. industrial countries, 63–64, 247 n64
emissions rates, 18, 45, 64, 137,
236 n27
reducing, 63–66, 68–69
role in global warming, 3–5, 7,
16, 44, 56, 62 (*see also* climate
change)
sources, 3
U.S. emissions, 64, 66, 69, 137, 184,
236 n27
See also Kyoto Protocol
Carbon Disclosure Project, 226
carbon sequestration, 65, 68
Cardoso, Fernando Henrique, 146
CARE, 208
Carnegie Endowment for International Peace, 224
Carson, Rachel, 50, 80(table), 82
Carter, Jimmy, 2, 6, 8, 9
Carter administration, 2–3, 129.
See also Carter, Jimmy
Carville, James, 119–120, 137
Cashore, Benjamin, 109–110, 145–146,
184–185
Catholic Relief Services, 215
Center for a New American Dream,
167–168, 218
Center for Development and
Population Activities (CEDPA),
211
Center for Environment and Population, 212
Center for Global Development, 214
Center for International Environmental Law, 223
Center for International Sustainable
Development Law, 224
CEQ. *See* Council on Environmental
Quality

CFCs (chlorofluorocarbons), 44,
54–55, 84, 92–94, 136. *See also*
Montreal Protocol; ozone: ozone
depletion
Charney, Jule, 3. *See also* Charney
Report
Charney Report, 3–5, 80(table),
84–85. *See also* National Academy
of Sciences
chemical pollution, 14, 46–50
in developing nations, 51–52
international agreements, 48,
81(table), 90, 107
move toward safer products, 167
resources, 226
See also persistent organic pollu-
tants; pesticides
Chertow, Marian, 161–162
Chicago, 184
Chicago Climate Exchange, 186, 226
Children's Health Center, Mount
Sinai School of Medicine, 48
China, 51, 53, 115, 177
ChooseClimate.org, 219
Christian Children's Fund, 215
Church World Service, 215
cities, 31, 51, 122
Clapp, Phil, 70
Clark, William, 170
Clean Air Acts, 45–46, 69, 72, 79
Clean Air–Cool Planet, 225
Clean Edge, 217
Clean Water Act, 23, 46, 79
Clean Yield Group, 226
climate change (global climate
disruption), 55–71
average temperatures (global),
56, 58
Charney Report, 3–5, 80(table),
84–85

climate initiatives, 186, 218, 225–
226 (*see also* Kyoto Protocol)
denial of, 6
education on, 170
and energy policy, 62–71
environmental effects, 6, 16, 32–34,
56–61
fossil fuel emissions' role, 3–5, 7,
16, 44, 56, 62 (*see also* carbon
dioxide and CO_2 emissions;
greenhouse gases)
governance failures, 5–6, 8–9, 96
international agreements, 55–56,
62–63, 81(table), 89–90, 96,
222–223 (*see also* Kyoto
Protocol)
1979 report, 2–3
public concern over, 100
rate of change, 60, 246 n59
societal and economic effects, 7–8,
56, 61
Climate Neutral Network, 226
Climate Tickets, 218
Clinton, Bill, 140
Clinton administration, 6, 123.
See also Clinton, Bill
coal, 68, 157
Coalition for Environmentally
Responsible Economies, 226
coffee, 219
Cohen, Joel E., 258 n3
Commission on Sustainable Develop-
ment, 105, 179, 180, 223
Commoner, Barry, 83
Compass of Sustainability (report),
225
*The Complete Guide to Environmental
Careers in the Twenty-first Century*
(Environmental Careers Organi-
zation), 207

Conference on Environment and Development. *See* Earth Summit

Conference on Population and Development (Cairo), 81(table), 90, 123, 212

Conference on the Human Environment (Stockholm Conference), 80(table), 86, 144

Congressional Office of Technology Assessment, 130

conservation. *See specific issues, such as* forests

Conservation Directory, 207–208

Conservation International, 185, 189–190, 208, 225

conservatives, political, 111–113

The Consumer's Guide to Effective Environmental Choice (Union of Concerned Scientists), 205

Consumers International, 219

consumption, 124–127, 134, 191–192. *See also* consumption, sustainable; market economy

consumption, sustainable, 166–169

green certification and ecolabeling, 89–90, 126, 167–168, 184, 187, 205, 218–219, 265 n31

individual choices, 188, 205–206, 217–218

resources, 218–220

contempocentrism, 138–139

Convention for the Protection of the Ozone Layer (Vienna Convention), 55, 88–89, 91–95. *See also* Montreal Protocol; ozone

Convention on Biological Diversity, 81(table), 90, 110, 223. *See also* biodiversity

Convention on Climate Change, 62, 81(table), 89, 96, 223. *See also* Kyoto Protocol

Convention on Long-Range Transboundary Air Pollution, 80(table), 90–91. *See also* air pollution

Convention on the Elimination of All Forms of Discrimination Against Women, 110

Convention on the Law of the Sea, 80(table), 90, 96, 107, 110. *See also* oceans

Convention on the Non-Navigable Uses of International Watercourses, 90

Convention on the Rights of the Child, 110

Convention on Trade in Endangered Species, 96. *See also* species extinction/endangerment

Convention to Combat Desertification, 81(table), 89, 96, 108, 223. *See also* desertification

Cool Companies, 215

Co-Op America, 218

coral reefs, 34, 57–58. *See also* oceans

corporations. *See* business; *and specific corporations*

Costanza, Robert, 27–28

Council on Environmental Quality (CEQ), 2–3, 79, 80(table), 85. *See also Global Future: Time to Act; The Global 2000 Report to the President*

Cradle to Cradle (McDonough and Braungart), 160–161. *See also* Braungart, Michael; McDonough, William

culture and consciousness, transition in, 191–201, 226–227

Daily, Gretchen, 27
Daly, Herman, 164
D'Andrea, Claudia, 40
Dasgupta, Partha, 121–122, 153
Dashboard of Sustainability (report), 225
DDT, 15, 47, 48, 50, 51, 82
deforestation and forest destruction, 14–15
  Amazon forest, 36–38
  and biodiversity loss, 6–7, 21
  and CO_2 levels, 16
  drivers of destruction, 38–42, 132
  international agreements, 89–90, 104
  logging, 32, 34, 37–40, 185
  Lomborg's analysis criticized, 115
  loss statistics, 6, 18, 30–31, 34, 36, 136
  in North America, 35, 185
  role in global warming, 56
  See also forests
Dell corporation, 168
democracy, development of, 173–174
Denmark, 66, 158
desertification, 7, 31, 85
  international conferences/agreements, 80(table), 81(table), 86, 89, 96, 108, 223
developing nations
  assistance to, 106, 108–109, 123, 153–157, 174, 189
  and the GEOpolity approach, 174–175
  greenhouse gas emissions, 18, 61, 63–64, 68–69, 247 n64 (*see also* carbon dioxide and CO_2 emissions; greenhouse gases)
  importance of development progress, 173–174
  and international environmental law, 107–109
  "leapfrogging" technology into, 260 n14
  pollution levels, 51–52
  population growth and demographic transition, 120–122, 152–153 (*see also* population and population growth)
  poverty in, 132 (*see also* poverty)
  solar energy, 159
  vulnerability to climate change, 61
  See also specific nations
development. *See* economic growth; poverty; sustainability and sustainable development
Development as Freedom (Sen), 213
domestic agenda(s). *See under* environmental governance
Doniger, David, 183
Dove, Michael, 115
Dow Jones Sustainability Index, 226
dsireusa.org, 220
Dubos, Rene, 84
DuPont corporation, 94, 186

Earth Charter, 193–195
Earth Day, 79, 80(table), 82, 224
Earth Day Network, 223–224
Earth Island Journal, 227
Earth Negotiations Bulletin, 223
Earth Policy Institute, 224
Earth Summit (Rio de Janeiro), 81(table), 88, 144, 226
  Agenda 21, 81(table), 108–109, 142, 157
  agreements signed, 89, 90 (*see also* Convention on Biological Diversity; Convention to Combat Desertification; Framework

Convention on Climate Change)
Earth Charter, 193–195
Rio Principles, 176, 181
EarthTrends, 209
Eco-Economy (Brown), 158–159
ecological economics, 158–159,
  161–166
Ecological Footprint (report), 225
ecological migration, 122
The Ecologist, 227
economic growth
  consumption, 124–127
  energy efficiency and, 63
  environmental benefits, 19, 237 n33
  environmental consequences, 14,
    45–46, 136–138, 141
  FROG philosophy, 172
  IPAT equation, 20, 120, 124,
    130–131
  pace, 136–137
  and poverty reduction, 155
  and sovereign autonomy, 99
  in the twentieth century, 13–14, 20,
    82, 124
  in the twenty-first century, 17–19,
    20–23, 192
  See also economy; globalization;
    market economy
The Economics of Welfare (Pigou),
  132–133
economy
  benefits of ecosystem services,
    27–28
  economic vs. environmental
    interests, 107
  environmentally honest prices,
    160, 161–166, 217–218
  global economic governance, 78
  market failure, 132–135
  nature-based economy, 29–30

nonmarket economic accounts,
  162–163
scale and rapid expansion, 135–138
See also economic growth
ecosystems
  ecosystem services defined, 27–28
  global capacity, 17, 35–36, 114
  Millennium Ecosystem Assess-
    ment, 221
  rationales for sustaining, 25–30
  threats to *(see also specific eco-
    systems, regions, and threats)*
  value of, 26–27
Ecotravel.com, 219
education, 169–171, 209, 220–222
EE-Link, 220
E. F. Schumacher Society, 226
Ehrlich, Paul, 27, 83, 124, 126,
  193–196
Ekins, Paul, 127
El Niño events, 57
emissions. *See* carbon dioxide and
  CO_2 emissions; greenhouse gases;
  nitrogen; sulfur dioxide emissions
endangered species. *See* species
  extinction/endangerment
Endangered Species Act (1973),
  23–24, 80(table)
endocrine disrupting substances
  (EDSs), 49–50
Energy, U.S. Department of, 3.
  See also United States: energy
  policies
energy and energy consumption
  energy efficiency, 63, 64–65, 67,
    70–71, 159
  international agreements, 112–113
    (*see also* World Summit on
    Sustainable Development)
  nuclear energy, 127–129

energy and energy consumption
(*continued*)
    production and environmental
      deterioration, 126, 134
    renewable energy technologies,
      65–67, 69–70, 158–159, 186,
      219–220
    resources, 218, 219–220
    rising consumption, 14, 20–21
    U.S. energy policy, 63–71, 111,
      159–160
    See also fossil fuels; greenhouse
      gases; sustainability and sustain-
      able development
Energy Star, 219
EnterpriseWorks, 214
Environment (periodical), 207, 220
Environmental Defense (organiza-
    tion), 79, 80(table), 207, 220, 223,
    225
environmental deterioration
    denial of, 6, 113–115
    difficulties in reversing global
      deterioration, 98–100
    drivers (principal threats), 30–36,
      99, 119–139 (*see also specific*
      threats)
    global agenda, 198
    globalization's effects, 145–146
      (*see also* globalization)
    production and, 125–126, 133–135,
      160, 162, 175
    rates, 33–35, 136–137
    transitions toward sustainable
      future, 151–171, 191–201 (*see also*
      GEOpolity; JAZZ; *and specific*
      areas of transition)
    twentieth-century expansion and,
      13–21
    See also specific ecosystems, regions,

and species
environmental governance
    alternative approaches proposed,
      105–106
    challenges and difficulties, 98–100
    domestic agenda(s), 79, 82–84,
      87–88, 99–100 (*see also specific*
      areas of concern)
    and economic growth, 19
    factors favoring treaty success, 106
    of forests, 39
    global agenda, 84–91, 99–100
      (*see also specific areas of concern*)
    global governance defined, 77–78
    global regulatory agency pro-
      posed, 105, 112–113
    international agreement and co-
      operation, 78–79, 86–87, 91–97
      (*see also* international environ-
      mental law; *and specific confer-*
      ences, treaties, and protocols)
    need for, 4–5, 19–21
    need to address drivers of destruc-
      tion, 119–120 (*see also* environ-
      mental deterioration: drivers)
    opposition to global agenda, 88
    problem-defined approach,
      101–102
    public access, 104, 181
    public demand for, 79, 82–84
    resources, 222–227
    standard regime model, 91–94
    transition to good governance,
      172–190
    See also GEOpolity; governance
      failures; JAZZ
Environmental Grantmakers Associa-
    tion, 168–169
Environmental Grant-making Foun-
    dations directory, 226

Environmental Law Institute, 111–112, 223

environmental legislation, U.S. *See also* Clean Water Act

environmental management training, 171

Environmental News Network, 209

Environmental News Service, 209

Environmental Protection Agency, U.S. (EPA), 69, 79, 80(table), 183
and chemical toxicity data, 47
and water pollution, 46, 50

"Environmental Research and Management Priorities for the 1980s" (Munro), 85

environmental responsibility. *See* ethics, environmental

environmental restoration, 200. *See also* sustainability and sustainable development

Environmental Sustainability Index, 224

EPA. *See* Environmental Protection Agency, U.S.

Esty, Daniel, 161–162

E–The Environmental Magazine, 218

ethics, environmental, 19–21, 24–25, 139, 192. *See also* Earth Charter

Europe and the European Union
chemical testing announced, 47
corporate approaches to global environmental issues, 107
environmental policies, 177, 197
and international environmental agreements, 62, 93–94
recycling, 168
renewable energy technologies, 66, 158

Exploring New Ethics for Survival (Hardin), 84

faith-based organizations, 214–215

Falk, Richard, 84

family planning, 211, 212. *See also* population and population growth

fertilizers, 71

fish
economic importance, 29
global catch rate decline, 33
international protections, 104–105, 107 (*see also* Convention on the Law of the Sea)
mercury levels, 49
overfishing, 15, 32, 33, 34, 86, 107
resources, 219
species extinction, 15
sustainability and certified products, 167, 186

food, 20, 30, 219. *See also* agriculture; fish

Foodroutes.org, 219

forests
Amazon forest, 36–38
certification/ecolabeling of forest products, 89–90, 184, 186, 265 n31
economic importance, 29
globalization's effects, 145
ownership and management, 39–40
protection and conservation measures, 37–38, 40–42, 97, 185–186, 189
resources, 219
sustainable forestry, 37, 40, 89–90, 167
threats to, 30–31, 53, 58 (*see also* deforestation and forest destruction)

Forest Stewardship Council, 167, 219

fossil fuels
coal, 68, 157
emissions, 15–16, 44–46, 49, 53, 90–91 (*see also* carbon dioxide and CO2 emissions; greenhouse gases)
fuel efficiency, 64–65, 67, 70–71
increased consumption, 124, 158
low-emission fuels, 65
oil, 69–70, 158
synthetic fuels, 3
taxes, 70
See also energy and energy consumption

Framework Convention on Climate Change, 62, 81(table), 89, 96, 223. *See also* Kyoto Protocol

freshwater and water conservation
acid rain and, 53
biodiversity loss, 33–34
drinking water, 50, 154 *(see also* water shortages/stress *subheading)*
freshwater release into oceans, 61
glacier melt, 58–59
growth in consumption, 31–32
international/regional agreements, 90–91
Lomborg's analysis criticized, 114–115
pollution, 46, 50, 51, 71–72
resources, 220
sewage, 51
true costs, 135
watercourse modifications, 32
water shortages/stress, 16, 18–19, 31–32, 85, 114–115

Friedman, Thomas, 140, 203

Friends of the Earth, 2, 80(table), 217, 223

FROG philosophy, 172

fuels. *See* fossil fuels; hydrogen fuel cells

FUSION, 188–189

Futrell, William, 111–112

Galbraith, John Kenneth, 125, 130, 192

Gasana, James, 122–123

gasoline, 15, 45. *See also* fossil fuels

GDP, measuring, 162–163

GEF. *See* Global Environment Facility

Gell-Mann, Murray, 170

GEOpolity
defined, 172–173
and JAZZ, 188–189
redesigning for success, 173–183
resources, 222–224
underlying principles, 175–176
See also international environmental law; World Environment Organization

Germany, 66, 158, 163, 177

Gibbs, Lois, 83–84

glacier melt, 58–59

Gleick, Peter, 114–115

global agenda. *See under* environmental governance

global climate disruption. *See* climate change

Global Environment Facility (GEF), 81(table), 89, 90, 174–175, 190

Global Future: Time to Act (U.S. Council on Environmental Quality and U.S. Dept. of State), 8, 85

global governance, 77–78. *See also* environmental governance

globalization
 and environmental decline, 136–
  138, 140–147
 and positive change, 197, 203–204
 and sustainable development, 111,
  141–147, 180–181
 See also economic growth
*Globalization and Environmental
 Reform* (Mol), 141–142
"The Globalization Backlash"
 (Micklethwait and Wooldridge),
 144
Global Network of Environment and
 Technology (GNET), 215
Global Reporting Initiative, 187, 226,
 265 n34
Global Scenario Group, 191–192, 193
*The Global 2000 Report to the Presi-
 dent* (U.S. Council on Environmental Quality and U.S. Dept. of
 State), 6–8, 80(table), 85, 121
global warming. *See* climate change
Go Mad! 365 Ways to Save the Planet
 (The Ecologist), 206
Gore, Al, Jr., 146
governance. *See* environmental
 governance; governance failures
governance failures, 1–2, 5–6, 8–9,
 98–117
 difficulties in reversing global
  deterioration, 98–100
 globalization (market) paradigm as
  cause of failure, 142–143
 (in)effectiveness of international
  treaties, 95–97, 100–101, 115–116,
  173
 policy and political failure, 134–135
 political challenges, 99–100, 103,
  106–115
 weaknesses of treaty negotiating

  procedure, 102–105
 See also environmental governance
Great Britain, 177
Great Work: Our Way into the Future
 (Berry), 227
Green@work, 207
GreenBiz.com, 206, 215–216
greenhouse gases
 atmospheric build-up, 52, 80–
  81(table)
 in developing vs. industrial countries, 18, 61, 63–64, 66, 68–69,
  137, 184, 236 n27, 247 n64
 reducing, 63–65, 68–69, 186, 196
  (*see also* fossil fuels: fuel efficiency; Kyoto Protocol; renewable energy technologies)
 resources, 219
 role in global warming, 3–5, 7,
  15–16, 44, 56, 62
 See also carbon dioxide and CO_2
  emissions; energy and energy
  consumption; fossil fuels; ozone
The Greening of America (Reich),
 82–83, 193
Greening of Industry Network, 216,
 226
Green Pages Online, 218
Greenpeace, 207, 223
Green Power Market Development
 Group, 186
Green Scissors, 217
Grist, 227
gross domestic product, measuring,
 162–163
Grundmann, Reiner, 182–183
Gulf Stream disruption, 60–61

Hague Declaration, 177
Hardin, Garrett, 84

Harvard Divinity School's books on world religions and ecology, 227
Hawkin, Paul, 165–166
Hayes, Denis, 223–224
hazardous waste, 14, 45, 81(table), 83–84, 90, 108. *See also* toxic wastes
health
    chemical threats and effects, 49–50, 86
    communicable diseases, 156
    life expectancy and child mortality, 154
    ozone depletion's risks, 15, 54, 93
Heinz Center, 224
Hempel, Lamont, 138
history of environmental movement/concern, 79–91
Hodel, Donald, 182
Hofmann, James, 183
Holdren, John, 83, 124
Home Depot, 90, 186, 265 n31
homepower.com, 220
Homer-Dixon, Thomas, 255 n21
HORIZON International, 214
hot spots for biodiversity, 189–190
Human Development Report, 213
The Human Future Revisited (Brown), 84
human rights treaties, 110
Hunter, David, 109, 181
hydrogen fuel cells, 67–68, 71, 158, 248 n75

ice and snow, 58–60
IIED. *See* International Institute for Environment and Development
IISD. *See* International Institute for Sustainable Development
India, 40, 51–53, 115, 153, 177

individual actions
    activism, 208–209
    association membership, 206
    conservation and eco-development, 208
    consumer purchases, 188, 205–206
    education, 209
    family involvement, 206
    and the future, 197–198
    investing, 205, 226
    NGO support/participation, 207–208 *(see also specific organizations)*
    voting, 188, 204–205
Indonesia, 39
industrial nations
    assistance to developing world, 106, 108–109, 123, 153, 157, 174, 189 *(see also* developing nations)
    and CFC production, 93–94 *(see also* Montreal Protocol)
    consumption, 124–127 *(see also* consumption; economic growth)
    greenhouse gas emissions, 18, 64 *(see also* carbon dioxide and CO_2 emissions; greenhouse gases)
    and international environmental agreements, 107–109 *(see also under* United States)
    and market globalization, 111, 142–143 *(see also* globalization; market economy)
    population growth and demographic transition, 120–121
    taxes, environmental, 70, 163
    See also specific nations
INFORM (organization), 226
Initiative on Science and Technology for Sustainability, 221
Institute for Agriculture and Trade Policy, 214, 224

Institute for Local Self-Reliance, 226
Institute of Ecosystem Studies, 221
InterAction, 215
Interagency Network on Women and
    Gender Equality, 210
Intergovernmental Panel on Climate
    Change, 170
International Center for Local Envi-
    ronmental Initiatives, 225
International Centre for Trade and
    Sustainable Development, 213
International Council for Local
    Environmental Initiatives, 184
International Council for Science,
    220
International Development Research
    Center (IDRC), 210
International Ecotourism Society, 219
international environmental law
    convention-protocol (standard)
        model, 91–95, 101
    increase in, 78
    (in)effectiveness, 95–97, 100–101,
        115–116, 173
    negotiating procedure weaknesses,
        102–105, 115, 174
    NGOs and, 181–182
    political opposition and conflicts
        affecting, 106–113
    readiness for next phase, 196
    reasons for adopting as main
        approach, 101–102
    redesigning for success, 173–183
    rulemaking and enforcement
        (proposed), 176–177 (see also
        IUCN—The World Conser-
        vation Union; World Environ-
        ment Organization)
    social and political context
        neglected, 106

and sovereignty issues, 99, 101, 103,
    106, 197
underlying principles (proposed),
    175–176
See also GEOpolity; and specific
    conventions, treaties, and protocols
International Forum on Globaliza-
    tion, 214, 224
International Geosphere-Biosphere
    Program, 60
International Institute for Environ-
    ment and Development (IIED),
    213, 214, 224
International Institute for Sustainable
    Development (IISD), 209, 214, 217,
    223
International Nitrogen Conference,
    72
International Society for Ecological
    Economics, 217
Inuit people, 48, 50
invasive species, 32, 145
investment
    in environmentally benign tech-
        nologies, 157
    environmentally responsible
        investing, 186–187, 205, 226
    to promote sustainable consump-
        tion, 168–169
Investor Responsibility Research
    Center, 226
Iowa, 66, 69
IPAT equation, 20, 120, 124, 130–131.
    See also affluence; population and
    population growth; technology
IUCN—The World Conservation
    Union (IUCN), 207, 208, 221, 223,
    224
    World Conservation Strategy,
        80(table), 85, 131–132

Jacobson, Mark, 66
Japan, 53, 62, 66, 104–105, 168, 177
JAZZ (green JAZZ), 173, 183–189,
    204–205, 225–227
Johannesburg Summit. *See*
    World Summit on Sustainable
    Development
Jones, Bryan, 198–199

Kates, Roberts, 170
Keeling, David, 2
Kellert, Stephen, 28–29
Kennedy, John F., 200
Kent, Jennifer, 126
Khor, Martin, 142–143
Kilimanjaro, Mount, 58–59
knowledge and learning, transition to,
    169–171
Kuznets curve, environmental, 237
    n33
Kyoto Protocol (1997)
    effectiveness, 96–97
    industrial nations regulated first, 108
    signed, 81(table)
    United States and, 55–56, 62–67,
        89–90, 104, 110, 113
Kysar, Douglas, 114

land degradation, 15, 30–31, 85, 132
Land Mine Convention, 110
land ownership, 38–39
Land Trust Alliance, 208
land use conversion, 30–31, 35, 85
law, environmental. *See* international
    environmental law; United States:
    environmental legislation; *and
    specific acts, conventions, treaties,
    and protocols*
lawsuits, environmental, 49, 79, 128,
    129, 184

lead, 15, 45, 51
League of Conservation Voters,
    204–205
Lebow, Victor, 127
Leopold, Aldo, 15, 24–25, 139
Letters to a Young Activist (Gitlin),
    209
Levin, Simon, 100
Levy, David, 107
Liberia, 155
Lieberman, Joseph, 69
The Limits to Growth (Meadows and
    Meadows et al.), 84
Living Planet Index, 224
Local Government Commission,
    226
logging, 32, 34, 37–38, 39, 40, 185.
    See also deforestation and forest
    destruction; forests
Lomborg, Bjorn, 113–115
Lovejoy, Thomas, 115
Lovins, Amory, 70–71, 165–166, 216
Lovins, Hunter, 165–166
Lowe's, 186
Lubchenco, Jane, 17
Lyautey, Marshal, 200

MacDonald, Gordon, 2
mammals, 15
*Man's Impact on the Global Environ-
    ment* (Report of the Study of Criti-
    cal Environmental Problems), 84
manufacturing
    energy-friendly techniques, 159
    and environmental cost, 125–126,
        133–135, 160, 162, 175
    recycling by manufacturers, 167,
        168
    See also automobiles; consumption
maple trees, 58

Marine Conservation Biology Institute, 208

marine environment. *See* oceans

Marine Stewardship Council, 167, 219

market economy

and environmentally honest prices, 161–162 (*see also* prices)

market failure, 132–135 (*see also* consumption)

See also business; economic growth; economy; globalization

Massachusetts, 68–69

Masters, Gilbert, 66

May, Robert, 34–35

McCain, John, 69

McDonough, William, 160–161, 217

McKibben, Bill, 15

McNeill, J. R., 137–138, 192

Meadows, Dennis and Dana, 84

Mean Genes (Phelan and Burnham), 127

mercury, 49

Mexico, 51, 153, 185

Mexico City Policy, 123

Micklethwait, John, 144

microcredit, 156, 215

Microcredit Summit Campaign, 215

Millennium Development Goals, 213

Millennium Ecosystem Assessment, 170, 221. *See also* Reid, Walter

Miller, Alan, 183

Mintzer, Irving, 183

Mitsubishi, 185

Mol, Arthur, 141–142

Molina, Mario, 54, 80(table), 84, 92, 182

Montreal Protocol (1987), 55, 81(table), 88–89, 93–95, 105, 108, 181–183. *See also* Framework Convention on Climate Change

Mooney, Harold, 27

Moore Foundation, 190

Mother Jones, 227

MoveOn.org, 227

multinational corporations. *See* business; *and specific corporations*

Muskie, Ed, 8

Myers, Norman, 126, 189

Nader, Ralph, 82

NASA (National Aeronautics and Space Administration), 93

Nash, Roderick, 24

National Academy of Sciences

on climate change, 3–5, 56, 60, 80(table), 84–85

nonmarket economic accounts recommended, 162–163

National Council for Science and the Environment, 221

National Environmental Education and Training Foundation, 221

National Environmental Policy Act (1969), 79, 129, 139

National Pollutant Release Inventory (Canadian), 226

National Pollution Prevention Roundtable, 216

National Religious Partnership for the Environment, 208, 226

National Wildlife Federation, 208, 223

natural capital, 164–166

natural gas, 157

Natural Resources Defense Council (NRDC)

established, 79, 80(table), 82

and GEOpolity, 223

and green JAZZ, 225

and the Montreal Protocol, 182, 183

Natural Resources Defense Council
(NRDC) *(continued)*
New Delhi conference attended,
207
organic foods suppliers listed, 219
The Natural Step (organization), 207
Nature Conservancy, 21, 105, 185, 208
Nelson, Gaylord, 82
Newell, Peter, 107
New Hampshire, 68–69
New Jersey, 69
NGOs. *See* nongovernmental
organizations
NIMBY ("not in my back yard")
principle, 100
nitrogen, 16, 71–72
nitrogen oxide emissions, 44–46,
53, 90–91 (*see also* acid rain)
Nixon, Richard, 127–129
nongovernmental organizations
(NGOs)
directories, 207–208
environmental protection efforts,
78, 89–90, 189–190
faith-based organizations, 214–215
and GEOpolity, 223
globalization feared/opposed,
141–142
and green JAZZ, 184–186, 187,
225–227
individual support/participation,
207–208
and international environmental
law, 104, 116, 181–183
and the Millennium Ecosystem
Assessment, 221
See also specific organizations
Nordhaus, William, 162
North-South differences, 107–108,
174–175. *See also* developing

nations; industrial nations
NRDC. *See* Natural Resources
Defense Council
nuclear energy, 127–129

Oates, Wallace, 132–133
Oceana (organization), 224
Ocean Dumping Convention, 96
oceans
climate change's probable effects
on, 56–58, 61
concern cited in 1980s reports, 86
coral reefs, 34, 57–58
"dead zones," 16
international agreements,
80(table), 90, 96, 104–105, 107,
110
sea-level rise, 56–57, 59–60
See also fish
OECD nations. *See* industrial nations
*The Official Earth Day Guide to Planet
Repair* (Hayes), 205–206
oil, 69–70, 157
O'Neill, Brian, 62
One Makes the Difference (Hill), 206
Only One Earth (Ward and Dubos),
84
Oppenheimer, Michael, 62
Oregon, 69
organic foods, 219
Organization for Economic Cooperation and Development (OECD).
See industrial nations
overharvesting, 32, 33. *See also* fish
Oxfam International, 208, 214
ozone
Antarctic hole, 55, 81(table), 94
history of scientific concern, 92–93
international protections, 55, 88–
89, 91–95, 105 (*see also* Frame-

work Convention on Climate
Change; Montreal Protocol)
ozone depletion, 16, 33, 44, 52,
54–55, 84, 85
and smog, 52, 72
See also air pollution; climate
change

packaging, 220
Pakistan, 59
Panayotou, Theo, 135
Parini, Jay, 58
Parris, Thomas, 207, 220
Pathfinder International, 212
PCBs, 15, 44, 48
Peck, Julia, 252 n26
People and the Planet (website), 210
permafrost thawing, 58
persistent organic pollutants (POPs),
48, 81(table), 86, 90–91, 107. *See
also* DDT; PCBs; pesticides
Peru, 51
perverse subsidies, 126, 135, 162
Perverse Subsidies (Myers and Kent),
126
pesticides, 14, 47–48, 50–51, 81(table),
86. *See also* DDT
pest management resources, 218
Peterson, Russell, 47
Pew Center on Global Climate
Change, 57, 184, 225, 226, 236 n27
pharmaceuticals, 29, 30
Phelan, Jay, 127
photovoltaic (PV) energy, 66–67,
157–158
Pigou, A. C., 132–133
Pimm, Stuart, 6–7, 21
Planet Ark, 209
Planned Parenthood Federation, 211
plutonium, 128

poaching, 32, 37
policy and political failure, 134–135
political involvement, 82–84, 204–
205
pollution, 43–73
gross insults vs. microtoxicity,
46–50
increase/decrease, 15, 44–46, 51–52
producers' payment of costs, 126,
134–135, 160, 162, 175 (*see also*
prices)
public concern over, 82–84
spills and accidents, 52, 80(table), 83
as threat to biodiversity and
ecosystems, 33
See also air pollution; chemical pollution; fossil fuels; greenhouse
gases; hazardous waste; ozone;
persistent organic pollutants;
pesticides; toxic waste
Pomerance, Rafe, 2
Population Action International
(PAI), 211
population and population growth,
85, 120–123
Cairo conference, 81(table), 90,
123, 212
declining fertility rates, 153, 196,
258 n3
environmental consequences, 14,
18, 122–123
international cooperation, 90, 95,
123
IPAT equation, 20, 120 (*see also*
IPAT equation)
resources, 210–213
transition to stable/smaller population, 152–154
in the twentieth century, 6, 13–14,
20, 120, 124

population and population growth
(*continued*)
  in the twenty-first century, 17,
    120–121, 152–154
Population Connection, 212
Population Council, 211
Population Reference Bureau, 211–212
Porter, Gareth, 95
poverty
  current world situation, 154–155
  effects of environmental degrada-
    tion on the poor, 36
  environmental decline linked to,
    7–8, 38–39, 131–132, 154
  reducing/eliminating poverty,
    154–157, 196, 213–215
  small loans (microcredit), 156, 215
  social services, 155–156
  urban poor, 122
Prescott-Allen, Robert, 225
prices
  environmentally honest prices, 160,
    161–166, 217–218
  producers' payment of costs, 126,
    134–135, 160, 162, 175
product certification and ecolabeling,
  89–90, 126, 167–168, 184, 187, 205,
  218–219, 265 n31
public-private partnerships, 189.
  See also nongovernmental
  organizations
Puerto Rico, 115

Rainforest Action Network, 226
Rainforest Alliance, 219, 224
Raskin, Paul, 191–192, 193
Raven, Peter, 6–7, 21, 115
recycling, 167, 168
regimes, 91–95. *See also* international
  environmental law

Reich, Charles, 82–83, 193
Reid, Walter, 26
Rejeski, David, 136–137
religion and religious groups, 124,
  214–215
renewable energy technologies,
  65–67, 69–70, 158–159, 186,
  219–220. *See also* energy and
  energy consumption
REP America, 227
Repetto, Robert, 134
reptiles, 15
responsibility, environmental. *See*
  environmental responsibility
restoration, environmental, 200. *See*
  also sustainability and sustainable
  development
Results (organization), 215
Revelle, Roger, 2
Rio Earth Summit. *See* Earth Summit
Rischard, J. F., 188–189
rivers. *See* freshwater and water
  conservation
Rocky Mountain Institute, 216, 217
Rowland, F. Sherwood, 54, 80(table),
  84, 92, 182
Russia, 177
Rwanda, 122–123

Sachs, Jeffrey, 143
SafeClimate for Business, 207, 216,
  219, 226
Safina, Carl, 29
Salmon Safe, 219
Sand County Almanac (Leopold),
  24–25. *See also* Leopold, Aldo
sanitation, 18–19, 51. *See also* fresh-
  water and water conservation
Save the Children, 214
Scholte, J. A., 138

science and policy
   and ozone depletion, 92–93
   public scientific understanding,
      169–171, 196
   resources, 220–222
   scientific uncertainty, 93, 175
   scientists and the environmental
      agenda, 83–85, 189
   *See also specific scientists, organiza-
   tions, and technologies*
Scientists' Institute for Public Infor-
   mation, 128, 129
sea-level rise, 56–57, 59–60
Second Nature, 221
Seidel, Steve, 183
Sen, Amaryta, 213
sewage, 51
Shell corporation, 186, 189
Shultz, George, 182
Sierra Club, 83, 207, 223
Silent Spring (Carson), 50, 80(table),
   82
Simon, Julian, 113
The Skeptical Environmentalist
   (Lomborg), 113–115
smog, 52, 72. *See* air pollution
snow and ice, 58–60
Social Investment Forum, 226
Socially Responsible Investing, 226
Society for Ecological Economics,
   217
Socolow, Robert, 72
solar energy, 159, 220
Solar Today, 220
solid waste, 45. *See also* hazardous
   waste; toxic waste
Song for the Blue Ocean (Safina), 29
South-North differences, 107–109,
   174–175. *See also* developing
   nations; industrial nations

sovereignty, 99, 101, 103, 106, 197
species extinction/endangerment
   aquatic species, 33–34
   climate change and, 32–33
   concern cited in 1980s reports, 85
   Endangered Species Act (1973),
      23–24, 80(table)
   extinction rates, 6–7, 15
   individual species defense, 25
   international agreements,
      80(table), 96
   invasive species and, 32
   large-scale extinction episodes,
      34–35
   Lomborg's analysis criticized, 115
   Red List, 221
   trade in endangered species, 162
   in the United States, 34, 35
   See also specific species and classes
spills and accidents, 52, 80(table), 83
Stiglitz, Joseph, 145
Stockholm Conference on the Human
   Environment, 80(table), 86, 144
Stockholm Convention on Persistent
   Organic Pollutants (POPs), 48,
   81(table), 90–91, 107
Stone, Roger, 40
Strong, Maurice, 144
subsidies, perverse, 126, 135, 162, 217
Subsidy Watch, 217
sulfur dioxide emissions, 44–45, 53,
   90–91. *See also* acid rain
Susskind, Lawrence, 183
sustainability and sustainable
   development
   corporate responses, 172–173,
      185–187, 196–197
   defined, 140–141
   education and, 169–171
   future scenarios, 192–193

sustainability and sustainable
development *(continued)*
GEOpolity approach, 172–183
(*see also* GEOpolity)
globalization and, 111, 141–147
international conferences/
agreements, 81(table), 112–113,
179–180, 189
JAZZ approach, 173, 183–189
natural capital and renewable resource management, 164–166
product certification and ecolabeling, 89–90, 126, 167–168, 184,
187, 205, 218–219, 265 n31
regeneration of environmental
resources, 156
resources, 208, 214–216, 220,
222–224
sustainable consumption, 166–169,
196, 218–220
sustainable forestry, 37, 40
See also technology
Sustainable Alternatives Network,
216
Sustainable Business.com, 226
Sustainable Communities Network,
226
Sweden, 54

Tata Energy and Resources Institute,
171
taxes, environmental, 70, 163
Taxpayers for Common Sense, 217
TechKnow, 215
technology, 127–131
biotechnology, 30
building design, 159, 161, 216
environmental impacts, 130–131
IPAT equation, 20, 120, 130–131
renewable energy technologies,
65–67, 69–70, 158–159, 186,
219–220
role in environmentalism, 149
spread of new technologies, 136,
260 n14
transition to environmentally
benign technologies, 157–161,
196, 215–217
Tellus Institute, 224, 226–227
Texas, 69
"Thinking Outside of the Box"
(Imhoff), 220
Third World. *See* developing nations
This Endangered Planet (Falk), 84
Thomas, Lee, 182
Tolba, Mostafa, 94
Tomorrow (periodical), 206–207
TomPaine.com, 227
tourism, 29, 34, 217–218, 219
Toxics Release Inventory (TRI), 185,
187, 226
toxic wastes, 45, 90. *See also* hazard-
ous waste
trade, 155, 180–181, 213–214, 218–219.
See also business; globalization
Train, Russell, 87
TransFair, 219
transportation, 67–68, 159, 217–218,
219. *See also* automobiles; fossil
fuels; greenhouse gases
treaties, environmental. *See* inter-
national environmental law
TRI. *See* Toxics Release Inventory
tropical forests. *See* deforestation
and forest destruction; forests
Trust for Public Land, 208
Turner, John, 67
Turning Point Project, 227
The Twenty-Ninth Day (Brown), 84

ultraviolet radiation (UV-B), 33, 54.
    See also ozone
UNDP. *See* United Nations Develop-
    ment Program
UNEP. *See* United Nations Environ-
    ment Programme
UNICEF (United Nations Children's
    Fund), 214
UNIFEM (United Nations Develop-
    ment Fund for Women), 210, 212
Unilever, 186
Union of Concerned Scientists, 224
United Nations
    environmental concerns recog-
        nized, 78, 80–81(table)
    funding, 143–144
    and global development, 212, 213,
        214
    and globalization, 142
    Millennium Assembly, 154
    and population issues, 80(table),
        212
    role in GEOpolity, 176–180, 222–
        223 (*see also* World Environment
        Organization)
    secretariats, 93, 104, 105 (*see also*
        specific secretariats)
    See also specific conferences, conven-
        tions, programs, and protocols
United Nations Association for the
    United States of America, 208,
    222
United Nations Development
    Program (UNDP), 173, 213
United Nations Environment
    Programme (UNEP)
    established, 80(table), 86
    and ozone depletion, 92–93, 94,
        183
    Production and Consumption

Branch, 216, 219
    reports, 40–41, 80–81(table), 85,
        131–132
    size and effectiveness, 88, 105,
        222–223
    as a WEO, 179
United Nations Population Fund
    (UNFPA), 212
United Nations University, 223
United States
    air pollution and emissions, 45–46,
        61, 64, 66, 68–69, 90–91, 137,
        184, 236 n27
    aquatic species endangerment/
        extinction, 34
    assistance to developing world,
        109, 123, 154, 157, 189
    CFC regulation, 54
    climate change's probable effects
        on, 16–17, 56–57, 58, 59, 60–61
    consumption, 125, 126 (*see also*
        consumption)
    corporate approaches to global en-
        vironmental issues (*see* business)
    deforestation, 115
    economic growth, 82 (*see also* eco-
        nomic growth)
    energy policies, 63–71, 111, 159–160
    environmental deterioration, 35
        (*see also specific ecosystems,*
        regions, species, and threats)
    environmental knowledge and
        understanding, 169–171
    environmental legislation, 23–24,
        45–46, 69, 72, 79, 80(table),
        103–104, 129, 139
    globalization paradigm embraced,
        143
    history of environmental concern,
        79–84, 111–112

United States *(continued)*
  and international cooperation
    generally, 103–104, 110–111
  international environmental gover-
    nance role, 87–88, 103–104,
    109–113, 116, 177, 200, 251 n21
  and the Johannesburg Summit,
    112–113, 189
  and the Kyoto Protocol, 55–56,
    62–67, 89–90, 104, 110, 113
  and the Montreal Protocol, 182–183
  and ozone depletion, 92, 93–94
    (see also Kyoto Protocol *sub-
    heading)*
  political and policy change, 198–200
  renewable energy technologies,
    66–67
  solid and toxic wastes, 45
  state/local environmental initia-
    tives, 184 *(see also specific states)*
  and the Stockholm Convention, 107
  values and habits of thought, 139
  water pollution, 46
  *See also specific presidents and
    administrations*
United States Society for Ecological
  Economics (USSEE), 217
universities, 220–222
U.N. Wire, 209
urbanization, 31. *See also* cities
U.S. Fund for UNICEF, 214
U.S. Green Building Council, 219
U.S. Public Interest Research Group
  (USPIRG), 217

values and habits of thought, 138–139
Vermont, 58
Vienna Convention (Convention
  for the Protection of the Ozone
  Layer), 55, 88–89, 91–95. *See*

also Montreal Protocol
Vitousek, Peter, 20
voting, 204–205

Ward, Barbara, 84
Wargo, John, 47–48
waste management, 51, 164, 226. *See
  also* hazardous waste; solid waste;
  toxic waste
water. *See* fish; freshwater and water
  conservation; oceans
Watson, Bob, 183
weather. *See* climate change
Wellbeing Assessment/Barometer
  of Sustainability, 225
The Wellbeing of Nations (Prescott-
  Allen), 225
wetlands, 31–32, 35
Where on Earth Are We Going?
  (Strong), 144
Wildlife Conservation Society, 221
wildlife trade, 32
Wilson, E. O., 24, 115
wind energy, 66, 70, 157
women, 121–123, 153, 210–212
Women's Environmental and Devel-
  opment Organization, 210
WomenWatch, 210
Woods Hole research organizations,
  60–61, 221, 224
Woodwell, George, 2, 35, 83
Wooldridge, Adrian, 144
"Working 9 to 5 on Climate Change:
  An Office Guide" (del Pino and
  Bhatia), 207
World Bank, 40, 78, 132, 142, 190, 213
World Business Council for Sustain-
  able Development, 224
World Charter for Nature, 80(table),
  251 n21

World Commission on Environment
and Development (Brundtland
Commission), 81(table), 87, 141
World Conservation Union (IUCN).
See IUCN—The World Conservation Union
The World Environment: 1972–1982
(Holdgate, et al.), 85
World Environment Organization
(proposed), 112–113, 176, 177–179
World Resources Institute (WRI)
environmentally critical technologies, call for development of, 159
established, 80(table)
and GEOpolity, 223, 224
global assessment on ecosystem
health, 35–36
Global Biodiversity Strategy, 25
and green JAZZ, 225
and international environmental
conferences/agreements, 146,
183, 207
on the need for technological
transformation, 130–131
projects, 214, 217, 222

World Resources Report (2000–2001),
26–27
World Social Forum (Porto Alegre,
2003), 186
World Summit on Sustainable Devel-
opment (Johannesburg), 81(table),
112–113, 179–180, 189
World Trade Organization (WTO),
81(table), 142, 162, 180–181, 213
World Vision, 215
Worldwatch Institute, 80(table), 85,
214, 224
World Water Development Report
(United Nations, 2003), 18–19
World Wildlife Fund (WWF), 40,
105, 185, 207, 208, 223, 224, 225
Wuppertal Institute, 217

Yale School of Forestry and Environmental Studies, 171, 222

Library of Congress Cataloging-in-Publication Data

Speth, James Gustave.
Red sky at morning : America and the crisis of the global environment /
James Gustave Speth.
p.   cm.
Includes bibliographical references and index.
ISBN 0-300-10232-1 (hardcover : alk. paper)
1. Global environmental change. 2. Environmental protection.
3. Globalization—Environmental aspects. 4. Environmental policy—
United States. 5. Environmental protection—United States. I. Title.
GE149.S64 2004
363.7'00973—dc22   2003020223